MW01055444

MAC COLLINS

FORMAFANTASMA

FRIDA FJELLMAN

PHILIPPE MALOUIN

CECILIE MANZ

SABINE MARCELIS

CASEY MCCAFFERTY

JAIME HAYON

MARTINO GAMPER

NIFEMI MARCUS-BELLO

YINKA ILORI

MATERRA-MATANG

MOISÉS HERNÁNDEZ

MIMINAT DESIGNS

HELLA JONGERIUS

NENDO

JONATHAN MUECKE

MISCHER'TRAXLER

MINJAE KIM

MARLÈNE HUISSOUD

SOMIAN DESIGN

GEORGE SOWDEN

SHAHAR LIVNE

STEPHEN BURKS MAN MADE

STUDIO LANI

INDIA MAHDAVI

MABEO

NAO TAMURA

TRIBUTO

FERNANDO LAPOSSE

TAF STUDIO

EREZ NEVI PANA

OBJECTS OF COMMON INTEREST

JULIE RICHOZ

JASPER MORRISON

PEDRO PAULØ-VENZON

MARZ DESIGNS

MASH.T DESIGN STUDIO

HUGO PASSOS

JONATHAN OLIVARES

MARIO TSAI

CHRISTIEN MEINDERTSMA

DANIEL RYBAKKEN

CAROLIEN NIEBLING

INGA SEMPÉ

STUDIO BRYNJAR & VERONIKA

SOFT BAROQUE

STUDIO JUJU

SINA SOHRAB

NICOLE MONKS

MULLER VAN SEVEREN

STUDIO URQUIOLA

JOMO TARIKU

WE+

BETHAN LAURA WOOD

TOOGOOD

TEENAGE ENGINEERING

ZAVIER WONG

THE AGENCY OF DESIGN

ZANELLATO/BORTOTTO

ZAVEN

MPHO VACKIER

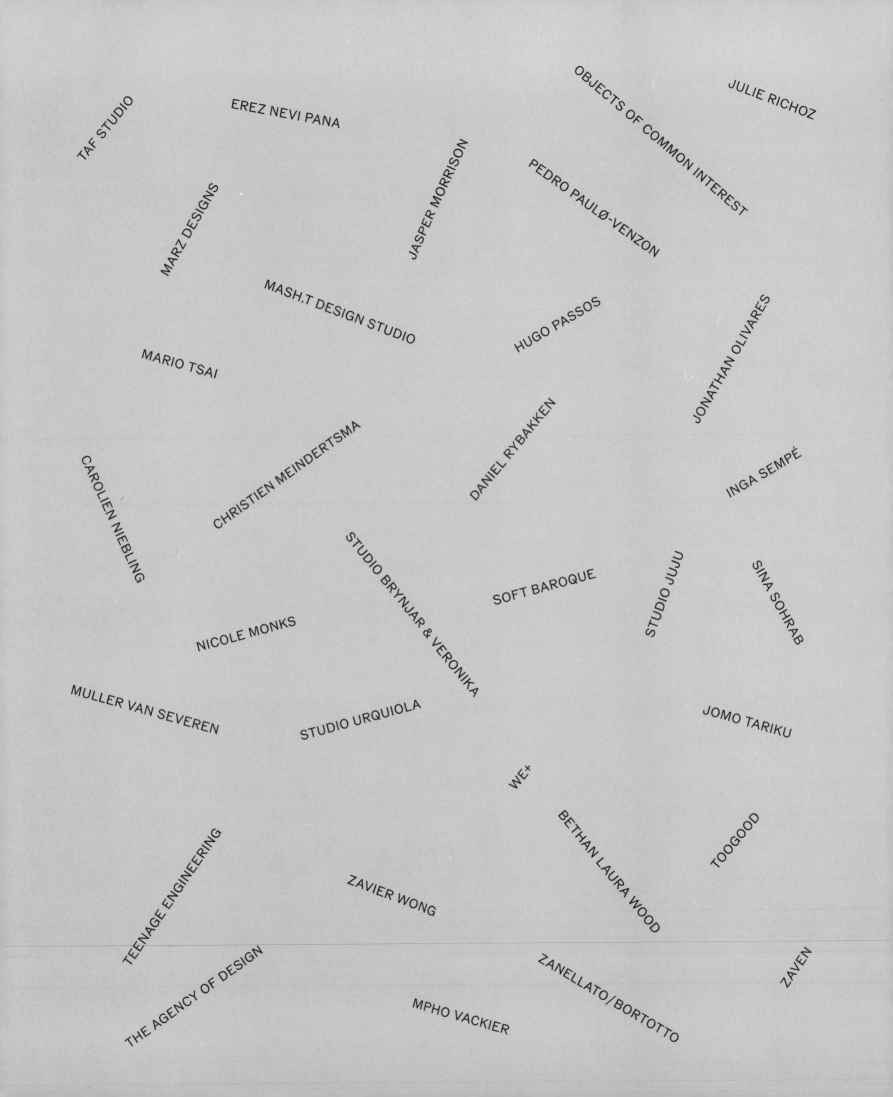

Designed for Life

Designed for Life

The World's Best Product Designers

Nominators

MARK ADAMS
Managing Director, Vitsœ
UK

GLENN ADAMSON
Curator, Writer, and Historian
USA

CHRISSA AMUAH
Designer, Curator, Editor,
and Design Consultant;
Founder, Africa by Design
UK / Ghana

SPENCER BAILEY
Writer and Editor;
Co-Founder and Editor in Chief,
The Slowdown
USA

MARC BENDA
Co-Founder, Friedman Benda
USA

ANDERS BYRIEL
CEO, Kvadrat
Denmark

ARIC CHEN
Critic; General and Artistic Director,
Nieuwe Instituut
the Netherlands

MARIA CRISTINA DIDERO
Design professional,
Independent curator, and Author
Italy

ALEXIS GEORGACOPOULOS
Director, ECAL
Switzerland

MARIANNE GOEBL
Managing Director, Artek
Switzerland and Germany

MARVA GRIFFIN
Founder and Curator,
Salone del Mobile.Milano
Italy

ANNIINA KOIVU
Design Writer, Curator,
and Consultant;
Head of Master Theory, ECAL
Switzerland and Italy

CECILIA LEÓN DE LA BARRA
Curator and Industrial Designer;
Director Zsonamaco Diseño; Chair
of Industrial Design at CENTRO.
Mexico

TUIJA MAKKONEN
Brand and Destination Manager,
Iittala
Finland

ANA ELENE MALLET
Professor and Curator
Mexico

TAPIWA MATSINDE
Author, Independent curator,
Consultant, and Storyteller
UK

JUSTIN MCGUIRK
Writer and Curator;
Director of Future Observatory,
Design Museum
UK

AMBRA MEDDA
Co Founder of Design Miami/;
Founder of Ambra Medda Office
(AMO); Co-Founder of AMO.shop
UK

ROSSELLA MENEGAZZO
Curator, Writer, and Associate
Professor of the History of
East Asian Art, University of Milan
Italy

JONATHAN OLIVARES
SVP of Design, Knoll
USA

FRANCESCA PICCHI
Architect, Curator, and Journalist;
CFO, Villa I Tatti, The Harvard Center
for Italian Renaissance Studies
Italy

MARCO SAMMICHELI
Curator of Design, Fashion
and Crafts, Triennale Milan
Italy

LIBBY SELLERS
Design Historian, Independent
Curator, and Writer
UK

ZHUO TAN
Event Director, Design Shanghai
China

MARIA VEERASAMY
CEO, Svenskt Tenn
Sweden

BEN WATSON
President, Herman Miller;
Chief Product Officer, MillerKnoll
USA

DEMETRIA WHITE
VP Global Storytelling and
Publishing Communications, Nike
USA

JANE WITHERS
Curator, Writer,
and Design consultant
UK

Introduction

"Good design." When that phrase was introduced into the vernacular—via the Museum of Modern Art in New York, which presented a series of exhibitions starting in 1950 that brought commercially available furniture and home goods into the museum environment—the question concerned "good." What makes something objectively good? At that time, "good" signified an object "intended for present-day life," made from "methods and materials [following the] progressive taste of the day." Several years later, in the 1970s, the industrial designer Dieter Rams took up the mantle by detailing ten principles of good design, chiefly that it "emphasizes the usefulness of a product whilst disregarding anything that could possibly detract from it."

Nowadays, the question is more often: *what* is design? Under its twentieth-century definition, design was distinctly not art. An object was designed for use, while art was made for decoration, display, provocation, and pleasure. This is no longer strictly the case. Blue-chip collectible design has commanded astronomical prices on the secondary market and is an ever-present element of art fairs worldwide. Design fairs have spawned weeklong, citywide takeovers of public plazas, showrooms, department stores, and convention centers—much of the design either being shown to the public as prototypes or created as site-specific work.

And yet, designed objects that blur the line with art still consider the person using them, even while rejecting or repelling or negating that person. One doesn't design a chair, no matter how conceptual, without considering the human who may sit on it.

However one categorizes the broadly ranging, often overlapping approaches to design in the twenty-first century, this user is ever-present, even more so within the triangular arrangement of manufacturer-designer-customer, or in the case of an independent operator engaging in the act of design to solve an imagined problem. As the selection of designers in this book should make clear, the wants, needs, and values of today's user differ from those of twenty, fifty, or a hundred years ago.

In the mid-century, democratizing design meant a focus on making better (things) for more (people) for less (cost). Problem-solving became a rallying cry for the corporatization of design, which in turn spawned the gigantic trade-furniture industry that has, until recently, driven the commercialization of product design. In the 1970s, a cadre of designers took an overtly optimistic tack in imagining a future free of societal stressors, paving the way for the complete rejection of formal Modernism in the 1980s. Depending on your camp, postmodernism is a philosophy that shattered the very idea of a predominantly rational approach to design, or a style to be contradicted, then embraced, in a seemingly endless cycle. Since then, the minimalism of the 1990s segued into the "supernormal" of the 2000s, followed by the frictionless perfectionism of tech-led design that has become so ubiquitous in the 2010s. All these historic movements and styles still exist in our minds and in our virtual shopping carts, thanks to the internet, a force so mighty that it has put centuries of knowledge at our fingertips and unlocked a turbocharged search engine of reference points, an instantaneous visual encyclopedia.

The design industry as we know it today both responds and reacts to market conditions. The consumer can now find, ogle, and purchase designed objects via auction houses, vintage resale websites, trade showrooms, retail catalogs, bricks-and-mortar stores, Facebook Marketplace, and Instagram direct messages. The trade show, as a concept, seems almost quaint in today's design landscape. Exhibiting a bunch of furniture prototypes to gauge their selling potential? An outdated idea, surely, when you can put almost anything on the internet and someone, somewhere, will want to buy it.

There is opportunity in this exposure. A designer's role has always been to consider a need, a new way of doing things, an ingenious answer to an existing question. If commercializing design looks a bit less like "what will sell?," all the more power to the people designing the things. In an idealized future, a designer might not be charged with making yet another iteration of the shell chair, but rather have the freedom to make the best (thing) with the most (creativity) with the least (amount of resistance).

The most established of today's design vanguard—among them Naoto Fukasawa (page 90), Hella Jongerius (p. 130), India Mahdavi (p. 160), and Muller Van Severen (p. 200)—are adept at designing the best possible example of an existing typology. Try to picture a chair without conjuring one (or many) of Jasper Morrison's (p. 194); attempt to imagine architectural lighting without thinking of Michael Anastassiades's work (p. 24) for Flos. Consider Ronan and Erwan Bouroullec's "Palissade" collection (p. 44), so quickly ensconced as a contemporary classic that one is hard-pressed to remember any other outdoor furniture. Even when Konstantin Grcic (p. 100) keeps us on our toes, as in the case of his ombréd rainbow treatment of ALPI wood veneer (2023), he's consistently delivering what one expects of Konstantin Grcic: technology-enhanced materials precision-engineered with quiet authority.

Others, who have followed this blueprint, will likely be the design stars of tomorrow. The Portuguese designer Hugo Passos's everyday objects (see the Cork Trivet, 2021; p. 216) seem almost offensively perfect in their ease and simplicity. Mario Tsai, who runs a multidisciplinary studio in Hangzhou,

China, worked in a furniture factory after university, which fittingly gives even his most traditional ideas a purely industrial bent ("Rough" collection, 2022; p. 268). Lagos-born Nifemi Marcus-Bello's handsome, streamlined pieces (LM Stool, 2018, and *Friction Ridge* bench installation, 2023; p. 172) contain highly specific cultural narratives. And Maria Jeglińska-Adamczewska, who works between France and Poland, manages a nearly impossible balance of versatility, expressiveness, and rigor in everything from furniture (Series 3, 2023) to portable walls (2019; p. 128).

But what is a burgeoning designer to do when the platonic idea of a table has already been made, and made again? Where to expend one's boundless energies? The overwhelming answer is in expanding the materials palette. This book features objects and products designed using silicone, glass, paper, polystyrene, polyurethane, aluminum, copper, steel, gold, bronze, brass, tin, plywood, cactus, cork, a multitude of hardwoods, silk, leather, sisal, cotton, wool, bamboo, rayon, hemp, alpaca, PVC, acetate, brick, resin, ceramic, nylon, enamel, rattan, sandstone, onyx, marble, fiberglass, LEDs, and recycled PET bottles. Even more novel are silkworm cocoons, recycled computers, carbon fiber, vegetable fibers, gel, seaweed, luffa, volcanic rock, bone, Cristalplant®, and Kevlar®.

For designers whose interest leans toward materials research over finished product, sustainability tends to be not a feature, but a starting point. The Tokyo design studio we+ (p. 274) has rendered foam upcycled from industrial waste into marble-esque stools (2023), while a closer look at a spare vertical lighting system bejeweled with emerald-hued disks reveals a material made from non-edible seaweed waste (2023). The Singaporean Zavier Wong (p. 276), who stayed on in the Netherlands after graduating from the Design Academy Eindhoven, seeks out the "imperfect, unwanted, or useless" in his efforts to prune the "industrial wilderness" in his work, such as lounge tables fashioned from brick and rebar rescued from a demolition site (2020). Another Eindhoven graduate, Shahar Livne (p. 156), combines social and ecological research with unusual materials to dramatic, nearly dystopian effect, such as tapestries made from wool, cotton, collagen, milk, iron, and blood (2022). London's Charlotte Kidger (p. 136) predicts the aesthetics of a future civilization, taking dust from waste polyurethane, reprocessing it with hand-dyed resin in princely colors—indigo, eggplant—and reforming the raw material into tables that recall architectural remnants.

Still others take a material and recontextualize it through inventive application. The American Jonathan Muecke (p. 196) trained as an architect, and his work takes a sharp, hyper-rational edge when it comes to exploring materials. His process involves so much research that the object itself, even something as sublime as the CTL (Carbon Tube Lounge Chair) of 2022, feels superfluous.

One cannot discuss raw materials without referencing craft. Fernando Laposse (p. 148) invokes his Mexican origins to champion local knowledge of crops, which make naturally functional materials. Materra-Matang (p. 178), a French design practice with three partners, uses ancient dyes and such time-tested craft techniques as paper cord construction, ironmongery, and the Japanese wood-preserving art of *shou sugi ban* in its highly site-specific furniture installations. India's Gunjan Gupta (p. 106) taps into regional symbolism and the tension between old and new, high and low, to explore the intersection of luxury and craft.

Still others subvert the definition of "good design" entirely. Misha Kahn, Sabine Marcelis, Bethan Laura Wood, and Soft Baroque all push and pull the discipline into the arena of art. Kahn (p. 132), an American who attended the prestigious Rhode Island School of Design, became a gallery darling thanks to his objects "of aggressive whimsy and compulsive maximalism." In London, Wood (p. 278) remixes historical design references (the Memphis Group, Meisen silk) to gleeful effect, while Soft Baroque (p. 228) cheekily translates virtual environments into glitchy, physical meta-furniture. Marcelis (p. 168) brings a more cerebral form to her spatial design; spare and self-contained, her approach to color and transparency prompts an emotional response through its restraint.

All that being said, the idea that categorizing such a large group of designers will help to define their very breadth is flawed. The 100 in these pages hail from every continent—save Antarctica—although many, if not most, live in a totally different place from their country of origin. At this point, in our globalized, highly connected, digitally fluent society, the lines of differentiation are less obvious than at any time in human history. The product designer of today is less concerned with traditional classifications that have tended to sort themselves into neat binaries: art furniture versus practical furniture, industrially made versus handcrafted, contract versus residential, formal versus informal. Instead, each constitutes one thread in a rich tapestry that is rapidly taking on dimensions. One might even call it the multiverse.

Kelsey Keith

"A chair is the first thing you need when you don't really need anything, and is therefore a peculiarly compelling symbol of civilization. For it is civilization, not survival, that requires design."

Ralph Caplan, 1982

"When the quality of form emerges, it goes straight to your heart. It has no need for justification."

Enzo Mari

Designers

AAKS

Weaving for Change Ihaya lamp. Straw, cotton, bronze, leather.
AAKS × UNHCR. 2017.

Can a basket turn into a purse or handbag? The designer Akosua Afriyie-Kumi, who grew up in Ghana, had always loved the country's basket bags, but wasn't satisfied with the available options. Returning there after several years studying fashion and working in the UK, she found that the bags she wanted to produce couldn't be made with the straws used in traditional Ghanian weaving. Undaunted, she turned to the fiber of the raffia palm, native to the African continent, and spent a year working with local women to craft the bags of her dreams. Shortly after the first AAKS collection was finished, Anthropologie got in touch—and she was off off, with the handbags reaching store shelves in 2015.

Sustainability is important to Afriyie-Kumi, who relies on local materials. The raffia handbags take about two weeks to weave, and are finished in the studio, where linings and details are added. Having started out with three weavers, Afriyie-Kumi now has eight studio employees and sixty weavers, who produce bags that will sell at international outlets, including Nordstrom and United Arrows. The bags themselves are bright and reassuringly sturdy. The bucket-shaped cross-body Baw Pot (2020), its shape inspired by clay cooking vessels, has become a hot-ticket item. The Baba Berry shopper (2020), its vibrant palette of red and orange created using natural dyes, has a decorative fringe and a sensible leather handle for transport with a touch of distinction.

Afriyie-Kumi is invested in the lives of people in the region, too. Through the Weaving for Change initiative, AAKS employs Tuareg artisans displaced from northern Mali to Burkina Faso. Working with the United Nations Refugee Agency, the brand hires weavers to handcraft wares such as the Bella and Oude lamps (2017), featuring textured shades crafted from straw and hand-dyed yarn. Basket, bag, or lampshade, these are objects produced with dignity and determination, and they radiate those qualities.

Hana Pompom bag. Raffia, leather, cotton. 2020.

Weaving for Change Bella lamp. Straw, cotton, bronze, leather. AAKS × UNHCR. 2017.

LINDSEY ADELMAN

LaLAB Illuminated Mobiles 01-07. Raw minerals, glass, ceramic, chains. 2023.

Lindsey Adelman's New York workshop is divided in two: the Department of Reality, where her team fabricates and sells made-to-order standard collections and custom work, as well as takes care of the daily operations; and the Department of Fantasy, which produces ideas, imagination, play, and inspiration brought to life through one-of-a-kind lighting, jewelry, ceramics, videos, paintings within the incubation studio LaLAB. Moving between these two spaces, she and her team craft chandeliers, mobiles, jewelry, tiles, furniture, even short films and music videos.

After graduating from the Rhode Island School of Design, Adelman opened her eponymous studio in 2006, and it blossomed into a showroom in 2012 and later a showroom in Los Angeles. She is always designing and never designing, an observer as much as a maker: of light on the sidewalk, shells on the beach, a stray hair caught under a piece of tape, Maasai ornamentation, the movies of David Lynch. Forms and ideas evolve through actual-size model-making and testing. The fixtures, many one-of-a-kind, balance industrial, meticulously finished metals with hand-blown, idiosyncratic, serendipitous glass, crocheted chain, chain fringe that resembles torn fabric, gold foil, and raw minerals, making the work as whimsical and glamorous as it is functional and rational.

The studio's seminal "Branching Bubble" collection of chandeliers (2006) paired organic globes of glass (blown by Brooklyn-based Michiko Sakano) with industrial brass swivel joints and elbows. Since then, the collections have become increasingly sculptural, collage-like, and layered with inspiration. "Knotty Bubbles" (2009), evoking windswept seascapes, light refracted through water, and Japanese buoys, are bound up in thick knots of heavy rope. "Cherry Bomb" (2014) was inspired by the ephemeral blossom, Spanish moss, and coarsely hemmed Alexander McQueen dresses. Playful and precious, the Illuminated Mobile lights (2023) add ceramic and jewel-tone glass globes, "barnacles," and torpedoes pierced with hand-knit chain and cast-bronze armatures. The Rock Lights melt over scintillating beds of selenite, pyrite, malachite, or jasper. They look like fragments of a dream—and dreaming is what they were made to inspire.

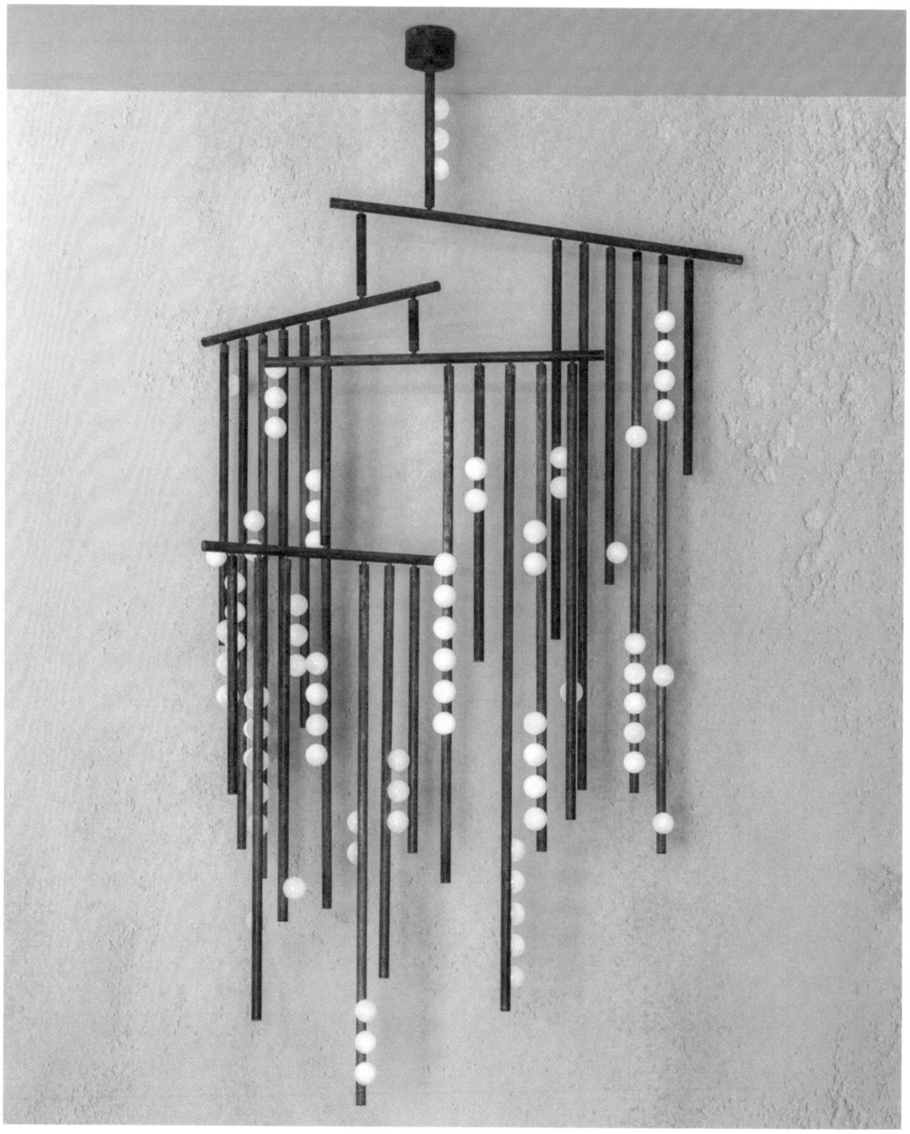

Drop System chandelier. Brass, glass. 2018.

Branching Bubble chandelier. Brass, glass. Jessica Helgerson Interior Design. 2006.

Cherry Bomb Fringe chandelier. Brass, glass, gold foil. Claude Missir Interiors. 2014.

LaLAB Cage Lights 01-04 and various LaLAB Rock Lights. Various materials. 2023.

AGNES STUDIO

Altar round table. Oak. 2022.

The designers Estefania de Ros and Gustavo Quintana-Kennedy founded Agnes Studio in 2017, and since then they have drawn on their backgrounds in interior design, furniture, and architecture to imagine an alternate past and an unparalleled future for Guatemalan interiors. Inspired by a trip in 2016 into the heart of the country to research the work of rural artisans for the exhibition *Simbiótica* held that same year in Guatemala, they work with local craftspeople to create collectible contemporary objects rooted in traditional practices. Their visions, in turn, help to unearth new possibilities for such materials as volcanic rock, which is plentiful in the region.

The artist Carlos Mérida and the architect and artist Efraín Recinos have been influential for the studio. Mérida and Recinos saw no contradiction in combining Mayan motifs with European Modernism, and Agnes Studio's projects take a similarly syncretic but distinct approach, operating as though the local aesthetic had evolved alongside the European one, in a situation of free exchange rather than colonial domination. Their Lana bench and chair, featuring virgin wool upholstery of the sort usually used for rugs, are inspired by the soft layers of cloud around the mountainous expanse of Momostenango in western Guatemala. The wool crowns *conacaste* (elephant-ear tree) or oak bases, giving the dream of resting in white or stormy clouds a gratifyingly solid foundation.

Other objects also make use of the landscape, both literally and metaphorically. The authoritative Obsidiana chair, with its many iterating oaken legs finished with iron vinegar dye, resembles a tree line as well as a futuristic throne, while the gorgeously curved Stelae chair (2022) seems at first glance to be an emanation of wood, to have come into being organically, without the touch of a human hand. The designers look forward to continuing to excavate tradition and weaving it into the designs of tomorrow.

"Lana" chair collection. Momostenango wool. 2018.

Códice cabinet. Oak. 2019.

Altar dining table. Volcanic rock, wood. With Marcelino Guoz for AGO Projects. 2019.

Códice Obsidiana chair. Oak, iron vinegar dye. 2020.

MICHAEL ANASTASSIADES

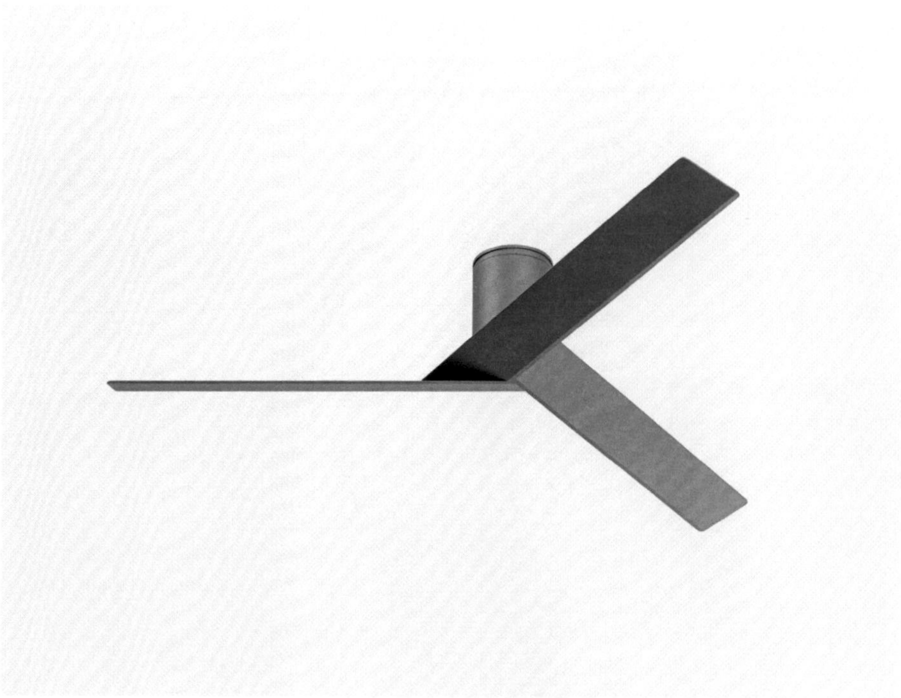

Superfan. Aluminum. Kettal. 2022.

Peaks pendant. Aluminum, LED. 2023.

Since establishing his London studio in 1994, Cyprus-born Michael Anastassiades has forged a distinguished path, attracting global clients and commissions for products, interiors, and experimental works. His approach reveals a passion for material expression and precise execution that has become his hallmark, yet this stellar career could easily have eluded him. Anastassiades revealed in a *The New York Times T Magazine* interview in 2018 that he realized the possibility of designing "everyday objects" only while studying civil engineering at Imperial College London. He subsequently graduated from the Royal College of Art and his designs—especially his lighting—quickly won attention.

The pendant series "Arrangements" (2017) for Flos exemplifies the appeal of Anastassiades's work. Composed of interconnecting circles, teardrops, and broken lines that can be added or subtracted at will, the delicate chandeliers evoke elegant trapeze artists suspended in midair. The slim aluminum forms delicately balance light, line, and gravity to create an arresting centerpiece, while reinforcing Anastassiades's view that light "can never be an isolated object but [is always] one that interacts with its environment."

For Bang & Olufsen's Beosound Edge (2018), precision and experimentation also come to the fore. From afar the sound system appears to be an elegant polished disk, but closer inspection reveals sleek, perfectly circular aluminum housing for a multi-room wireless speaker. While its form incorporates innovative sound engineering and functions, the design draws on the classic chunky shape of the 1980s British pound coin. This is trademark Anastassiades: adapting a traditional reference to a cutting-edge interpretation.

Anastassiades was made a Royal Designer for Industry by the British Royal Society of Arts in 2015. His work is exhibited internationally and held in permanent collections at the Victoria and Albert Museum in London, MAK Vienna, the Museum of Modern Art in New York, the Art Institute of Chicago, and the Frac Centre-Val de Loire in Orléans, France.

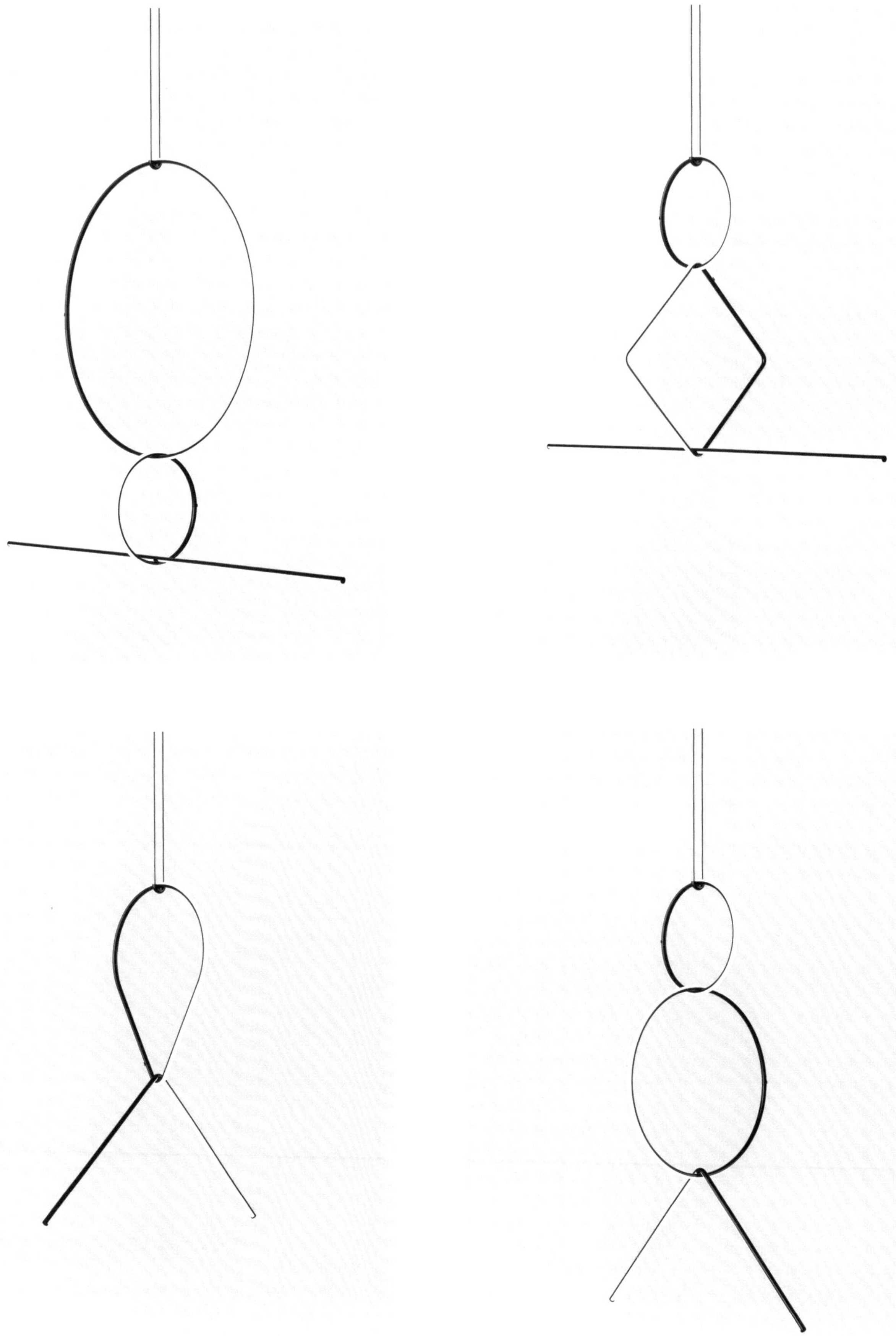

Arrangements LED lighting. Aluminum, platinum optical silicone. Flos. 2017.

Fringe tiles. Porcelain stoneware. Mutina. 2023.

Besound Edge speaker. Aluminum, fabric. Bang & Olufsen. 2018.

Jack room divider bookcase. Various materials. B&B Italia. 2018.

OMER ARBEL

"87" pendant. Glass, electrical components. 2017.

A performance unfolds. Several glass artists prepare molten glass bubbles, which are then collectively smashed together, giving rise to an unpredictable new formation of interlocked glass. Welcome to the creative collisions that fill the world of Omer Arbel. This performative act, called "100" (his innovations are numbered chronologically), reflects how Arbel's thinking surpasses conventional paradigms of design, beauty, and making.

Like his creations, the Vancouver-based designer transcends categorization. Omer Arbel Office, established in 2005, describes itself as a hub for a "constellation" of experimentation, straddling architecture, sculpture, invention, and design. A recurrent theme is a questioning of the meaning of materials, with many works excavating and reforming the intrinsic mechanical, physical, and chemical qualities that define them.

Light is another elemental focal point, particularly through Arbel's role as artistic director of Bocci, the lighting and glass-blowing studio he co-founded in 2005 in Vancouver. Project "87" (2017) explores the boundaries of light and glass. A matrix of hot glass is stretched and folded back on itself numerous times as it cools, with trapped air creating pearlescent microfilaments through which light subtly filters from an LED source at one end. The result is a glowing sculptural multi-light suspension of gently stretched looping ribbons with a delicately ribbed texture, evoking a softness of form far removed from the angular rigidity usually associated with glass.

Project "113" (2018) is no less innovative. An ongoing series of experiments, it aims to manipulate the qualities of copper alloys and glass by first blowing a glass form, into which a liquid alloy is poured before the glass shatters, leaving a metallic shadow of itself. Each piece by Arbel explores how creating something new and timeless from the broken, the combined, and the reformed might be a metaphor for gaining a deeper understanding of the wider world.

"113" sculptural objects. Copper. 2018.

"100" pendant. Glass, electrical components. 2022.

INI ARCHIBONG

Galop d'Hermès watch. Rose gold, quartz, grained silver, leather. Hermès. 2019.

For Ini Archibong, design is inextricable from a broader spiritual and artistic practice. Living and working on the shores of Lake Neuchâtel in Switzerland, he spends solitary days dreaming up pieces that range from watches through furniture and installations. In every medium and scale, his works draw on elements of his Pasadena childhood and lifelong obsessions: colorful low-rider cars and world religions, Sun Ra, comic books, and sci-fi literature. Each of Archibong's creations is intended to function as an artwork. And for him, no work of art is merely decorative or frivolous. Whether mass-produced or intended for the luxury market, each has a definitive function: to engage and elevate the user.

To lift people out of their everyday lives and inspire contemplation, Archibong relies on serious craftsmanship and a breadth of cultural reference. His Orion table, named for the great hunter of Greek mythology, whose name appears in Hesiod and Homer, features a hand-carved Carrara marble top and three colored glass legs that are shaded blood-red at the top, fade to lavender, and finally deepen to a Mediterranean blue. Debuting during Milan Design Week in 2016, the table is now part of the New York Metropolitan Museum of Art's collection, as is Archibong's vibrant Vernus 3 chandelier, a work of glass and galvanized steel inspired by the playful forms of Ettore Sottsass. Designed and produced for Friedman Benda, Vernus 3 was later acquired by The Met's permanent collection, and was debuted during their long-term installation *Before Yesterday We Could Fly: An Afrofuturist Period Room*.

The multitudes that Archibong contains also include a watchmaker. A collaboration with Hermès in 2019 yielded the Galop d'Hermès watch, with a polished or diamond-studded case referencing the shape of a stirrup, in a nod to the brand's origins as a manufacturer of equestrian products. Yet Archibong's works have a way of suggesting that we are not delimited by time. By striving for an unforced and unexpected beauty, his objects and spaces become occasions for catching a glimpse of the sublime.

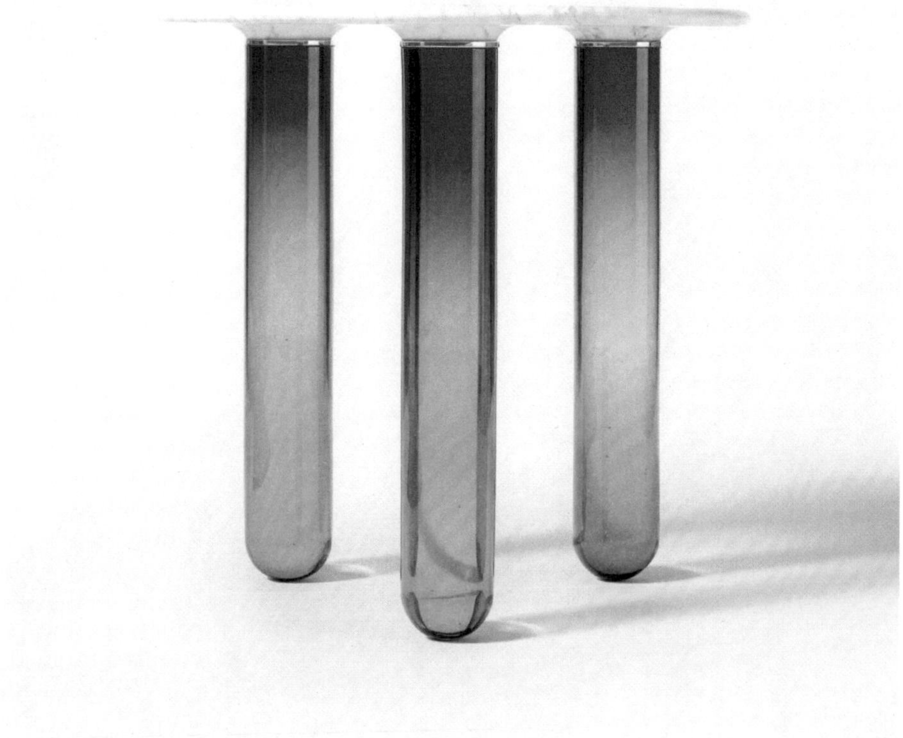

Orion table. Glass, Carrara marble. With Glassworks Matteo Gonet. 2021.

Vernus 3 chandelier. Glass, galvanized steel. With Glassworks Matteo Gonet. Friedman Benda. 2020.

ATLASON STUDIO

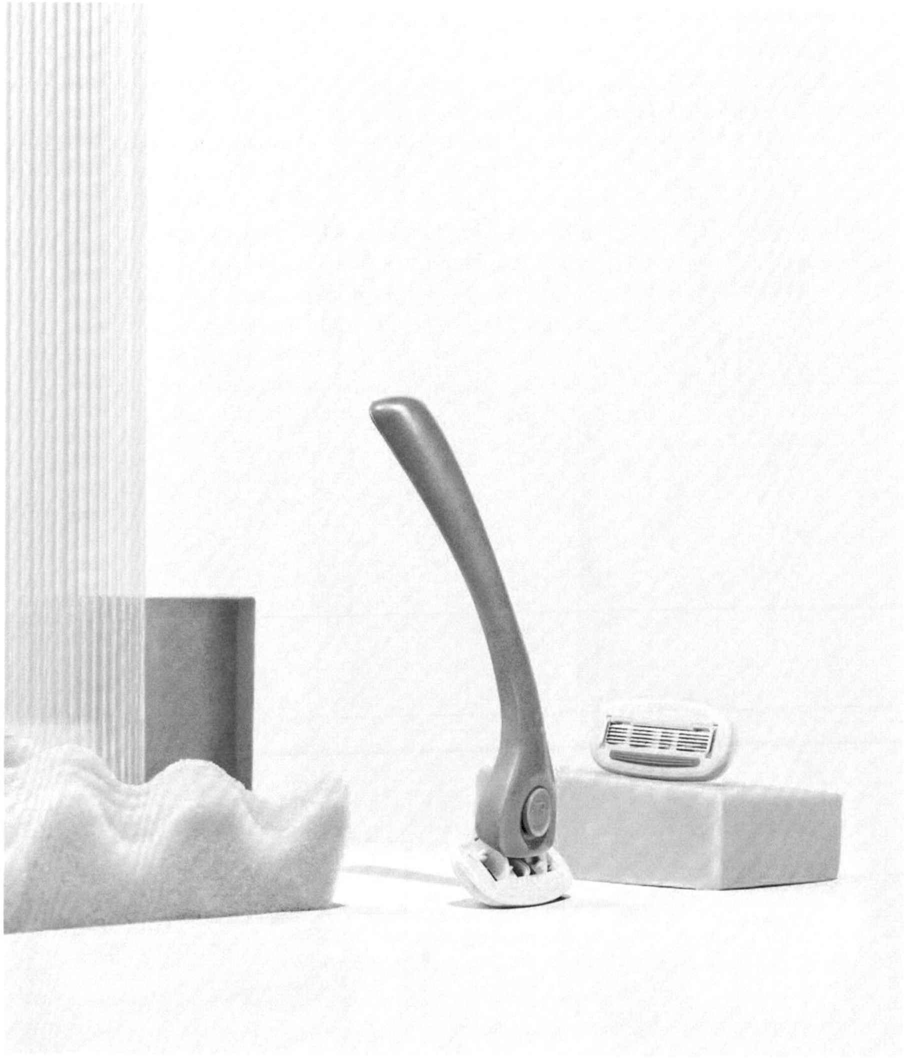

Ergonomic Razor. Various materials. Billie. 2019.

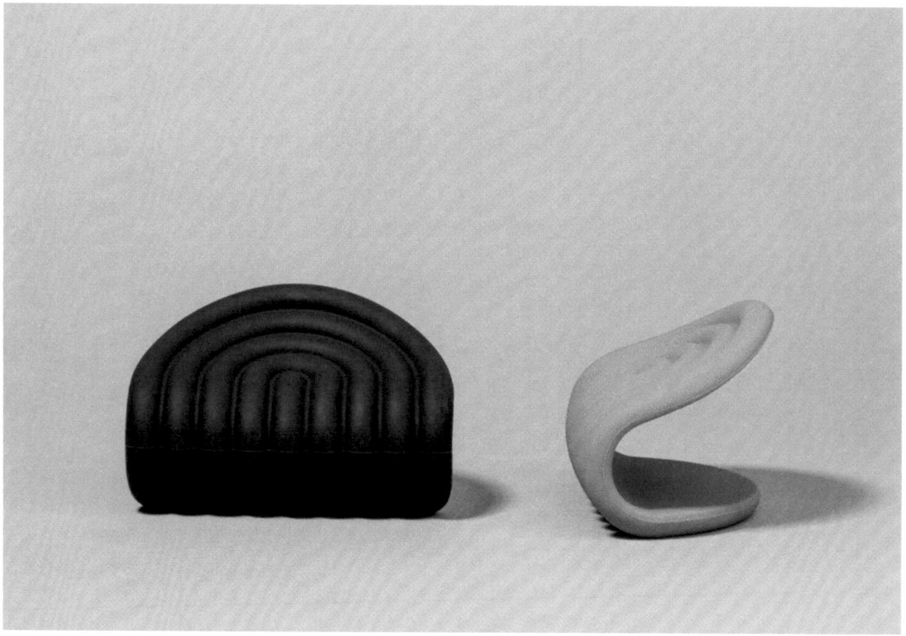

Our Place Kitchen Hot Grips. Silicone. Our Place. 2021–23.

Does the world need another (fill in the blank product)? Omnidesigner Hlynur Atlason would say it needs a *better* one. Born in Reykjavik, Iceland in 1974, Atlason graduated in industrial design from Parsons School of Design in New York in 2001. A year later, IKEA included his oversize Tuno Clock in its PS Collection. Two years later, he opened his Manhattan office to create a broad spectrum of design—from kitchen tools and a razor redesign to furniture and sustainable packaging—for the likes of Heller and L'Oréal. The work starts with questioning the status quo and how it evolved, learning voraciously: new brand languages, materials, consumer habits, technology, processes. Atlason—an eternal student—embraces these opportunities.

The Ergonomic Razor (2019) for Billie looks simple but warm and fresh, with a form that flows between ergonomic touchpoints. At a different scale, the sinuous, fully recyclable, indoor/outdoor Limbo Chair (2023) is equally welcoming of the human form. But it took a lot of effort to make it look so effortless. The "Pastille" seating system (2022) showcases its low-slung architecture, but without the discomfort of a low seat. The team used sleight of hand—down toppers, for example, offer a sense of sinking in without making it difficult to stand up again—to create horizontal proportions and an impression of floating.

Vala (2020) is a collaboration of contradictions that focuses on the act of sitting itself, not the seat. It's a recliner that's gender- and age-neutral, crisp and soft, compact on the outside but stuffed with functionality within. As one leans, its lozenge-like shapes float apart to mask the mechanisms. To do this, the team 3D-printed models of components at full size to determine proportions and the precise placement of parts. With this ever-adaptive approach to design, it seems hopeful, as the studio's tagline says, that "everything we imagine can be made."

Limbo Chair. Post-consumer-recycled polyethylene blend. Heller. 2023.

Vala Recliner. Aluminum, foam, fabric. MillerKnoll / DWR. 2022.

Pastille upholstery collection sofa. Various materials. MillerKnoll / DWR. 2022.

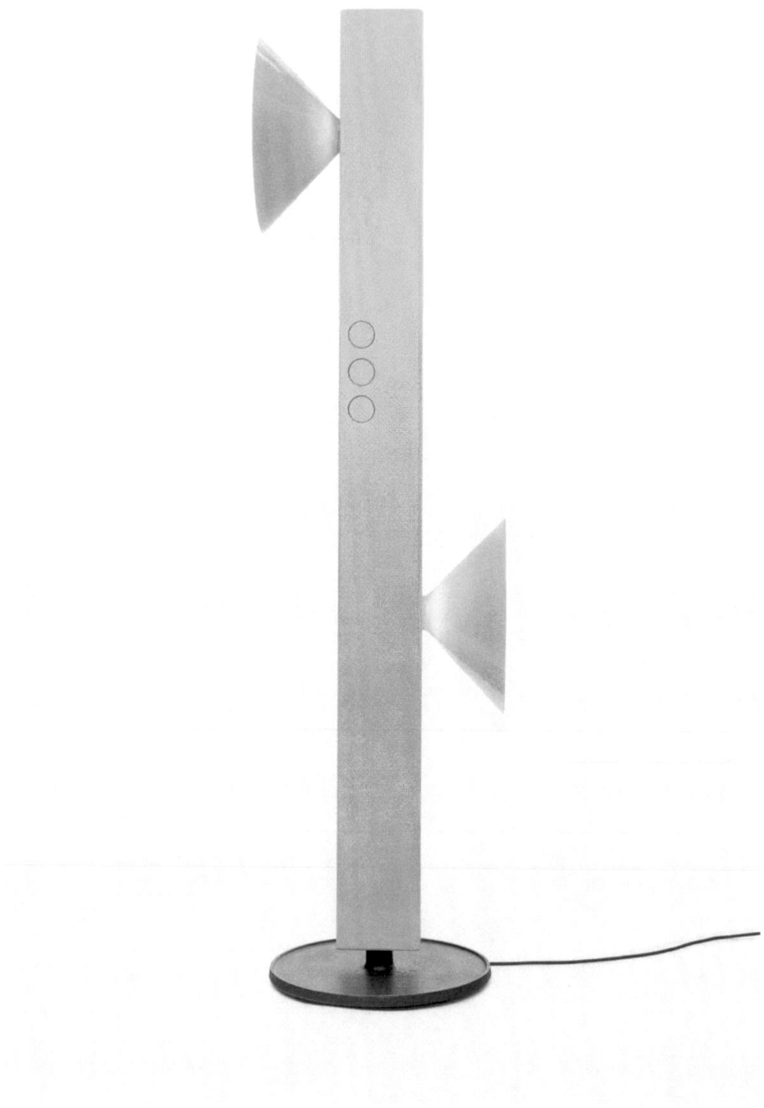

BARBER OSGERBY

The British design duo Edward Barber and Jay Osgerby need little introduction, having scooped numerous accolades over their twenty-six years of practice, including OBEs, Royal Designers for Industry, and the Jerwood Prize. From beginnings fabricating cardboard maquettes in an apartment in London's Trellick Tower for their breakthrough Loop table for Isokon Plus in 1996, their eponymous business has grown steadily, following a design sensibility that blends humor, material curiosity, and elegance of line. Their spare yet tactile approach is seen in architecture, exhibition design, interiors, sculpture, and products. One such is their Bellhop table lamp (2017) for Flos, for London's Design Museum, conceived as a "modern candle" that would cast a warm wash of light. The injection-molded polycarbonate shade deflects light from the bulb to give a soft reflected glow.

"Soft Work" (2018) for Vitra answers a different challenge: to create robust yet inviting furniture systems for new ways of working. Rather than cramped desks and flimsy partitions, this collection reconsiders the sofa as a starting point: a comfortable place for thinking and working. The result is a sinuous upholstered seating system, with paneled spaces for quiet work, adjunct circular tables for team collaboration, and neatly integrated side tables for coffee and laptops to perch on.

Similarly adaptive to contemporary needs is the seating family "On & On" (2019) for Emeco. Incorporating recycled PET, glass fiber, and non-toxic pigment, the cheerful, stackable seating—a reinterpretation of the classic bentwood chair—is designed to weather everyday use and can be fully recycled.

Such quiet, thoughtful work has made Barber Osgerby an exemplar of British contemporary design. Its pieces are held in permanent collections at the Victoria and Albert Museum and the Design Museum in London, the Metropolitan Museum of Art in New York, and the Vitra Design Museum in Weil am Rhein, Germany.

Signals lighting. Aluminum, glass. Venini for Galerie kreo. 2022.

Bellhop table lamp. Polycarbonate. Flos. 2017.

On & On chair. recycled PET, glass fiber, non-toxic pigment. Emeco. 2019.

Tobi-Ishi striped marble table. Marble. B&B Italia. 2022.

BIG-GAME

Giroflex 150 chair. Japanese oak, stainless steel, aluminum, plastic. Giroflex & Karimoku New Standard. 2022.

Established by Augustin Scott de Martinville, Grégoire Jeanmonod, and Elric Petit in Lausanne in 2004, BIG-GAME is a design studio for the people. The founders met while studying at ECAL (École cantonale d'art de Lausanne), and are united by the belief that designs should rise to the occasion, foregrounding utility and appealing both to art-lovers and to people who may not think about design at all. The collective has worked on furniture and other products, art direction, scenography, exhibitions, and research. Often characterized by its apparent simplicity, their work is the result of deep thinking, prolonged experimentation, and a preternatural knack for tweaking existing constructions just so.

Collaboration with international companies and local manufacturers has been key for BIG-GAME since its inception. Its now legendary BOLD chair (2009), a sculptural composition of two curved, foam-wrapped metal tubes, came into being once a sock manufacturer was found to produce coverings for the tubes. The EXTRA BOLD armchair (2021) is a plusher version of the original. And the studio's winsome Giroflex 150 (2022) is a charming homage to the classic swivel office chair, reimagined in Japanese oak. The designers were inspired by the original chairs' longevity and aimed to make something just as durable, as well as gratifyingly streamlined and socially responsible, using wood from young-growth trees that might otherwise have been pulped.

The brief, as BIG-GAME perceives it, is always to make objects that are reliable, effective, unobtrusive, and beautiful: things that make both private and public life a little easier, and infinitely more pleasant. The studio's Castor Lobby Sofa (2022) for Karimoku New Standard is part of a modular system that allows socializing as well as solitary waiting. And Les Forgés 1890 (2019), a set of cooking knives for Opinel, is a gleaming five-piece invitation to make oneself just as comfortable in the kitchen as in one of BIG-GAME's infinitely agreeable chairs.

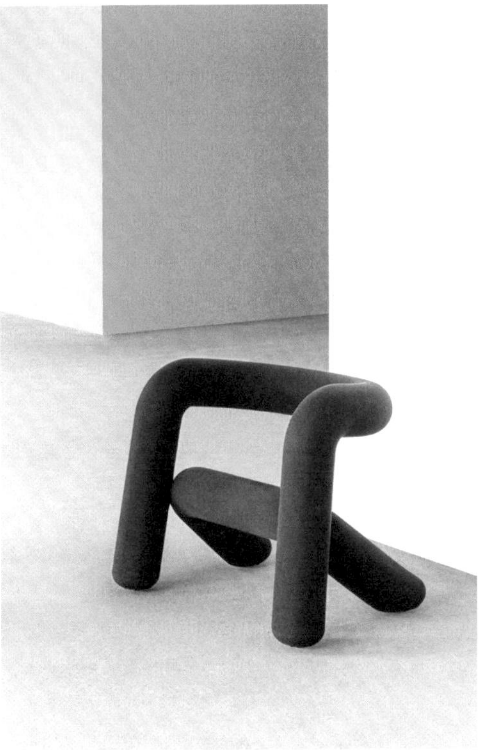

EXTRA BOLD armchair. Stainless steel, foam, fabric. Moustache. 2021.

Les Forgés 1890 knives. Stainless steel, beech. Opinel. 2019.

Castor Lobby Sofa. Japanese oak, fabric, foam. Karimoku New Standard. 2022.

AGUSTINA BOTTONI

Calici Milanesi glassware. Borosilicate glass. 2018.

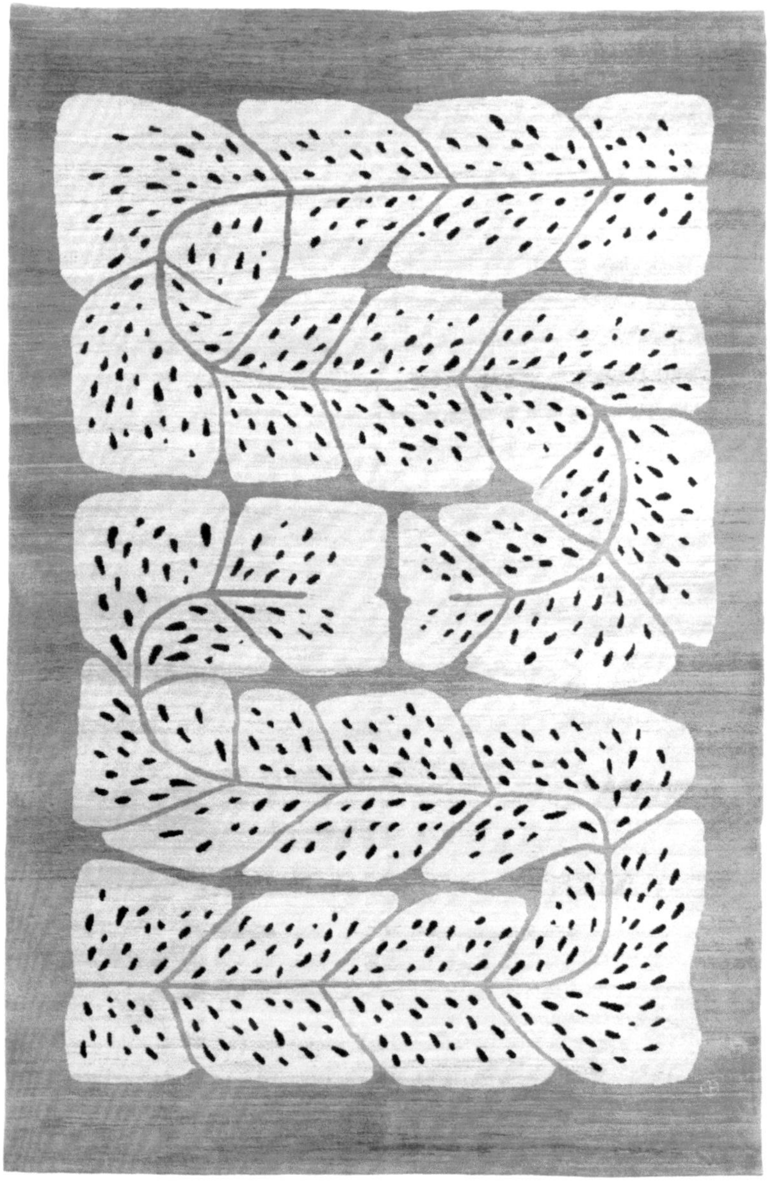

Foliage rug. Wool, natural pigments. Galerie Chevalier Parsua. 2021.

Agustina Bottoni's elegant, inspired designs gently alter the space around them. Whether products, furniture, textiles, sculptures, or installations, they are an unexpected touch that transforms. Born in Buenos Aires, Bottoni studied fashion in Argentina, then made her way to Milan's Nuova Accademia di Belle Arti for a master's in design, opening her studio a year after completing the program. Making it a point to work with local artisans and workshops, she draws on Milan's tradition of craftsmanship and its built environment, creating products that echo the region's aesthetic history in a major key.

Bottoni, who thinks of her designs as delicate, has gone to great lengths to ensure that they're also long-lasting. Her Calici Milanesi set of glasses (2018)—martini glass, wineglass, and champagne coupe—for instance, is made with borosilicate glass, which can withstand shifts in temperature and is thus able to hold freezing or hot drinks. The three pieces are inspired by Milan's 1930s Villa Necchi Campiglio, designed by the architect Piero Portaluppi, once a private villa and now a museum, as well as a setting for Luca Guadagnino's film *I Am Love* (2009). The glasses are likewise cinematic, making a small, festive production of every sip.

Levity and lightness are key to Bottoni's works, as with her piece *Melodicware* (2017). This kinetic sculpture made from solid brass with a satin finish, grounded in a black Marquina or white Carrara marble base, has brass chimes that sing in the wind, bringing forth the airy tune it is already so tempting to ascribe to Bottoni's creations. And her Presenza lamps (2021) are a delightful, slightly comic duo: brass frames dressed in light hemp fabric that resembles old-fashioned women's underclothes. Unassuming yet full of personality, the lamps are testament to the charm of Bottoni's vision.

Presenza lighting. Hemp fabric, brass, LED. 2021.

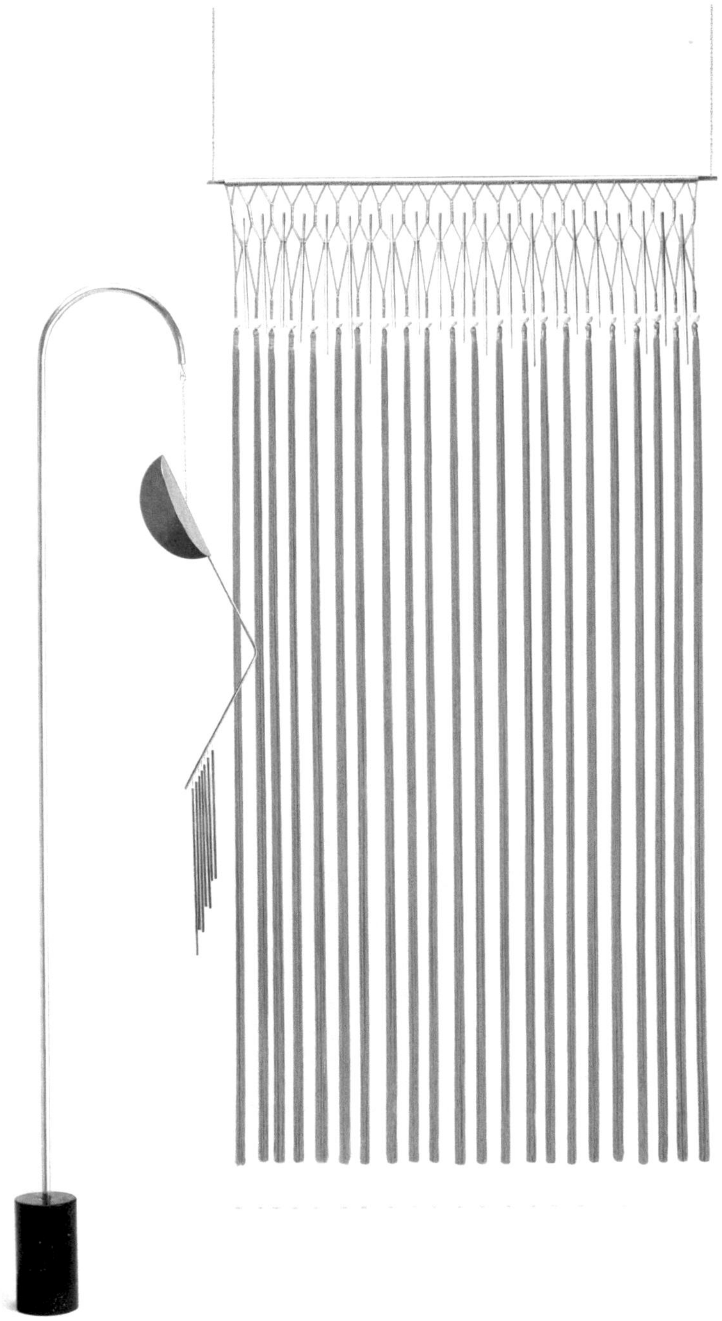

Melodicware sculpture and curtain. Brass, rayon, marble. 2017.

BOUCHRA BOUDOUA

While studying spatial design at London's Central Saint Martins, the Moroccan-born designer and artist Bouchra Boudoua found inspiration in the contrast between the century-old building and the avant-garde ideas and energies reverberating inside its walls. The pottery she produces in collaboration with artisans in Morocco is similarly inspired by a confluence of traditional geometric patterns and contemporary forms. Fueled by her love of this storied craft, yet firmly rooted in the contemporary, Boudoua is committed to sustainable production. Non-toxic, lead-free glazes lend a healthy shine to handmade terracotta bowls, vases, plates, and other decorative and functional objects enlivened by her bright painted lines.

Born in Casablanca and now splitting her time between her hometown and Marrakech, Boudoua is also drawn to Morocco's rural areas, where a centuries-long tradition of pottery-making survives. Returning from her travels with a trove of images, from a particular textile stitch to an interesting architectural flourish, she constructs a personal iconography for her work, eventually sending these relics of hyperlocal culture all over the world. Ceramics—among them the deep red Jouj vase (2022)—are available through the Conran Shop in London, and tall vessels inspired by bogolan cloth, a handmade cotton fabric from Mali, are sold online through Boudoua's studio. Visitors to Morocco, meanwhile, encounter her cups and plates when they dine at Marrakech's historic La Mamounia hotel. In 2022, Boudoua worked with Palestinian refugees in Lebanon to create a set of ceramics embroidered with traditional Palestinian cross-stitching for the "Autumn Harvest" project, exhibited in Abu Dhabi.

Boudoua's ceramics are vivid yet contained, as useful as they are playful, manifestly sturdy and endlessly charming, some incorporating whimsical touches of raffia or combining rattan with clay. They are a worthy embodiment of the designer's desire to "make a place for tradition in modern life."

Ceramics Set 2 art collection. Terracotta clay. 2022.

Ceramics Set 1 vases. Terracotta clay. 2022.

RONAN & ERWAN BOUROULLEC

Le Belvédère pavilion. Various materials. 2020.

Since first collaborating on a small table at ages twenty-four and nineteen respectively, the brothers Ronan and Erwan Bouroullec have experimented, researched, and creatively reconsidered the role of design. Their response translates across many fields, with commissions that range from televisions and room dividers through chairs, lamps, and books.

One of the Bouroullecs' strongest motivations is to create good design that is widely accessible. This is reflected in the "Palissade" collection of outdoor furniture (2018), commissioned by HAY and including tables, benches, chairs, and stools of powder-coated steel that sit as easily on a private patio as in a busy public space. Colored in subtle, natural hues, they are designed to blend in rather than compete with their surroundings.

Bouroullec design traits of simplicity and rigor underpin Rope (2020), a chair produced by Artek and designed to weather marine conditions. Its deceptively simple outline is rendered in tubular-steel framing, and it has a beech plywood seat with rope creating an unexpected detail for arm- and backrests. The tactile, pliable rope wraps around the steel, allowing the chair to flex to the height and shape of each user.

"Belt" (2019), the Bouroullecs' adaptable lighting collection for Flos, also concentrates on the flexibility of textiles. Composed of leather or fabric straps that support and link suspended strips of light, the piece is a sophisticated interpretation of everyday industrial bands. In the designers' hands, buckles and straps are reworked to create a streamlined pendant or wall lamp.

The Bouroullecs' long-standing vision to use good design as "a way to change the world, to create beauty in mass-production," is seen across their broad spectrum of work. Celebrated worldwide, their uncompromising and playful approach has won countless awards, commissions, and a major retrospective in 2015 at the Musée des Arts Décoratifs in Paris.

Palissade park bench. Powder-coated steel. HAY. 2022.

Rope chair. Steel, beech plywood, ash, flax or polyester. Artek. 2020.

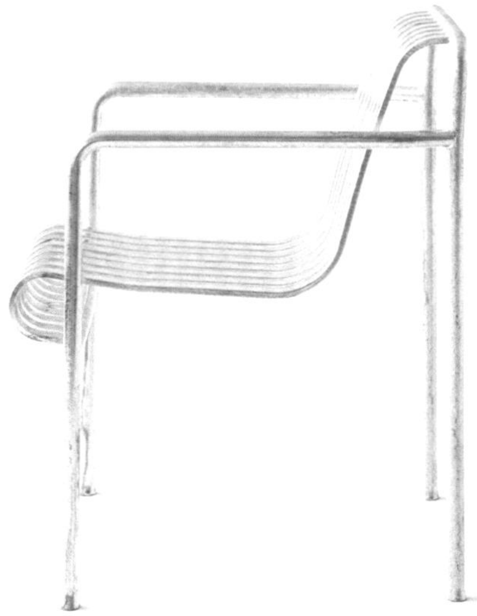

Palissade dining armchair. Powder-coated steel. HAY. 2018.

Belt, lighting line. Aluminum, leather or textile fabric. 2019.

RODRIGO BRAVO

AFB (artifact for birds 01) bird table. Aluminum. With Clemente Mackay. 2023.

Picture *Combarbalita*: a rare volcanic rock found only in the mountains of Chile, long used by Indigenous artisans drawn to its patterns, textures, and shades, from pinks and whites to reddish browns. It is the protagonist in the clean-lined geometry of the "Monolith" series (2019) by the Chilean designer Rodrigo Bravo, who smoothly balances its layered mineral-rich tones and textural irregularities in objects with a sculptural simplicity. The series is a typical reflection of both the aesthetics and the processes of the Chilean designer behind the studio Bravo, set up in Santiago in 2005, whose creative vision shifts between interior, product, and furniture design.

The concept of harnessing the power of nature in a human context often seeps into Bravo's projects, added to a methodology rooted in the melding of material, process, and technology, finished with the geometric curves and sculptural minimalism of physical form. One example is AFB 01 (artifact for birds 01) (2023), a piece inspired by the work of the iconic Japanese sculptor Isamu Noguchi, created with the aim of harmonizing nature and urbanism. A jigsaw puzzle of vertical and horizontal aluminum planes interlock to create a geometrical installation that provides a timeless contemporary feeding sanctuary for birds.

Another highlight is Bravo's "Tube Mutation" series (2020), which explores the creation of objects, both simple and ambiguous, through the modification of steel pipes. The results are abstractions of minimal curves and lines that glean beauty from the industrial, hovering somewhere between furniture and art. The collection includes the TM1 Bench, which taps into the simplicity of its tubular form to embody a piece that is both functional as furniture and sculpturally decorative.

For all its creative and conceptual abstraction, Bravo's work often feels accessible, usable, and rooted in the modern world. He explains: it's about "innovation driven from common sense."

"Monolith" series No. 08. Combarbalita stone. Luis Aldays. 2019.

E Table. Fresno timber, teak oil. Teks. 2021.

"AL" series table and chair. Aluminum. With Diego Soria for Verso. 2021.

"Tube Mutations" series TM1 bench. Metal, electrolytic zinc bath finish. Metal DG. 2020.

THILO ALEX BRUNNER

On Cloudnova. EVA, rubber, various textiles. On. 2020.

The product designer Thilo Alex Brunner is a proponent and innovator of Swiss design. Born in Biel/Bienne and taking his master's degree at ECAL (École cantonale d'art de Lausanne), where he later ran the product design program, he also co-founded the agency Brunner Mettler, more recently called BMCO. Since 2010, BMCO has been a fixture in European design, working with companies including Swatch, Wenger, and Sigg. Since 2018, Brunner has focused solely on his work with On, the Swiss sneaker and sportswear brand that's a runaway favorite of celebrities and athletes worldwide, from Dwayne "The Rock" Johnson to Roger Federer. On's THE ROGER tennis shoe (2020) was made in collaboration with the record-setting player.

Brunner appreciates the Swiss tradition of collaboration at every step of the design process, but he's not interested in amassing options until the product is so multifunctional as to be overwhelming, another iteration of the proverbial Swiss Army knife. His preference for simplicity informs the line of Cloud sneakers he designs for On, beloved of professional athletes and diverse movement enthusiasts, all of whom appreciate the shoes' soft landing and firm push off, not to mention the unencumbered silhouette. For such recent editions as the On Cloudnova (2020) and On Cloudmonster (2022), Brunner sought to create running shoes that answered only to necessity, a lightweight option made in part from recycled materials in an effort to avoid a surplus of waste or decoration.

Brunner believes that the beauty of a product stems from its usefulness, which is true both of his shoes and of the athleticwear he produces with On, including the On Weather Jacket (2016).

On Cloud 5. EVA, rubber, various textiles. On. 2022.

On Weather Jacket. Various textiles. On. 2016.

On Cloudmonster. EVA, rubber, various textiles. On. 2022.

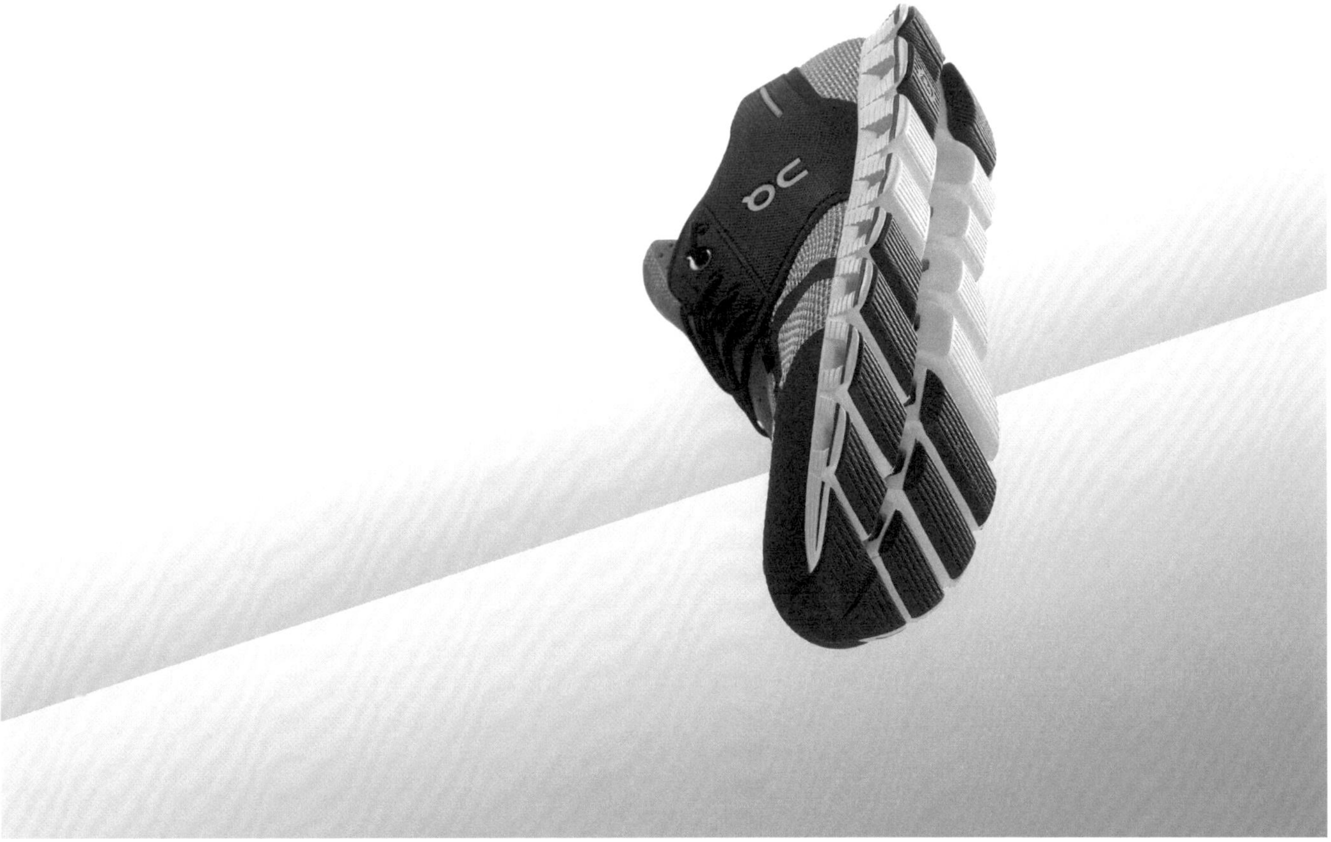

On Cloud 1st Generation. EVA, rubber, various textiles. On. 2014.

On THE ROGER Centre Court. EVA, rubber, various textiles. On. 2020.

FABIEN CAPPELLO

Mesa Milagros table. Steel, mosaic. AGO Projects. 2022.

A watering can born from a mapping of tin artisans in Mexico. A cobalt-blue curve of outdoor seating. A desk lamp with candy-bright pink and yellow glass panels. Locality, materials, color, playfulness: all are defining ingredients in the work of Fabien Cappello, whose designs span the spectrum of modern living, from household products and limited-edition furniture to public spaces.

The French designer aims to understand design "not as an isolated exercise, but as the connection point between people and their life, production and culture, places and identities." Key to this is an intuitive sensitivity to location: in addition to residencies in Italy, Portugal, and Korea, he launched Studio Fabien Cappello in London in 2010, relocating to Mexico in 2016, first Mexico City then Guadalajara. There, he explores the layers of narrative that define the role of design in homes, public spaces, and society at large. Recent projects include a minimalist sweep of blue outdoor seating for Mexico City's new cultural space LagoAlgo (2022).

Cappello's skills at mapping local resources through artisans and materials shine through in his tin creations. An unraveling of the threads of Guadalajara's local *hojalata* (tinware) industry resulted in a homeware collection (2020), including myriad watering cans, crafted from thin embossed tin sheets by named artisans: Arturo and Maria Vega; Alejo and Antonio Perez.

The singular form of Cappello's beech Molino Grinder (2022), a "functional sculpture" for the tabletop with boldly hand-painted stripes, reflects his playful relationship with color (the designer in fact has some degree of color vision deficiency—an irony that is not lost on him). Sun-drenched color mixes light up many other designs, from the graphically checkered custom-made furniture textile Ventana (2023) to the glass panels of his brass-framed lights. Connecting many of these creations is a recalibration of contemporary notions of beauty and comfort, by spotlighting elements of culture and materials that society often overlooks.

Molino salt and pepper grinders. Hand-painted beech. Hem. 2022.

Regaderas de hojalata watering cans. Tin. 2020.

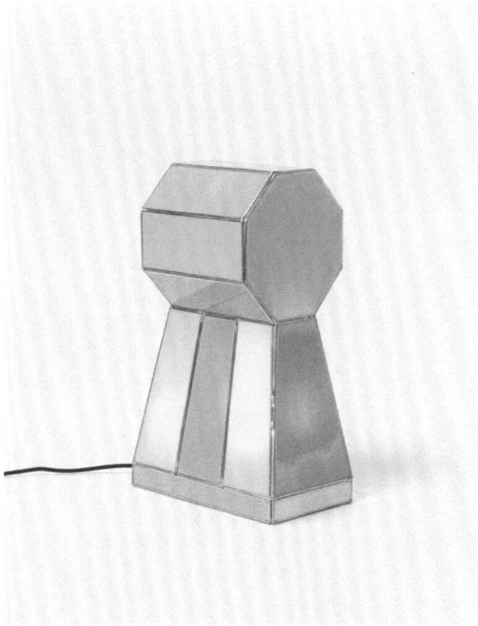

Toni lamp. Brass, glass. AGO Projects. 2022.

Sillón Bulky sofa. Various materials. AGO Projects. 2023.

ALVARO CATALÁN DE OCÓN

Alhambra Terrazzo vase and bowl. Glass, concrete, pigments, marble, resin. ACdO. 2018.

Ceramics Cu vases. Ceramics, copper, silica. ACdO. 2019.

Capturing attention for its vast, floating form, *Ramingining* (2016–17) is one of the most ambitious iterations of Alvaro Catalán de Ocón's lamps, which reuse waste materials creatively. Commissioned for Australia's National Gallery of Victoria Triennial, *Ramingining* caught public attention for its woven cloud of dyed fibers, floating above visitors' heads and pierced by tiny points of light. On closer inspection, it becomes clear that each lamp is framed by a plastic bottle carefully woven into the large fixture, created in collaboration with the Yolngu weavers of East Arnhem Land.

Collaboration and techniques of craft are a familiar part of Catalán de Ocón's work. *Ramingining* (named after the remote Northern Territory community that helped to produce it) brought together Indigenous weaving practices that included the collection of pandanus fibers and local dyeing techniques to produce gradated rings of ocher, straw, burgundy, and red. Uniting each artist's circular woven piece into one larger form, *Ramingining* tells the unique and collected stories of local kinship systems.

The installation builds on Catalán de Ocón's most famous design, his joyful PET Lamps (2012), with tentacular arms connecting a family of colorful woven shades. These creative light fixtures debuted at Milan's esteemed Galleria Rossana Orlandi in 2013 and quickly won acclaim for their overarching objective: the responsible use of materials and the diversion of landfill for productive purposes. Catalán de Ocón was an early adopter of such approaches, and in PET, working in collaboration with artisans from various countries, he reuses discarded plastic bottles in each fixture. The bottles are interwoven with plant fibers to create bright, eye-catching lamps that are as resourceful as they are playful. For multi-award-winning Catalán de Ocón, design is a tool to highlight the power of collaboration and Indigenous knowledge, and the joy that can be found in the recycling and reuse of materials.

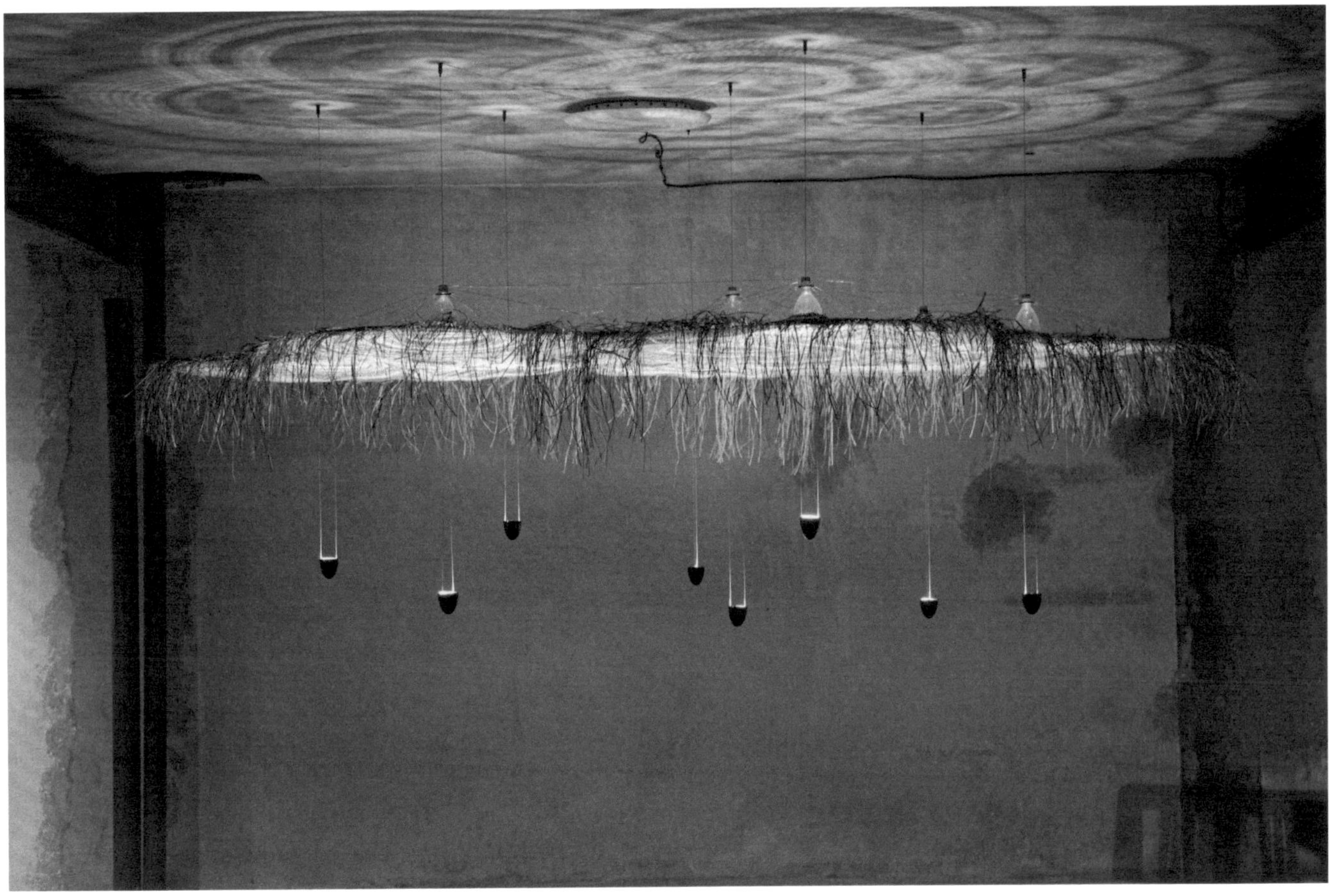

Ramingining PET Lamp. Pandanus, natural dyes, reused PET plastic bottles. ACdO. 2016–17.

Home/Office. Chair by Charles and Ray Eames, 1958. ACdO with Vitra and local artisans in Madrid. 2014.

Plastic Rivers rug. Yarn from recycled PET bottles. ACdO with GAN's team of local artisans in India. 2022.

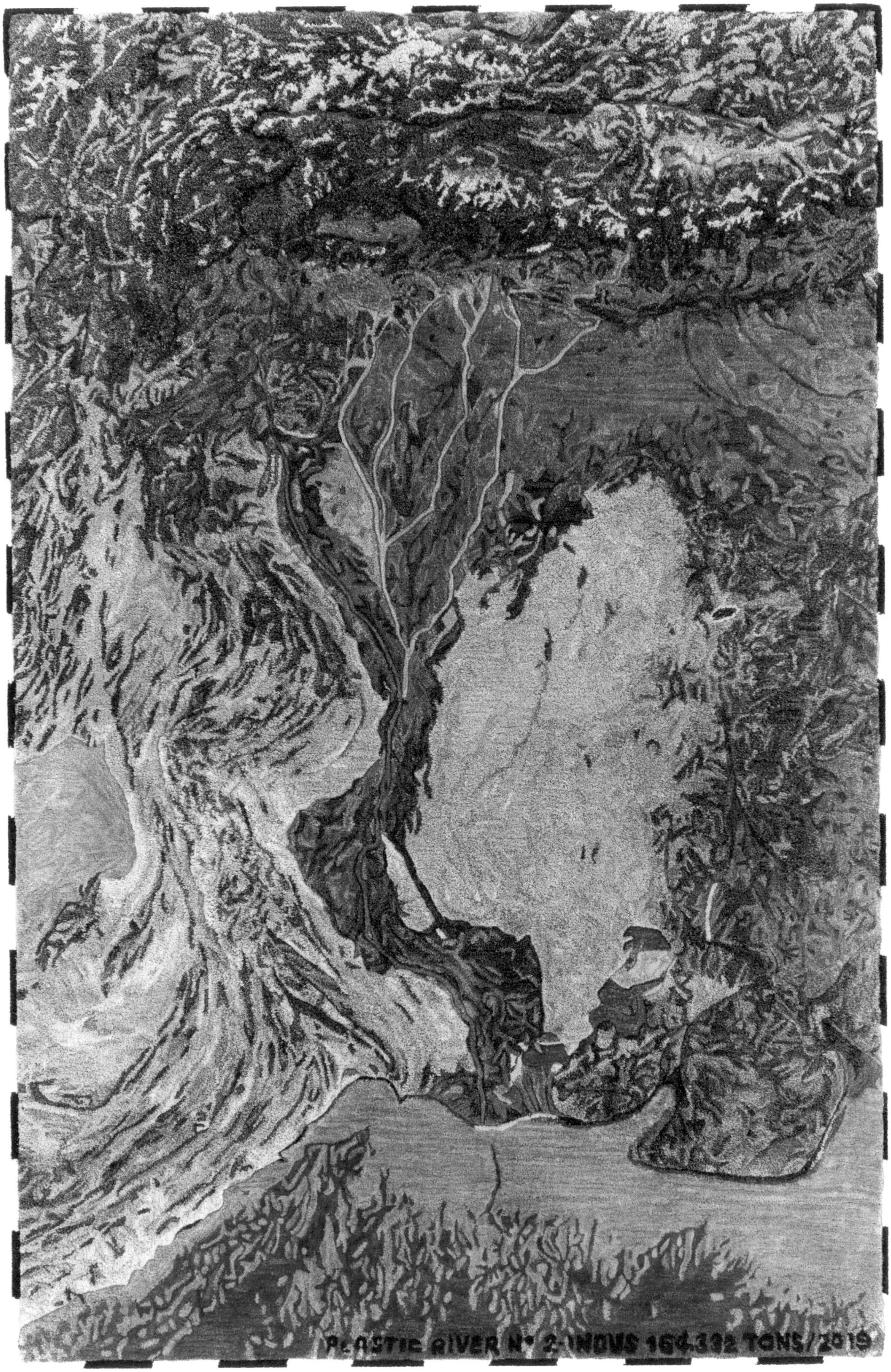

Plastic Rivers rug. Yarn from recycled PET bottles. ACdO with GAN's team of local artisans in India. 2022.

MARISOL CENTENO

Beneath the color-soaked surfaces of Marisol Centeno's contemporary textiles lie myriad questions—from design's role in contemporary society to how it can be a tool for change. Centeno, a textile designer based in Mexico City, has long been creatively fueled by an interest in exploring the stories, processes, and rituals embedded within everyday textiles. A desire for design to leave a positive imprint on society led her to spend a year with the artisan Zapotec community in Oaxaca, resulting in the launch in 2012 of Bi Yuu (Air and Earth). The brand produces traditional handwoven organic flatweave rugs, many with sunbursts of color and motifs inspired by Mexican Modernist architecture.

Centeno's creative explorations—and questioning—deepened in 2016 with the opening in Mexico City of Estudio Marisol Centeno, a space she views as a "laboratory" for textile experimentation. The studio has undertaken a raft of localized collaborations with high-profile brands, from hole-punched textile street installations for Adidas to elegantly woven vegetable fiber and metallic thread panels inspired by pre-Hispanic dancer headdresses for Cartier's Mexico City flagship.

Cochineal—and traditional Indigenous insect-dyeing techniques associated with it—is another focal point of Centeno's research, resulting in the woven wall piece *h22 c20 013* (2019). The textile displays a minimalist geometric motif connected to the molecular structure of cochineal, all in a vivid spectrum of naturally dyed shades of pink.

Meanwhile, the multicultural impact of design as a tool for social change remains at the forefront for Bi Yuu, which recently collaborated with weaving communities in Bhadohi, northern India, through GoodWeave International, a network of organizations that works to end illegal child labor in the textile industry. This collaboration evolved into "Anhelo," a capsule collection of hand-knotted and hand-tufted wool and bamboo-silk rugs made in Bhadohi, the craftsmanship balanced by designs inspired by late 1960s Mexican artworks.

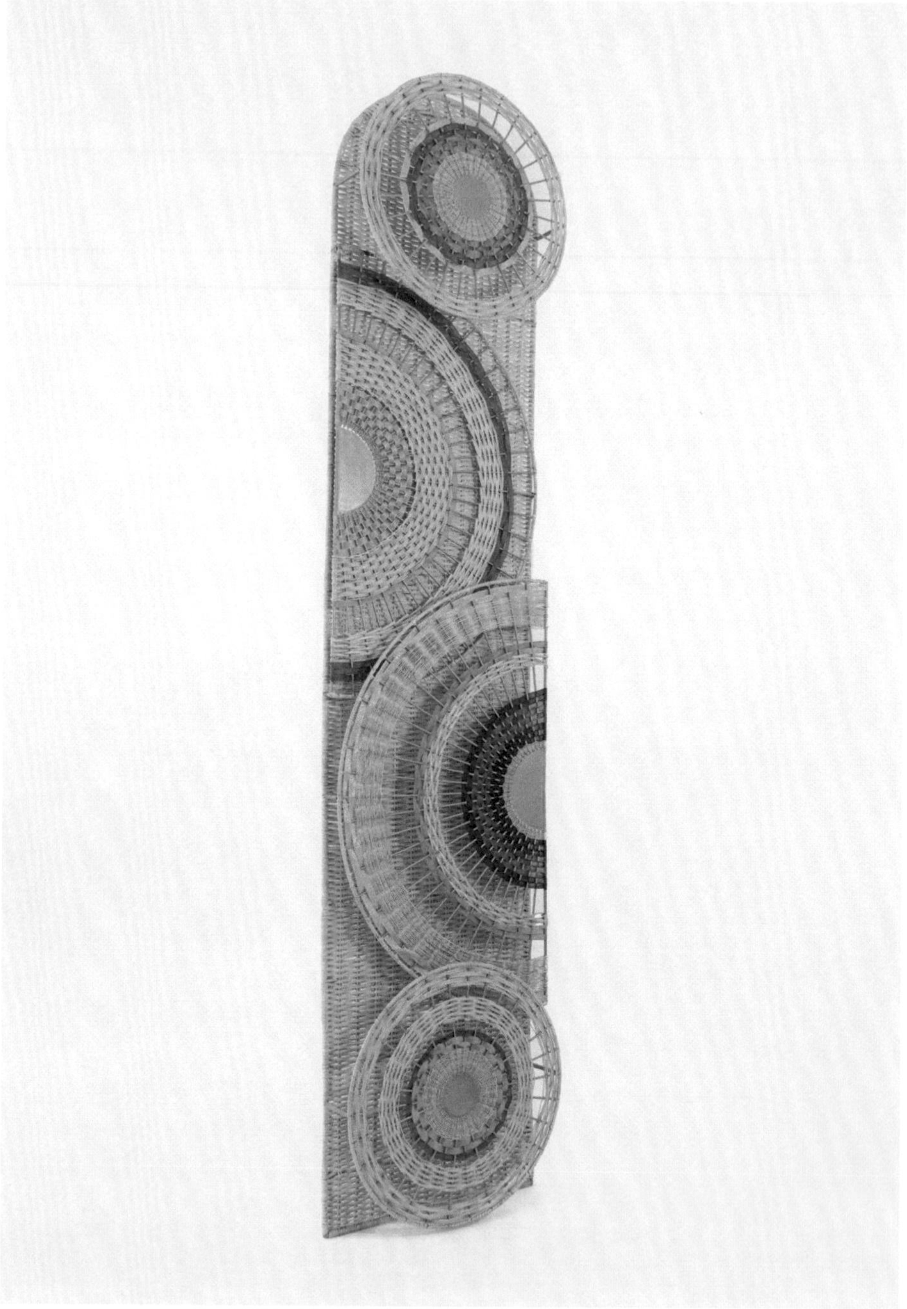

Chichini installation. Metal, vegetable fibers, cotton, metallic thread. Cartier. 2019.

"Quimera" tablecloth collection. Recovered cotton yarn and recycled PET bottles, jacquard weave. Bi Yuu. 2022.

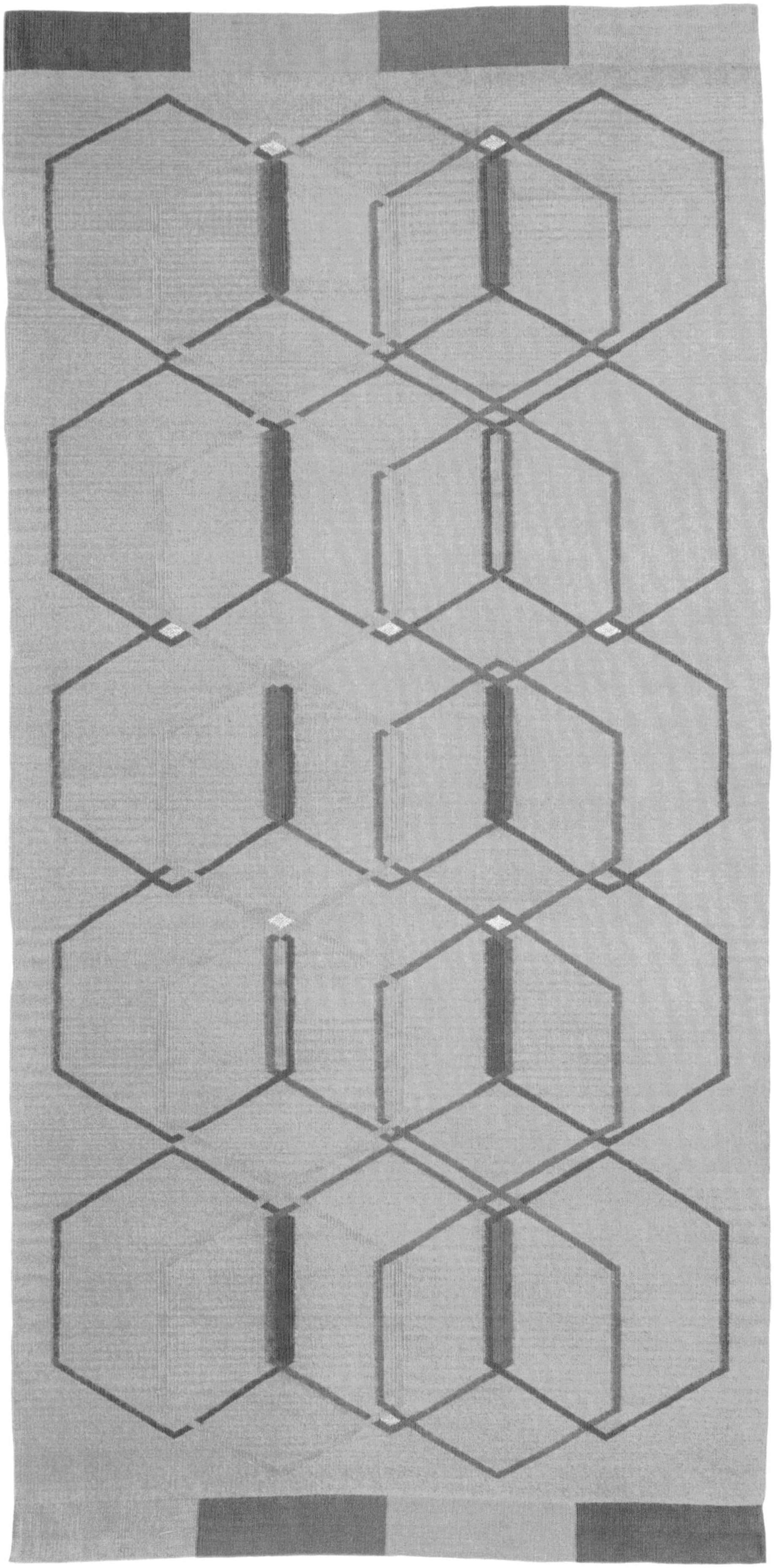

h22 c20 013 wall hanging tapestry. Alpaca, silk, cochineal dye. 2019.

“Anhelo” rug collection. Wool, bamboo. Bi Yuu. 2019.

MICHEL CHARLOT

PALMA chair. Beech. Sipa Sedie for Camper Goods. 2023.

Michel Charlot's work is informed by his faith in the principles of industrial design, belief in the efficiency of both product and process, and, finally, an almost dogmatic observance of Swiss tradition: methodical organization, formal rigor, and clean lines. Since graduating from ECAL (École cantonale d'art de Lausanne), in 2009, he has followed a considered path that has led him to design objects for the most important companies in European design. His collaboration with Jasper Morrison (p. 194) was an important chapter in his career. Viewing the world of the English master accelerated the development of Charlot's approach to design and helped him to achieve the professional maturity that today makes him a respected designer with a signature style.

Charlot's studio is in Porto, Portugal, and there, in 2019, he curated *Portugal Industrial* for the city's biennale. This experimental exhibition was dedicated to a series of successful episodes in the country's industrial production, and included designs by big brands and unknown designers alike.

Design, as a discipline, tames wild intuition and connects it to a system of objects that can help and support certain actions and encourage particular behavior. Charlot adheres strictly to this doctrine, to the extent that he has never worked on projects for galleries or created art editions. His research and practice are devoted to industry. The fields of application range from office and domestic furniture through utensils and accessories. In 2013 the U-turn lamp system (2012)—a sophisticated disc of LEDs with concave elements on the back that accommodate a supporting pivot topped by a sphere to move and adjust the direction of the light—won Charlot the prestigious Swiss Design Award.

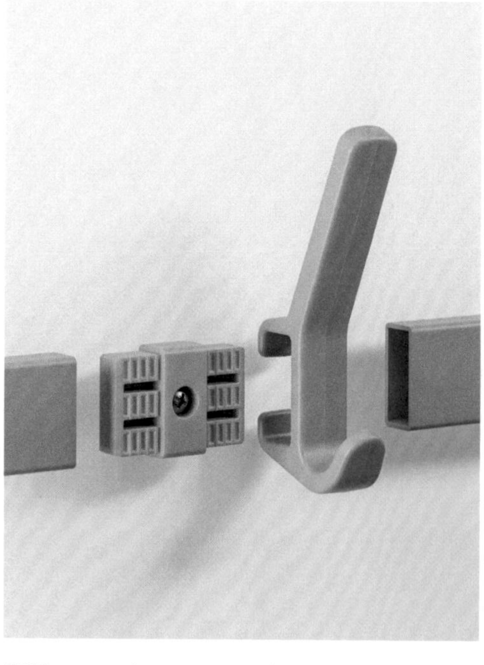

JUST coat rack. Aluminum, plastic. Van Esch. 2022.

Flokk Giroflex office chairs. Various materials. Flokk / Giroflex (not in production). 2019.

WALL display board. Various materials. Faust Linoleum. 2023.

PIERRE CHARPIN

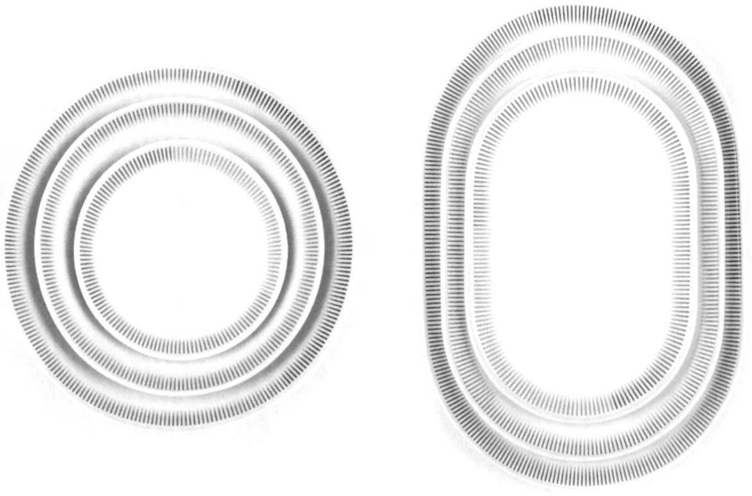

Outline tableware. Ceramic. Project assistant Aurélie Vial. 2018.

Be it a plate, a chair, or a spatial intervention, the poetics of color and geometry, infused with a softly sensual minimalism, are often threaded through the works of Pierre Charpin. The Paris-based creator found his way into the world of design in the early 1990s after training as an artist, a path that left an enduring imprint on his creative expression. Since then, during a decades-long career creating furniture and objects with countless creative partners—from Alessi to Hermès—he has consistently blurred the line between art and design.

Whether it's a limited-edition commission or an industrial product, the start of the creative process is always the same for Charpin: drawing. Elemental shapes and signature palettes are often the result of meticulous research into form and color, alongside a tactile warmth, as he explains: "I always imagine an object being touched." One example is the Astair armchair (2019) for Ligne Roset, the inspirational springboard of which was the mix of geometric simplicity and comfort in the Tre Pezzi armchair (1959) by the twentieth-century Italian designer Franco Albini with Franca Helg. The Astair, complete with ottoman, is defined by an integration of independent elements all softly padded.

Meanwhile, "Similitude(s)," showcased at Galerie kreo in Paris in 2020, is an exploration of color and geometry through a medley of products—vases, tables, mirrors—in a textured mix of materials, from glazed earthenware to metal. Among them is Translation, a coffee table with a clean-lined top of enameled lava stone in a deep ocean blue with abstract white and black inserts, on an aluminum frame.

Charpin has cast his creative gaze on almost every element of daily life, lighting included, as reflected in his popular "PC Lamp" series (2016–19) for HAY, which smoothly meshes a functional minimalism with his signature sensitivity to form and color.

Astair armchair. Steel, leather. Project assistant Florent Jullien for Ligne Roset. 2019.

Translation coffee table. Lava stone, metal. With Florent Jullien. 2020.

Cadence tableware. Crystal. Project assistant Aurélie Vial. 2018.

Self-produced chair. Painted plywood. Galerie Yvon Lambert. 2023.

“PC Lamp” series. Aluminum, steel, PC, silicone. With Mathieu Peyroulet Ghilini and Florent Jullien for HAY. 2016–19.

Lento armchair. Wood, leather, wool, and fabric. 2020.

FRANK CHOU

The Beijing-born designer Frank Chou has been making strides in the industry since founding his eponymous design studio in 2012. Named *GQ*'s Lifestyle Designer of the Year 2022, he recently partnered with Louis Vuitton to create furniture for the brand's travel-inspired collection "Objets Nomades," drawing inspiration for the organic silhouettes of his pieces from the topography of China's mountainous Yunnan province and the sandstone sweeps of Arizona's Antelope Canyon. These dramatic, weathered landscapes are natural correlates for Chou's design philosophy, since the designer's greatest wish is to make pieces that will stand the test of time.

Consequently, Chou is not afraid of putting the time in. Having worked in China and elsewhere, he decided to base his studio domestically, and found himself working in a start-up environment, organizing manufacturers and brands to create a streamlined, harmonious production process. The studio has a wide remit, encompassing product and space design as well as brand consultation and curation. The furniture Chou produces is sturdy, minimalist, and seemingly modular, although upon closer inspection each piece reveals a startlingly unique foundation.

An immediate eye-catcher among Chou's creations is the Balance dumbbell (2022), a relic of the ancient Greeks' pursuit of beauty and fitness, but also an undeniably modern object, a sleek cultural signifier in brass or polychrome. His Lento armchair (2020) offers a post-workout respite in restful green or tranquil ash-gray, with a wooden frame encased in luxuriously textured velvet or leather. But Chou's interest in designs of the past is entirely in the service of his commitment to making objects that are manifestly contemporary while promising to last. To this end, he believes that a designer should be at least in part an engineer, as well as an empathetic and observant collaborator—and, when the time comes, someone who insists on the strength of their vision.

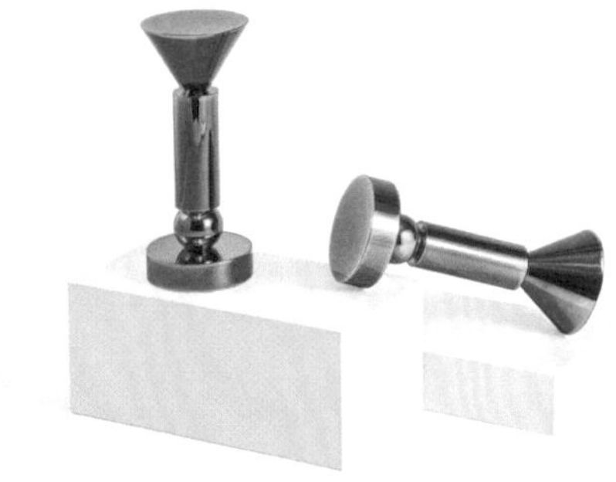

Balance polychrome dumbbells. Metal. 2022.

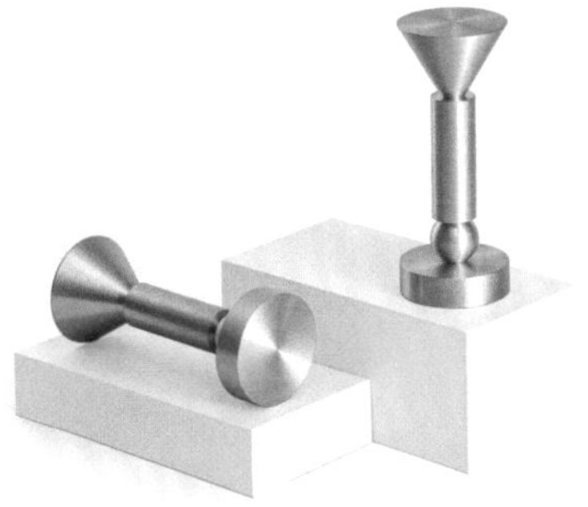

Balance brass dumbbells. Brass. 2022.

“Align” collection. Ceramic, thick glaze covering. 2021.

Performance Rearranged lighting installation and furniture. Steel, glass, LED. 2021.

PAUL COCKSEDGE

Paul Cocksedge is particularly recognized for creating illuminating work that surprises and delights. An appetite for mathematics, science, and design led him to carry out early experiments into electrical components, welding, and light, an interest that developed during his training at the Royal College of Art in London. Echoing the playful experimentation of his venerable tutor Ron Arad, Cocksedge is also animated by the capacity for materials and processes to shape design. Rather than conforming to a particular house style, his studio—which he founded in 2004 with Joana Pinho—recognizes the fundamental properties unique to each element. The broad appeal of his work transcends language and culture, and is reflected in clients and accolades that span Asia, Europe, the United States, and the United Kingdom.

Poised (2013) illustrates the designer's material exploration perfectly. Created from half a ton of sheet steel, the cantilevered table balances perfectly on a single surface. Despite the seemingly effortless way the thick slab of burnished steel hovers in midair, intensive calculations were required to wrangle gravity, mass, and equilibrium into an elegant industrial form.

Process is particularly evident in *Performance Rearranged* (2021). Here, contrasting materials unite in an integrated, performative piece in which the CNC-routed cherrywood mold for a mouth-blown glass lampshade is reworked and rearranged to create a burnished piece of furniture to sit beneath it.

The sense that a material has "come alive" in Cocksedge's hands also radiates from *Bourrasque* (2022), a permanent installation for Dior's venerable showroom at 30 avenue Montaigne in Paris. Reworking a commission for Lyon city council in 2011, *Bourrasque* creates a dramatic, performative element. The work, formed of acrylic and LED, resembles sheets of paper drifting on a breeze: a dynamic foil to Peter Marino's luxurious interiors. By night the laminated sheets glow, creating a captivating flight of fancy.

Poised table. Steel. 2013.

Slump Rock Table. Glass, rock. 2020.

Slump Bubble Table. Glass, mild steel. 2020.

Bourrasque Dior lighting installation. Acrylic, aluminum, LED. 2022.

MAC COLLINS

009 bowls. Finnish pine. Vaarnii. 2021.

The award-winning young artist and designer Mac Collins makes histories visible. He spent the early part of his time at university looking to European and Japanese furniture design, but became increasingly interested in mining his own British-Jamaican heritage. The brilliant result was his senior project in 2018, the stained ash Iklwa chair, inspired by Afrofuturism as much as an enthusiasm for the warmth and tactility of wood. With an oversize, shield-like wooden back and armrests resembling the Zulu iklwa spear, the chair is striking, a site to ennoble the sitter.

For Collins, the chair was a way to offer comfort and empowerment while keeping in mind generations of people who were denied these things. The design was picked up for mass-production by the furniture maker Benchmark, and Collins was off, winning the London Design Museum's inaugural prize for emerging designers in 2021 and participating in the UK pavilion at the 2023 Venice Biennale. His love affair with wood continues with such projects as the cherrywood Concur chair (2022) and its matching, multifunctional companion—footrest or side table—which invite the sitter to engage in relaxed yet rigorous contemplation. The 009 pine bowls Collins designed for Vaarnii in 2021 exemplify his usual sureness of line, the shallow concavity of the bowl sitting atop squat legs and showcasing the unique grain of the Finnish wood.

Collins, who cites the British artist Chris Ofili and American artist Theaster Gates as influences, is driven by a powerful sense of responsibility to his tradition and his peers as well as a love of creation, pushing him to engage with new materials and ideas. Most recently, he has been trying his hand at sand-casting aluminum and upholstering new pieces. He now teaches first-year students on the course he once took at Northumbria University in northeastern England, nurturing a host of visions for the future.

"Iklwa" collection side table. Oak. Benchmark Furniture. 2020.

"Ikiwa" collection statement lounge chair. Ash. Benchmark Furniture. 2020.

Concur lounge chair and companion. American cherrywood. Benchmark Furniture. 2021.

STEFAN DIEZ

Flexible and functional with a minimalist industrial design edge and an unwavering commitment to sustainability: these are all qualities that underpin products created by the German industrial designer Stefan Diez, whose output ranges from furniture and lighting to architectural elements. Diez is at the forefront of transforming ways of designing in today's world. This is reflected in his 10 Circular Design Guidelines, which highlight how commercially successful products can be environmentally and socially responsible.

For Diez, who founded Diez Office in Munich in 2002, the focus lies not only on form, function, and beauty, but also on the wider context of how contemporary objects can be developed and manufactured for the circular economy. This was the case with Costume for Magis (2021), which aims to rethink the meaning of a sofa in a sustainable context. The easily adaptable singular-unit modular sofa was designed with removable fabric covers on a structure 5⁄32 in (4 mm) thick made from recycled and recyclable polyethylene. To enhance sustainability, the studio explored the development of a new business model, which would enable Costume sofas to be returned by consumers before being recycled into new products.

Other products include Plusminus, a flexible lighting system with industrial simplicity designed for Vibia in 2021. A simple conductive textile ribbon that can be cut or adjusted enables the free placement of the luminaires through simply clicking and connecting. "Ayno" (2020) is another highlight—a contemporary riff on the iconic 1920s Midgard TYP 133, featured at the Bauhaus. The adjustable joint-free lighting system is defined by a slim curved rod of flexible fiberglass, to which two adjustment rings are attached, resulting in a smooth arc to which ultra-light cone-shaped lampshades can be attached.

The key thread connecting these creations is sensitivity to the climate and context surrounding the way everyday products are made and used today.

Boa table and Fuld chair. Various materials. Boa table: HAY; Fuld chair: Herman Miller. 2023.

Costume modular sofa system. Recycled propylene, fabric, and elastic. With Dominik Hammer for Magis. 2019.

Ayno lamp. Various materials. Midgard. 2020.

Plusminus lighting system. Various materials. With Karina Wirth and the Textile Prototyping LAB for Vibia. 2021.

Plusminus lighting system. Various materials. With Karina Wirth and the Textile Prototyping LAB for Vibia. 2021.

FRIDA FJELLMAN

Rök (Smoke) carafes. Glass. Svenskt Tenn. 2022.

I Himlen chandeliers. Glass and brass. Hostler Burrows. 2022.

It's entirely appropriate that the stopper in Frida Fjellman's Rök (smoke) glass carafe (2022) is shaped like a cloud of vapor or a plume of smoke. The carafe can be used as a pitcher or a vase, but in any configuration, it'll become a centerpiece. The tension between ethereal and material, the challenge of fixing something that's fundamentally in flux, is key to Fjellman's imaginative works. The multidisciplinary artist trained as a ceramicist and now works with glass, wood, and neon, creating fixtures, sculptures, and installations that offer an alternative to the pared-back minimalism that has come to be expected of Scandinavian design.

Recognized for her work at home in Sweden as well as elsewhere, Fjellman works on products for the historic Kosta Boda glassworks, while exhibiting her artwork and executing public and private commissions. Her jewel-like, prismatic chandeliers—including Pastellogrosso (2023), pendant lights reminiscent of aquatic lifeforms or video-game gems—set the scene for magic, a trip through a fantastic grotto or giant's cave. Depending on their installation, the colors, and the texture of the glass, the prisms "can be punk or romantic, classical or new," the designer says.

In drawing on Sweden's natural environment and its folkloric tradition, Fjellman has recourse to a rich range of moods and aesthetics, from the mildly mystical to the thrillingly intense. She also values the fantastical possibilities inherent in the material itself; her other series include glass animal vases and decorative statuettes of spirits, such as the emerald-green Ghost (2016). *She's Lost Control* (2019), an installation for the European Fine Art Fair in New York that suspends a network of hand-blown glass lightning bolts from the ceiling, is both a hovering reminder of the power of nature and a remarkable piece of artifice.

Venus in Glass sculpture. Glass, wood, argon tubing, steel. Swedish National Museum. 2017.

FORMAFANTASMA

Cambio exhibition furniture. A single tree blown over in a storm in northern Italy in 2018. 2020–21.

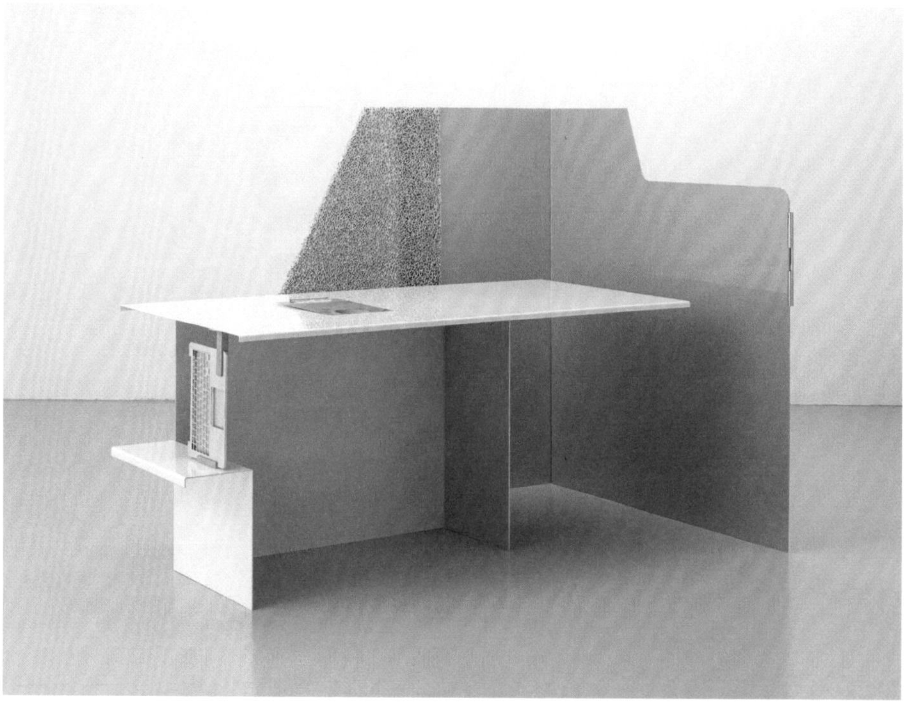

Ore Streams cabinet. Recycled iron, aluminum, computer cases, recycled electronic components. 2017–19.

Deep research and curiosity about material culture informs the work of Andrea Trimarchi and Simone Farresin of the award-winning practice Formafantasma. Their work is distinguished by a fusion of tactile and intellectual, with a motivation to use elements that are often considered waste.

Graduating from Design Academy Eindhoven in 2009, the pair had early breakthroughs including adaptations of scaly fish skin, cow bladders, and cork for Fendi's *Craftica* show (2012), and "De Natura Fossilum" (2014), a furniture collection for Libby Sellers (p. 7) created from Mt. Etna's basalt rock. A focus on the sustainable use of resources reads across their work, intersecting with "social, economic, geopolitical, and territorial" concerns.

The exhibition *Oltre Terra* ("Transhumance"), commissioned in 2023 by the National Museum of Norway, illustrates the interdependency of natural and built environments. The show set out historic and contemporary relations between humans and sheep—and, by extension, wool—through film, objects, and instruments. Mounted on tables to invite engagement, artifacts ranged from Norwegian sails and an ancient woolen tunic to Formafantasma's rug newly created with cc-tapis, using wool-fiber waste in four hues.

An examination of electronic waste occurs in *Ore Streams*, which debuted at the National Gallery of Victoria, Australia, in 2017, with a second iteration in *Broken Nature* at the 2018 Venice Triennale. A response to e-waste, *Ore Streams* presented research into the problematic accretion of this type of waste. Careful analysis was accompanied by a collection of office furniture composed of typical dismembered waste objects. Phone components, computer entrails, and aluminum casings were reassembled and transformed into cubicles, desks, file cabinets, and chairs, creating a refined suite of discarded materials.

Formafantasma continues to educate and fascinate with its thorough research and crafted design responses, working from its Rotterdam and Milan studios.

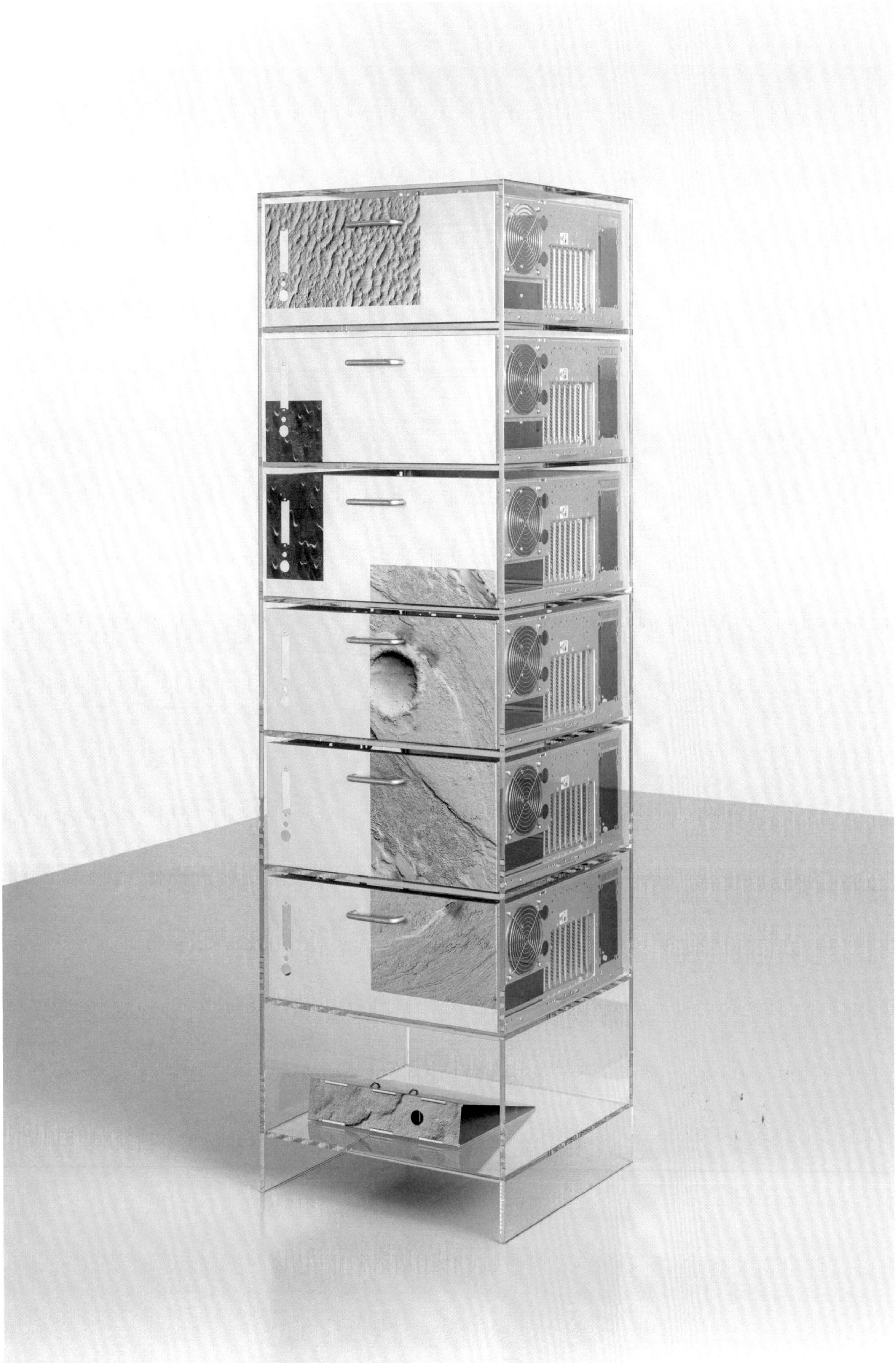

Ore Streams cabinet. Recycled iron, aluminum, deadstock of computer cases, and recycled electronic components. 2017–19.

Oltre Terra exhibition. Various materials. 2023.

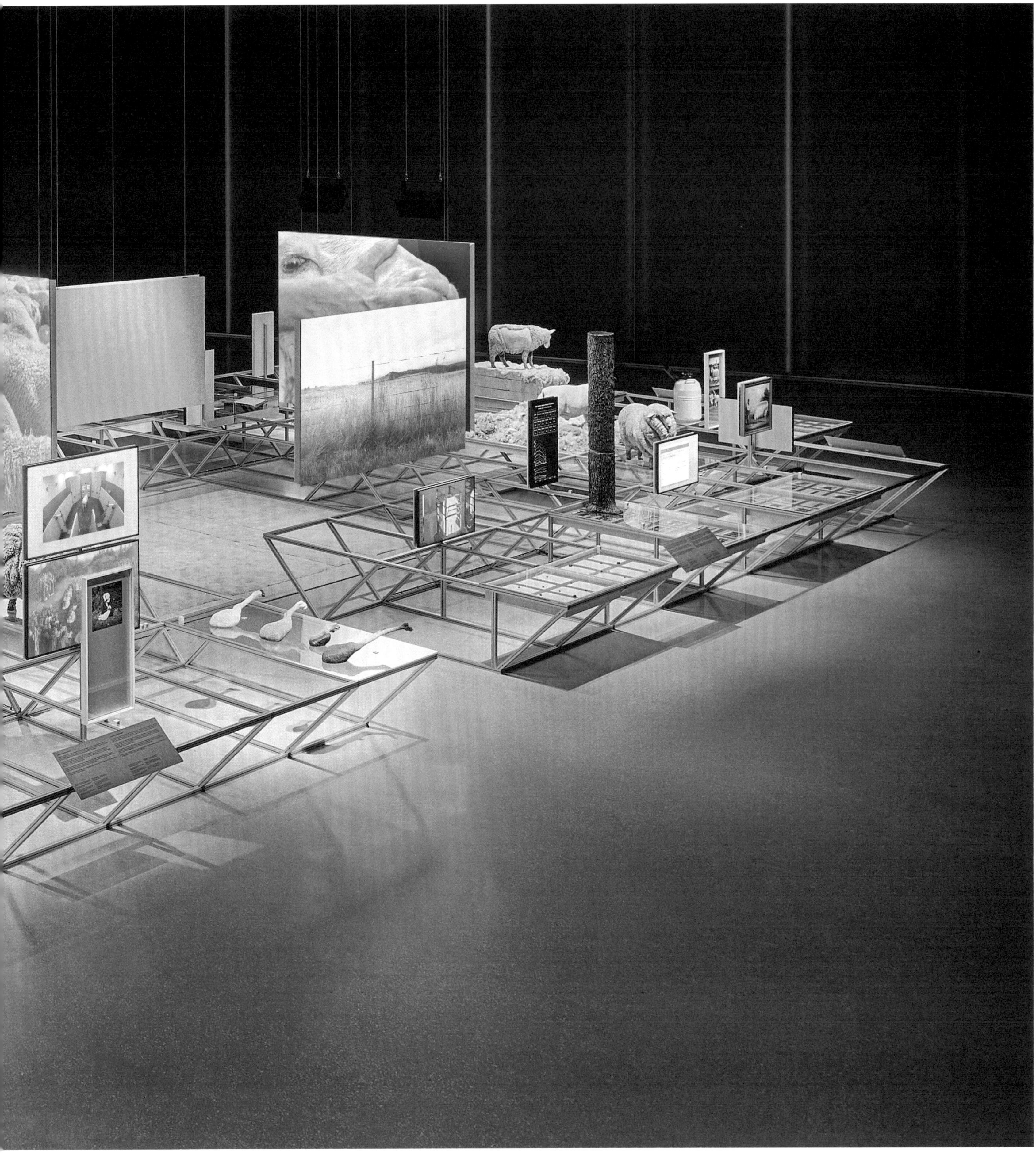

FRONT

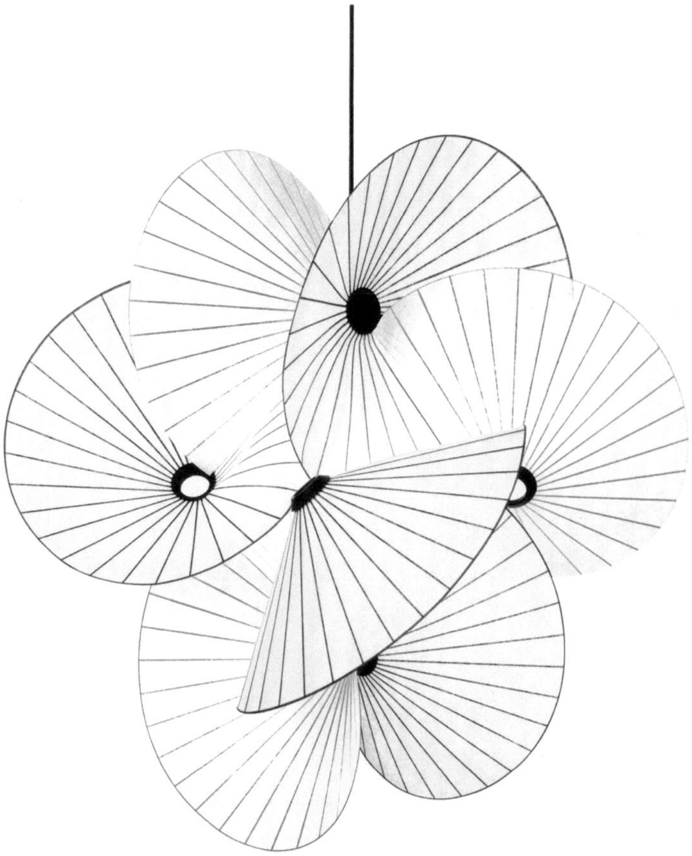

Serpentine Light. Printed non-woven PES, steel. Moooi. 2022.

Front, the Stockholm design studio Sofia Lagerkvist and Anna Lindgren founded with two other designers in 2003, is a front only for talent and an abiding belief in magic, which Lagerkvist and Lindgren share and which animates their work. The two met as students of industrial design at Konstfack (University of Arts, Crafts, and Design), Stockholm, where they bonded over their sense of humor and curiosity; their first project involved letting animals define the parameters of clothes hangers and wallpaper.

Front's lifelong fascination with the natural world gave rise to the "Pebble Rubble" collection of furniture (2022), produced by Moroso, which aims to bring people inside the designers' process of taking solace in nature. Through paintings, drawings, and 3D scans of the natural environment, Lagerkvist and Lindgren seek to re-create not just the colors and textures but also the atmosphere of a forest glade. Their fifteen-module set, along with three additional footstool pieces, can be arranged in a near-infinite number of configurations, once more allowing adults the childhood pleasure of playing with stones. Other rock-like furniture pieces are upholstered with the Arda textiles (2022) the duo designed for Kvadrat, echoing the fine gradations of color caused by minerals, or imitating the soft layers of moss and freshly fallen snow on a rocky surface.

Front's designs now sit in museum collections, public spaces, and private homes. But even when limiting itself to the indoor, domestic space, Front still exercises an enormous amount of freedom, roaming in time. The Bronze Mirror, exhibited in 2021 at the Parisian Galerie kreo, is inspired by small mirrors worn in ancient China, and the frame is crafted at the Marinelli Bell Foundry in Agnone, Italy, which has been operating since the fourteenth century. The Serpentine Light (2022) looks to paper-folding, its twisting form implying an eternally playful and beneficent dance of light.

Seven Stories About Mirrors, Obsidian Mirror. Various materials. Limited edition, Galerie kreo. 2021.

Design by Nature, Rock Pieces. Various materials. Moroso / More-So. 2021.

Design by Nature, Wilderness Sofa. Various materials. Moroso / More-So. 2021.

Seven Stories About Mirrors, Bronze Mirror. Various materials. Limited edition, Galerie kreo. 2021.

Seven Stories About Mirrors, Convex Mirror Vase. Various materials. Limited edition, Galerie kreo. 2021.

Pebble Rubble sofa system. Various materials. Moroso. 2022.

Seven Stories About Mirrors, Water Reflection Side Table. Various materials. Limited edition, Galerie kreo. 2021.

NAOTO FUKASAWA

Pao light. Polycarbonate. HAY. 2020.

Without thought. If there were just two words that summed up the quiet fusion of simplicity, beauty, and function that imbues the work of Naoto Fukasawa, it would perhaps be these. The influential Japanese designer is behind a decades-long output of intuitive products for the quotidian—from toasters and clocks to sofa systems—all fusing a low-key minimalism with seamless functionality.

Fukasawa, who launched his studio in 2003 and is globally acclaimed for his prolific Muji product development, has long highlighted the human-focused design philosophies that lie at the heart of his creations. Among them is the idea of "without thought"— tapping into the belief that the starting point of any design for daily life should be the observation of unconscious human behavior, in order to create a truly intuitive product. One celebrated example is his clean-lined wall-mounted CD player for Muji, a minimal white box operated by a simple tug of a cord.

Fukasawa's furniture design is no less intuitive. The Harbor Laidback lounge chair (2021) for B&B Italia balances an elegant presence with a sculptural lightness, reduced through its clean and minimal flowing lines to its essential form. The sensory experience of human comfort is another layer in Fukasawa's creative formula, as embodied by the Cinnamon armchair (2023) for Molteni&C. Inspired by "the feeling of being wrapped in a warm embrace," owners are invited to cocoon themselves in a seat that seemingly hovers inside a deep, minimal U-shaped curve of cushioning.

Meanwhile, Fukasawa's "Pao Portable Lamp" lighting series (2020) for HAY consist of lights in a trio of smooth, high-gloss shades (gray, red, black), their lit form echoing the glow of a Mongolian *pao* tent after dark. Ease of use is, as always, quietly intuitive, and the efficiently concealed light source and compact battery operation enable users to enjoy it effortlessly—and without thinking.

Cinnamon armchair. Various materials. Molteni&C. 2023.

Harbor Laidback lounge chair. Various materials. B&B Italia. 2021.

GAMFRATESI

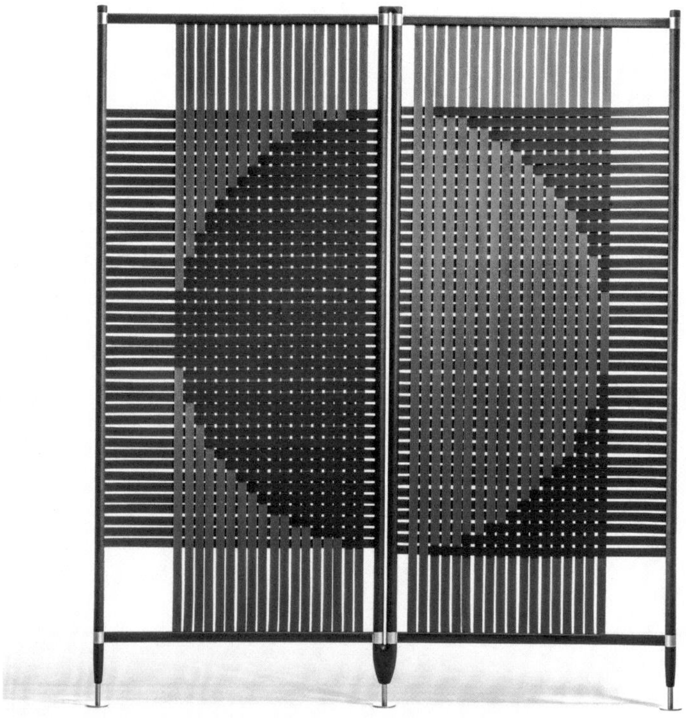

Plot room divider. Aluminum, moka ash finish. Poltrona Frau. 2021.

The stylistic trademark of GamFratesi is careful, measured minimalism. The fusion of two worlds—the Danish tradition of furniture and craft, and an intellectual and conceptual approach that is typically Italian—has marked out a clear path for the studio's design methods and production.

It was destiny that united both life and work. Enrico Fratesi and Stine Gam developed their method by studying and training in Italy, Denmark, and Japan. They are now based in Copenhagen, and these stylistic influences and a European flavor are still evident in their work. The Doric coffee table (2022), for example, is a response to the architectural traditions of the Classical era, taking its name from the Doric order of ancient Greek, and later Roman, architecture.

The main areas of the studio's work are furniture, interiors, and accessories, and its output includes a collection of objects that constitute the landscape of many restaurants, hotels, and residences it has designed around the world. Among these items of furniture is the Beetle chair (2013), a design that has been an enormous commercial success, with an ergonomic, organic form inspired by the shape of a beetle's forewings. Fratesi and Gam draw on nature and the world around them, borrowing codes and color palettes that they convey in their projects, particularly in the spaces they design, which always evoke the warmth and emotion of domesticity.

As a champion of understated elegance, GamFratesi has often been invited to collaborate with international luxury brands. Wood, combined with upholstery and fabrics, is undoubtedly one of the studio's favorite materials, although it is not afraid to venture into technology and consumer electronics. Indeed, the Beosound A5 (2023), another of the studio's works, is one of the most powerful and acoustically advanced speakers currently on the market.

Beosound A5 portable speaker. Aluminum, polymer, paperweave, oak. Bang & Olufsen. 2023.

Miau armchair. Oak. KOYORI. 2022.

Doric table. Travertine. GUBI. 2022.

Shelley armchair. Various materials. Minotti. 2019.

Violin chair. Various materials. GUBI. 2021.

MARTINO GAMPER

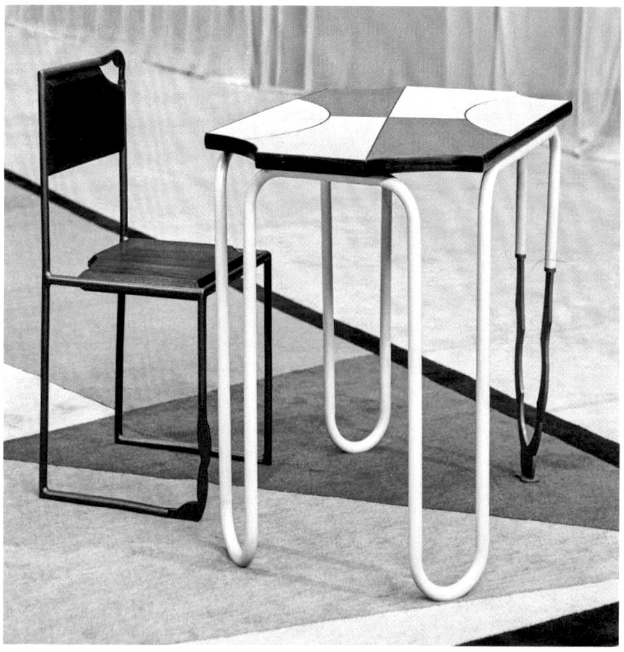

Innesto Furniture: Cathedra Equisetifolia, Tabula Floridum, and Tapete Entrance Carpet. Various materials. 2021.

Martino Gamper's designs and exhibitions have a sketch-like immediacy, dreamed up and swiftly manifested using a near-infinite variety of methods, materials, and techniques. *I Am Many Moods*, an exhibition held at Anton Kern Gallery, New York, in 2023, featured just short of 1,000 hooks and vases, crafted from the expected materials, such as glass and metal, as well as more surprising ones, among them branches, cork, and stones. It constituted a designer's sketchbook in three dimensions, a collection of iterations on a platonic ideal that this merry array brought into question.

Gamper was born in South Tyrol, Italy, apprenticed there, and traveled the world before studying at the Academy of Fine Arts Vienna and London's Royal College of Art. He now works on interior and product design and commissions for clients through his East London studio, established in 2000, but the freedom to wander is still crucial for him. In his design universe, the best objects aren't necessarily the perfect ones but rather those that will remain in use long after their making. Sheer numbers, in that case, are on his side—in a frenzy of experimentation, surely such objects will arise.

Gamper burst onto the scene in 2007 with a spree of chairs. In the project "100 Chairs in 100 Days," he used found and donated objects in a daily making practice (he has kept the spirit of the project going by making a new chair each time the group is exhibited). Bricolage remains central to his work, but the chairs he admires most are Gio Ponti's classic, lightweight Superleggera (1951–7) and Enzo Mari's minimalist, nylon-and-aluminum Tonietta (1985). Gamper's own Aloïse Chair (2021), a reconsideration of Christian Dior's Louis XVI-inspired Medallion chair, suspends the upholstered dual-color back panel, making a bezel of the chair's frame. This playfulness combined with an appreciation for classicism is a testament to Gamper's range.

I Am Many Moods hooks and vases. Various materials. 2023.

AlpiNN restaurant design. Various materials. AlpiNN. 2018.

“100 Chairs in 100 Days” project. Discarded chairs and found materials. 2007.

KONSTANTIN GRCIC

Noctambule lamp. Blown glass, LED. Flos. 2019.

The Bell chair (2020) has an eggshell-like seat, four C-shaped legs, and a lightweight injection-molded form of 100 percent recyclable polypropylene repurposed from the producer's own industrial waste. It is meticulously designed to be affordable and sustainable, with a smoothly clean and minimal silhouette.

The Munich-born designer Konstantin Grcic has spent more than three decades designing—and redesigning—the objects that fill daily life. With a focus on function before form, his designs are often defined by rigorously researched technology, a near-spartan efficiency, and an elemental sensitivity to the manufacturing process and its social context—typically packaged in a minimalist simplicity of form.

Trained first as a cabinetmaker, Grcic went on to study design at the Royal College of Art in London before setting up his own studio in 1991 in Germany. Today, Konstantin Grcic Design in Berlin is behind a powerhouse constellation of creative projects, including industrial products, design editions, exhibitions, and architectural and fashion collaborations. For all its functionality, his work often has an element of playfulness—as reflected in Arcobaleno (2023), a sunshine-burst of brightly colored indoor wooden wall tiles for ALPI. The name, Italian for "rainbow," taps into the wood veneer's layered tonalities, with gradated shades carefully engineered through a programmed sequence following in-depth research and development.

Much of Grcic's work blurs the boundaries of art and technology, as is the case with the Noctambule lamps (2019), a series of six blown-glass lighting modules for Flos, inspired by night owls. Stacked on the floor or suspended collectively as chandeliers, these clear cylindrical lights are almost invisible by day, yet dramatically transform spaces with their delicately sculptural illuminated forms after dark.

Grcic's is a creative vision that results in a beauty born from efficiency, simplicity, and meticulous attention to process, whether it's an art installation-like lighting system or a recyclable polypropylene chair.

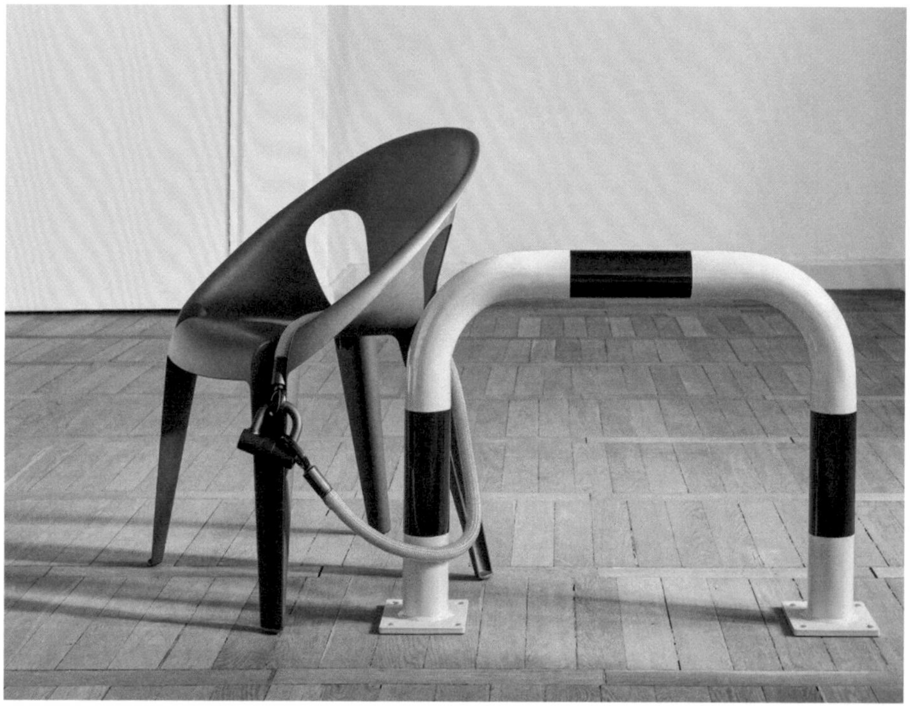

Bell chair. Recycled polypropylene. Magis. 2020/2022.

Arcobaleno and Raggiosole veneers. Wood. ALPI. 2023.

GT2P

The topography of the Chilean Andes is the creative starting point for "Remolten" (2019), a series of products ranging from chairs to tables, crafted from a reformation of volcanic rock harvested from the mountain range. This is one of myriad exploratory research projects masterminded by gt2P ("great things to People"), a studio collective based in Santiago.

The studio was founded in 2009 by a quartet of creatives—Guillermo Parada and Tamara Pérez, who met studying architecture, alongside Sebastián Rozas and Victor Imperiale. Since then, the team have carved a singular, experimental path through the creative world, by applying a methodology they have dubbed "paracrafting," referring to a parametric intersection of art, science, cultural, and material context plus modern production processes.

The results range from materials to public space. Among them is *Suple: Connecting Form* (2018), an abstract nodular installation inspired by the Chilean construction industry slang word "supple," loosely translated as an element that connects or functions in an improvised, flexible manner. With an array of angular linear elements intersecting at a single point, its molecule-like form was calculated from a 3D convex hull polygon before being rendered in bronze, cast by lost wax from a digitally carved mold. Its versatility fuels countless forms and functions, including the *Suple: Connecting Form* bench permanently installed in the garden of the Design Museum, London.

Meanwhile, the playfully poetic series "Imaginary Geographies" (2018) aims to embody a "geometric and material reconstruction" of the Andes. The starting point is an audio composition mingling mountain sounds with a poem. Sound frequencies are digitally transformed into lines, then brought to life through wood carving, with surfaces that reflect the undulating peaks of the Andes. The resulting pieces include a circular coffee table in the Chilean wood *lenga* (Patagonian cherrywood) with a lake-like expanse of black basalt on its surface, around which the wood rises up like the Andes.

Suple: Connecting Form. Bronze, stainless steel, volcanic rock. 2018.

Conscious Actions installation. Powder-coated steel. 2020.

Less CPP N2 Porcelain vs Lava Lights. Porcelain, volcanic lava rock, LED, brass. 2014.

Imaginary Geographies Coffee Table. *Lenga* and black basalt. 2018.

Remolten Monolita Chair. Stoneware, volcanic lava. 2019.

Monople Sideboard. Lacquered ash. 2021.

GUNJAN GUPTA

Ikkis tea set. Terracotta-coated copper. Studio Wrap. 2020.

Gunjan Gupta's New Delhi-based Studio Wrap is named after the traditional Indian craft of silver-wrapping furniture. Establishing the studio in 2006 to work on luxury interiors and product design, Gupta took inspiration from the perceived purity of silver and the deft handling necessary to "wrap" it. Her studio's creations likewise strive for unity of concept and masterful execution. Born in Mumbai, India and trained at Central Saint Martins in London, Gupta draws on an international archive of design but works chiefly with local materials, including bamboo, tin, jute, terracotta, and stone, to express her vision in sustainable terms.

The Matka Table (2013) is a perfect synthesis of Gupta's entrepreneurial mindset and loyalty to place. Fashioned from copper, wood, and red sandstone, it features a tabletop resting on a water pitcher, a solid structure that transforms a familiar object into a surprisingly functional *objet d'art*. But the *pièce de résistance* may well turn out to be her Mudawalla Bicycle Throne (2016). Simultaneously delicate and bombastic, it is composed of bamboo stools and bicycle parts, supported by a steel frame. It gives the royal treatment to the relics of a legion of cycling salespeople, once ubiquitous but perhaps soon to disappear from India's city streets. Gupta's Boriwala Bicycle Throne (2008), now part of the permanent collection of the Vitra Design Museum, is another paean to a humble profession, constructed of found parts and referencing the outsize loads regularly transported by tradespeople in India.

Gupta also founded Ikkis (2019), a design brand supplying objects for contemporary homes. From a copper-and-terracotta kettle (Chai Surahi; 2020) to the limited-edition Shatranj chessboard (2020), crafted in collaboration with a pair of local artisans from metal and earth found at the site of the historic Bidar Fort in central India, the brand provides thoughtful and unique touches, always in line with Gupta's overarching vision.

"Tantra" collection. Glass, brass, enamel. Studio Wrap. 2020.

Mudawalla Bicycle Throne. Bamboo, steel, recycled bicycle parts. Studio Wrap. 2016.

Matka Mix Coffee Table. Red sandstone, copper, wood. Studio Wrap. 2013.

Aloo Bori sofa. Jute, foam, steel. Studio Wrap. 2016.

JAIME HAYON

Spanish-born and -based Jaime Hayon creates designs that are "made for humans" with the hope of provoking happiness in those who use his pieces. This benevolent attitude has created a spirited oeuvre that spans art, interiors, and products. He broke onto the design scene in the early twenty-first century with glossy, vibrant interpretations of Spanish culture, and these early works—particularly the ceramics—drew attention for their distinctive ability to interpret and broadcast Iberian sensibilities through contemporary design. His work also conveyed a revived interest in fusing craft with industrial design, an approach that has since burgeoned.

Local culture, artisanal techniques, and a strong dose of humor continue to read across Hayon's work. For BD Barcelona's "Dino" series (2020), he created an irreverent take on the wingback chair, disrupting the classically serious character of such a seat. With a long neck, a squat body, and short arms, the chairs recall the proportions of a brontosaurus and perch on skinny powder-coated legs of cast aluminum. Rendered in ocher, taupe, and umber hues, as well as classic charcoal and teal, the shape and detailing are typically Hayon.

Likewise, the "T-Bone" series (2021) for Ceccotti Collezioni, Italy, renders Hayon's irrepressible spirit in a refined language of natural materials. Composed of ash or walnut "bones" fleshed out with upholstery pads and backrests in leather or wool, the armchairs bear expressed T-shaped timber joints. Smoothly finished and tapering to almost cartoonish proportions, the frames are a cheeky nod to the beefy skeleton after which the series is named.

Having enjoyed commissions from some of the world's largest and most respected producers—Bisazza, Zara, Fritz Hansen, and Cassina, to name a few—Hayon has a reputation cemented by accolades from *Time* magazine, *Wallpaper**'s Top 100 and several *Elle Decoration* awards.

Frames chairs. Rattan. Expormim. 2019.

Vuelta lounge chair. Wood, fabric. Wittmann. 2017–23.

Dino lounger seater. Wood, fabric. BD Barcelona. 2020.

T-Bone lounger seaters. Wood, fabric. Ceccotti Collezioni. 2021.

MOISÉS HERNÁNDEZ

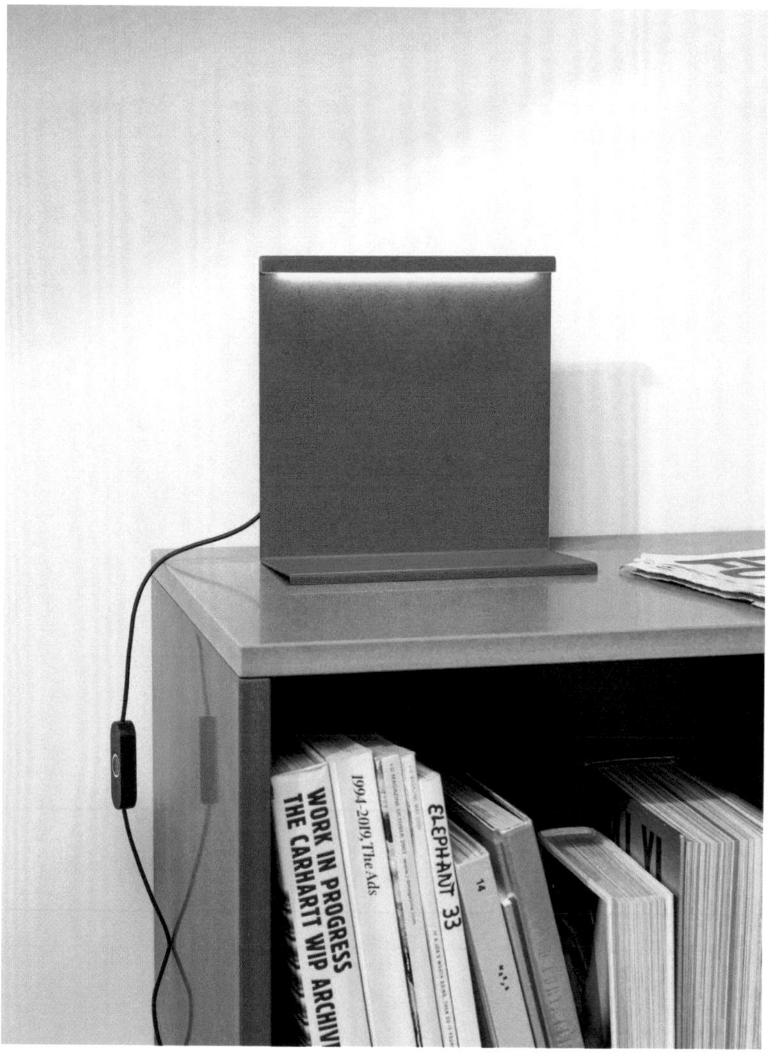

LBM Table Lamp. Steel, LED. 2022.

For Moisés Hernández, color—as etched in many shades across his vibrant Mexican homeland—is often the starting point. He set up his studio in Mexico City in 2014, after graduating from ECAL (École cantonale d'art de Lausanne) as a Master of Product Design. The vivid tones and high tempo of the city seep into many of his creations for daily life, tempered by a signature simplicity of form and a contemporary aesthetic, plus a sensitivity to ancestral Mexican culture and traditions. Grana Chair (2021)—a color study in the medium of wood—is one such highlight. Hernández experimented with immersing different woods in hot water with cochineal beetles, in an echo of traditional Mexican textile dyeing methods. He discovered that alkaline elements resulted in the color evolving into purples and scarlet, while acid elements created vibrant red-orange tones. This led to a collection of two clean-lined maple chairs: one dyed a warm fusion of shades created by both alkaline and acid elements; the other a boldly monotone pink.

The colorful monolithic structures synonymous with the iconic Mexican architect Luis Barragán inspired the creation of LBM Table Lamp (2022), for HAY. A reflection of Hernández's fascination with the dynamic between color, light, and shadow, the lamps are crafted with minimalist simplicity from a simple, thin plane of vertical sheet steel. They are available in an inventive array of colors, from Titanium Yellow and Clay to Luis Pink.

Textures, traditions, and craftsmanship are also key ingredients in Hernández's studio's creative vernacular, as embodied in Mestiza (2020), an elegant chair with curved lines, a U-shaped base, and woven textile all inspired by the traditional Mexican *equipale* chair. Exploring the world of color remains a key focus for Hernández, who since 2021 has been working as a color designer for Apple in California.

Mestiza chair (left). Steel, nylon cord, palm leaves. Mexa. 2020.

Grana Chair. Maple, cochineal dye. 2021.

MARLÈNE HUISSOUD

From Insects vases. Propolis. 2014.

"Cocoon" collection bench. Silkworm cocoons, honeybee bio resin, oak. 2017.

Please Stand By insect hotels. Unfired clay, natural binders, wood. With Robert Francis and Brandon Mak. London. 2019.

It's no typical beehive. Instead, picture a log-shaped body on four legs, crafted from red oak scorched black, engraved, and varnished with propolis, a resinous material produced by bees to seal gaps in hives. This is Beehave (2019), one of many creations that make up the singular and unwaveringly inventive world of Marlène Huissoud.

The French designer and artist is increasingly renowned for her progressive imaginings of the natural world and the challenges it faces today. The foundation of her attraction to the ever-shifting dynamic between humans and nature is perhaps rooted in her childhood, spent in the French Alps, the daughter of a beekeeper. It was while she was studying material futures at Central Saint Martins in London that a signature project was born: "From Insects," a deep dive into the materials that make up insects.

Other highlights include "Cocoon," an exploration of silkworm cocoons as a material. In a consciously slow process, thousands of cocoons were accumulated and varnished with natural honeybee resin, resulting in otherworldly black, organic abstractions.

In *Mamá* (2022), bees are not only the focal point, but also co-creators. This site-specific work at SFER IK in Tulum, Mexico, spotlights endangered native stingless Melipona bees, which are regarded as sacred in Mayan culture. Huissoud sculpted seven beehives from a local vine known as *bejuco*, and finished them in dung, ash, clay, and cactus wax. She then encouraged the participation of the bees in the artwork's evolution.

"Please Stand By" (2019) consists of "hotel" refuges for London's insect pollinators, crafted from primitive unfired clay, natural binders, and wood, with perforations up to 4 in (10 cm) deep to accommodate visiting insects. As with many of Huissoud's projects, the poetic form of the hotels is underpinned by an acute awareness of humankind's imprint on nature.

Mamá bee habitat. Various materials. With AZULIK Workshops for SFER IK. 2022.

YINKA ILORI

Visitors enter Yinka Ilori's studio in the industrial neighborhood of Park Royal, west London, through brightly colored, arched doorways. Amid the area's former munitions factories, concrete, and corrugated metal, it's like walking into Candyland: powder-puff-pink brick, diaphanous curtains, scarlet industrial shelving, technicolor walls, and, above the kitchen sink, the message "Love Always Wins" in a 1970s bubble font. Unapologetically optimistic, Ilori tells stories and brings people together through color, pattern, light, and joy.

Of British and Nigerian heritage, Ilori was raised on a council estate in Islington and studied art and design at London Metropolitan University before working in the studio of the British designer Lee Broom. Inspired by West African textiles, Nigerian fables, and oral tradition (and, at first, by upcycling second-hand furniture), he went solo in 2011 and launched his studio in 2015. Today, he and his "color-obsessed" team make architecture, sculpture, furniture, playgrounds, pop-ups, interiors, and graphic design for clients ranging from Courvoisier and Adidas through Lego, Pepsi, and Pinterest.

Colour Palace (2019), a temporary, flexible pavilion for the Dulwich Picture Gallery during the London Festival of Architecture (made in collaboration with Pricegore architects), was constructed from thousands of pieces of hand-painted wood, its facade layered with bold patterns that shifted as visitors moved around it. The *Launderette of Dreams* (2021), using 200,000+ LEGO bricks, was an interactive art installation and play space that echoed Ilori's childhood efforts to make adventures out of the everyday. Transforming common objects from ordinary to enchanted, he turned laundry drums into kaleidoscopes and added murals, hopscotch flooring, and vending machines that dispense LEGOs instead of detergent. *Listening to Joy* (2022) at the V&A Dundee was another interactive playscape. Walls sewn from zippable mesh formed a reconfigurable maze, and visitors played two circular xylophones, recording and mixing a soundtrack that captured the joy elicited inside.

Colour Palace pavilion. Hand-painted timber. With Pricegore. 2019.

If Chairs Could Talk. Upcycled chairs. 2015.

Launderette of Dreams interactive art installation and play space. Various materials. 2021.

YES TO
BALL GAMES

INDUSTRIAL FACILITY

Collaborating between London and California, Industrial Facility is the transatlantic duo of Sam Hecht and Kim Colin. Of British and American descent respectively, the pair have built their career working closely with industry to refine and rethink products. This approach has won them a roster of eminent clients that includes Thonet, Muji, Google, and Herman Miller. Their calling card is simplicity of line paired with technical innovation, producing wholly contemporary design solutions with a quiet aesthetic.

A commission from the British company Pure Audio, for instance, involved revisiting the humble radio—a small product with diminishing appeal in the smartphone age. Internet radio (2022) is the result: a compact, stripped-back box with a subtle tilt that answers the basic principles of broadcasting radio. Restraint is the key to its appeal. Instead of including myriad functions, the design focuses on producing excellent sound and integrating navigation buttons seamlessly, while the digital channel finder and C-shaped cylindrical aluminum handle fold away neatly.

The S 220 chair for Thonet (2022) is another instance of Industrial Facility reworking and updating references to a beloved product. Continuing Thonet's tradition of molded plywood seating, S 220 combines a gently curving bentwood arm, a molded one-piece plywood seat and back, and tubular-steel legs. Its comfortable, stackable form is freshly modern, but also recalls the sinuous details of Thonet's 214 and 209 chairs, as well as the plywood classics of Norman Cherner and Arne Jacobsen.

In Industrial Facility's skilled hands, less is never a bore, but rather a quiet celebration of design essence. This consistent, careful approach has distinguished them as Royal Designers of Industry and Royal Society of Arts Fellows, while their works feature in significant collections, among them the Museum of Modern Art and the Cooper Hewitt in New York, the Victoria and Albert Museum and the Design Museum in London, and Centre Pompidou in Paris.

Hover sit-stand table. Various materials. Herman Miller. 2023.

Internet radio. Various materials. Pure Audio. 2022.

Powerbox. Lithium phosphate battery. Herman Miller. 2023.

S 220 chair. Plywood, walnut veneer. Thonet. 2022.

Palco outdoor sofa. Water-dispersing cushioning, teak. Kristalia. 2021.

ISPA (NIKE)

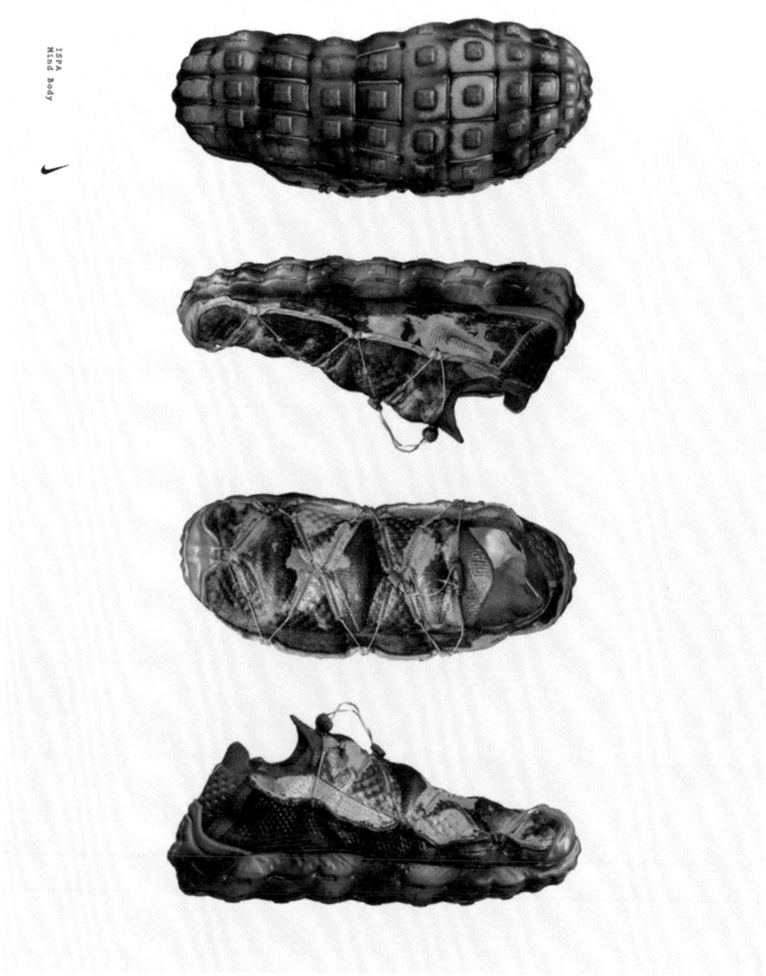

Nike ISPA MindBody footwear. Flyknit, algae inks. Nike. 2023.

ISPA is a creative engine driving experimentation across the athletic brand Nike. Part of the Nike Design department, the ten-person "micro-collective" works to challenge the status quo, fuel innovation, simplify production, and increase sustainability. ISPA is an acronym that describes the team's values and methods: Improvise. Scavenge. Protect. Adapt. Team members constantly test their assumptions, thinking, searching, and working hands-on to find the best materials, whether conventional or unconventional. Then they improve, adapt, evolve, and reuse their solutions to achieve the broadest possible applications.

Evolving old materials and methods while drawing new inspiration and typologies into the mix, ISPA designed Nike's Drifter footwear (2021). Drifter takes cues from the Japanese *tabi* workman's boot and the brand's Air Rift (1996), a sneaker-sandal hybrid. Drifter's split-toe construction, lightweight upper, and responsive foam technology make it agile, while external webbing gives it stability. Recycling one of Nike's proprietary foams for the first time, the team iterated and reiterated to find its optimal chemistry and form. Finally, after doing some skillful "scavenging," they tapped the Japan-based company BUAISOU, which creates indigo from cultivation through hand-dyeing, to give the shoes an artisanal finish, ensuring no two Drifters are alike.

ISPA's Universal (2020) used artificial intelligence to create a mash-up of four heritage footwear silhouettes. That form was then built from sugarcane-based Bio-EVA foam with cork insoles and fully replaceable components that allow customers to extend the life of their shoes. Among other reused materials, the Link Axis shoe (2023) has a 100 percent recycled upper and TPU tooling made from Nike air bag scrap material, reducing waste from the get-go. But it can also be completely disassembled at the end of its life, making it easier to recycle and reuse its components once more. When done right, the shift to a circular economy leads to greater creativity and innovation, not less. Just ISPA it.

Nike ISPA Drifter footwear. Recycled Nike Grind ZoomX foam. With BUAISOU for Nike. 2021.

Nike ISPA Overreact Flyknit footwear. Flyknit, React foam technology. Nike. 2020.

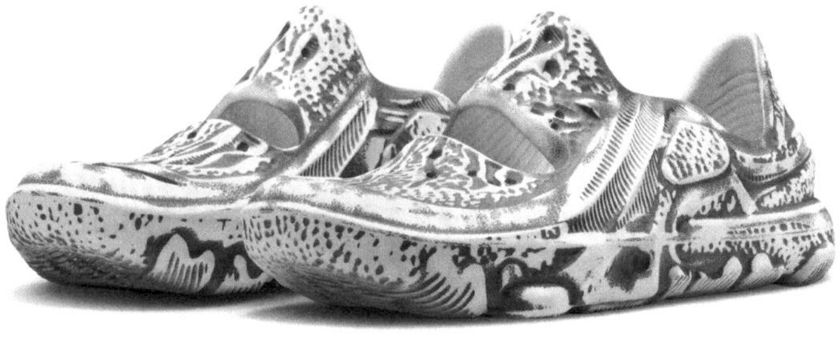

Nike ISPA Universal footwear. Bio-EVA foam technology, cork. Nike. 2023.

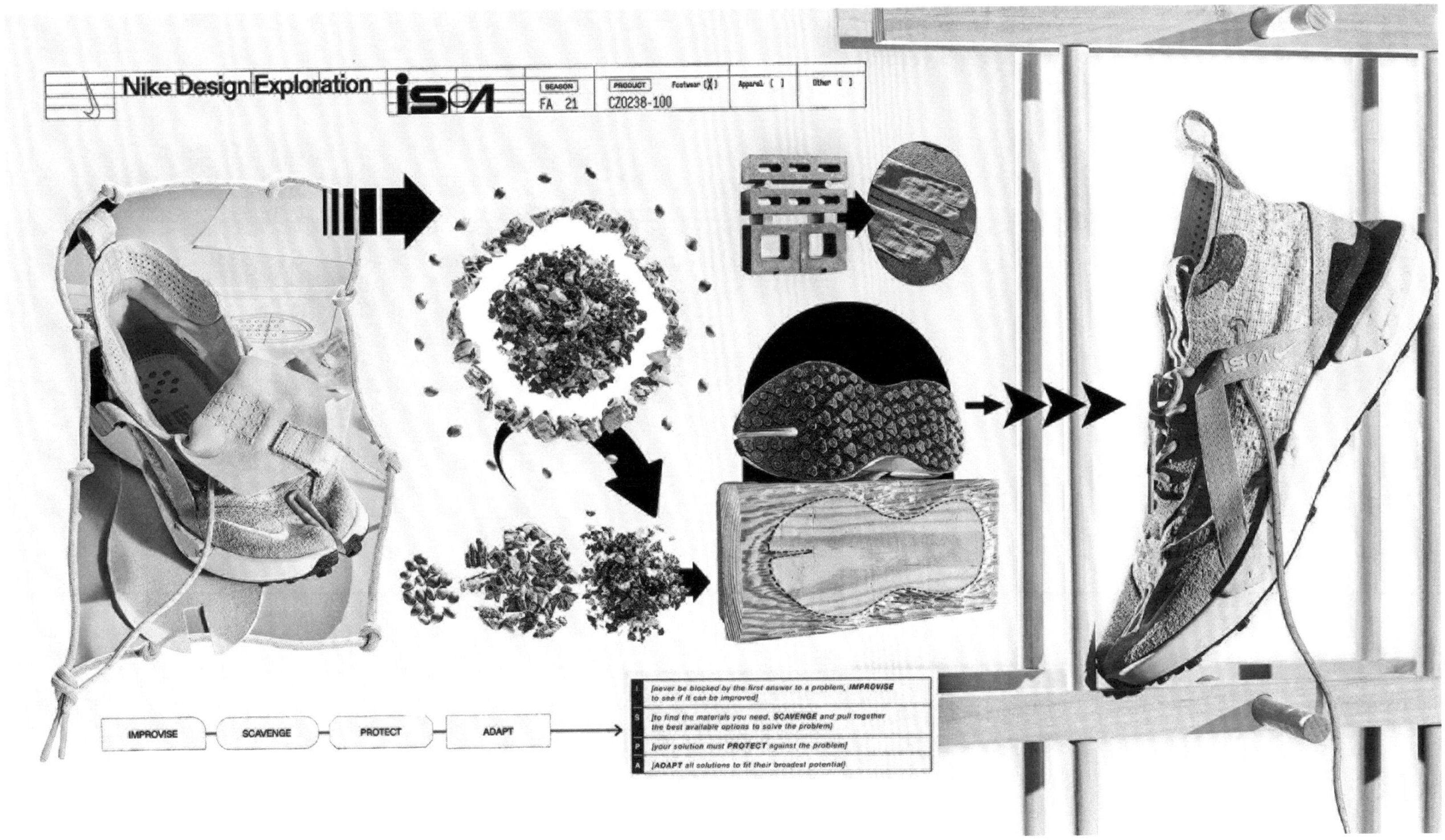

Nike ISPA Drifter footwear. Recycled Nike Grind ZoomX foam. With BUAISOU for Nike. 2021.

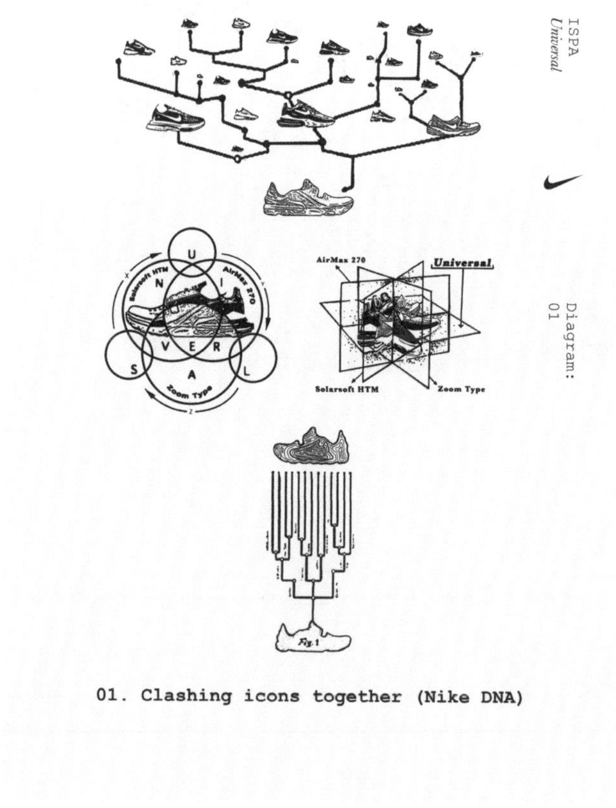

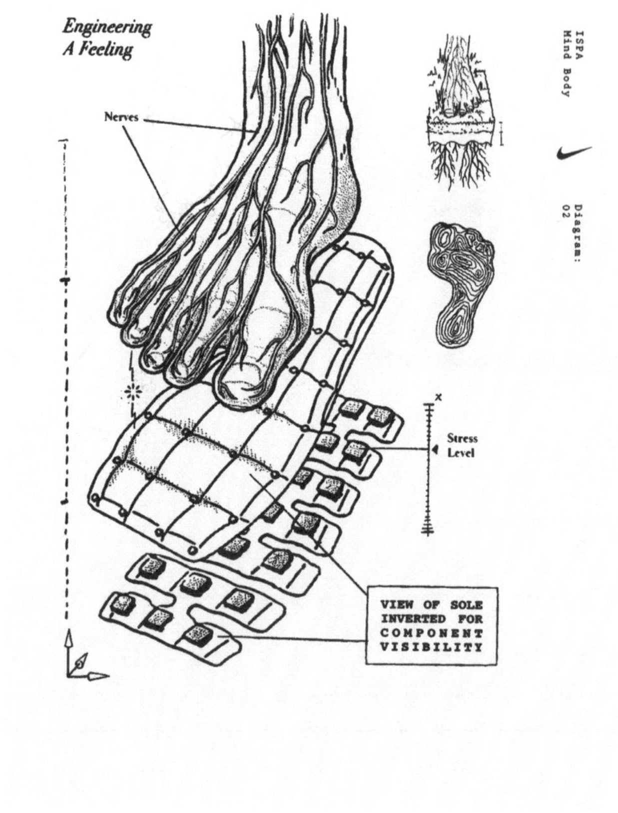

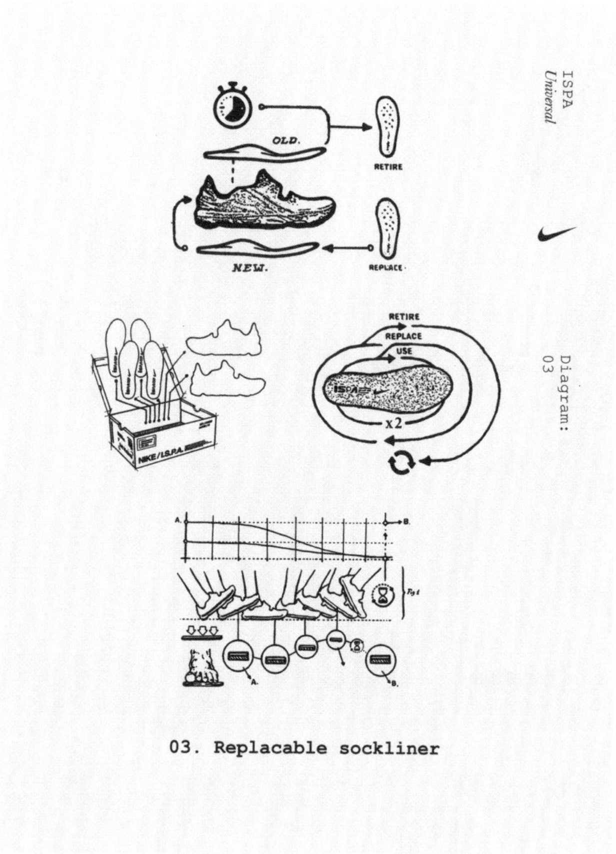

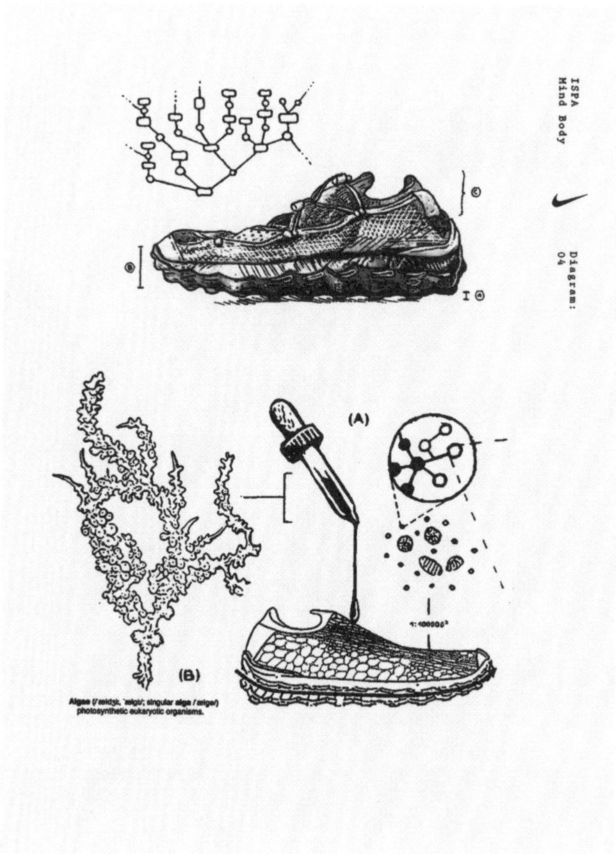

Nike ISPA MindBody footwear. Flyknit, algae inks. Nike. 2023.

Nike ISPA Link Axis footwear. Various recycled materials. Nike. 2023.

MARIA JEGLIŃSKA-ADAMCZEWSKA

It is the often nomadic nature of the background and education of contemporary designers that feeds their creativity. It also gives them courage and flexibility, preparing them for the uncertainty of a fragile industry. Maria Jeglińska-Adamczewska has lived between France, Switzerland, and Poland. For some time, she has been based between France and Poland, where she opened her studio in 2012 and has built a career working on many different scales, from furniture and objects (most famously those designed for the luxury hospitality chain Puro Hotels) through art-directing commercial events and curating exhibitions.

Jeglińska-Adamczewska has designed projects for the Saint-Étienne Biennale, the London Design Biennale, and the Łódź Design Festival. She has also been the creative director of the Polish fair Arena Design in Poznań. These projects were not just useful commissions but also, perhaps more importantly, served as research platforms and provided her with the opportunity to test new ideas and prototypes through ephemeral architectural structures.

Playing with color, mobility, and transparency, Jeglińska-Adamczewska's furniture pieces are characterized by a casual use of materials, such as recycled fabrics, industrial glass, and pigment. They are versatile objects, often informal, on wheels, such as her multifunctional Portable Walls (2019), or with staggered surfaces. Storage units can be moved around and used to divide spaces as if they were domestic film sets. The recurrent use of curves and surfaces in sequence lends her work an underlying expressiveness. This is the case in the "Arco" collection (2020), where the seats are a contemporary version of the *sgabelli* stools of the Renaissance and the structure that supports the table and the legs themselves is designed not merely for stability or comfort but to give that added burst of energy that has become the designer's signature. Such projects make hers one of the loudest voices in European design today.

Series 3 furniture. Textured glass, aluminum, wood. PLATO. 2023.

"Arco" collection seat and table. American cherrywood. American Hardwood Export Council. 2020.

Portable Walls. Wood, aluminum. Museum of Applied Arts, Budapest. 2019.

HELLA JONGERIUS

Woven Cosmos exhibition. Various materials. 2021.

Breathing Colour exhibition. Various materials. 2017.

Since the 1990s, the work of Hella Jongerius has challenged ideals of design perfection. Her approach brings material enquiry and a human touch to industrial efficiencies through processes that disrupt the usual techniques of production and instead introduce a sense of craftsmanship.

Born in the Netherlands, Jongerius was part of Droog, the pioneering Dutch collective established in 1993 by Renny Ramakers and Gijs Bakker. This formative period set the tone for the works of creative disruption for which Jongerius has become known and that have won her a global list of clients, including KLM, Vitra, Maharam, and IKEA, as well as a place for her works in the permanent collections of major museums.

Since she established her studio, Jongeriuslab, in the same year, her material manipulations have been seen in such exhibitions as *Breathing Colour* at London's Design Museum (2017), which explored the perception of color through different materials and its changes through light and seasons. The centerpiece of the show was a ring of 300 porcelain pots arranged in gradated hues colored by mineral and chemical glazes, a collaboration with the Dutch porcelain experts Royal Tichelaar Makkum. The vases experiment with historical recipes and modern techniques to glaze ceramics, creating vibrant, original chromatic juxtapositions.

Similarly, Jongerius's Vlinder Sofa (2019) for Vitra expresses her particular skill with color and textile production. Although the sofa follows a traditional form, the design breaks from archetype with its plump, cushiony cover created from jacquard weave. Its rich, expressive surface translates a handwoven method into an industrial textile by uniting eight colors of two varied thicknesses to create a subtle 3D finish.

Jongerius once said, "Materials are my first love." As her career heads into its fourth decade, that continues to ring true. Her reputation as a progressive designer with exquisite material sensibility and an appetite for innovation is as strong as ever.

Bovist floor pillow, stool, ottoman. Fabric, synthetic beads. Vitra. 2019.

Vlinder Sofa. Foam, downy overlay. Vitra. 2019.

Windswept table. Stainless steel, glass. 2022.

MISHA KAHN

As a kid in Duluth, Minnesota, Misha Kahn would pester his mother to take him to yard sales. Today, he elevates garbage and garage sales to the world of the art gallery.

Kahn studied furniture design at the Rhode Island School of Design, then took a Fulbright Fellowship in 2012 to make footwear at the Bezalel Academy of Arts and Design in Jerusalem. His first job was men's window displays at Bergdorf Goodman in New York City. By 2016, he'd signed with Friedman Benda gallery in the same city, and begun to exhibit at the Whitney Museum of American Art and at the Walker Art Center, Minneapolis.

Messy, charismatic, and extroverted, Kahn taps the spectrum of materials and methods: nylon and down feathers, cactus and bone, what he describes as "crap from the sea," and assemblage, glass collage, metal-casting, handweaving, digital modeling, salvage. The results are objects of aggressive whimsy and compulsive maximalism: a handwoven mohair tapestry inspired by Jell-O molds, jewelry made by casting inflated vinyl in resin, large inflatable outdoor sculptures, and a cabinet crafted by Swaziland basket weavers from trash, grass, and stained glass.

In virtual reality, Kahn accretes clinging, overripe forms that he then fabricates in plastic or resin and *Playboy*-perfect automotive paint. He collages 3D scans onto digital forms to make globular, multi-component upholstered sofas or bronze chairs that look molten. He grafts human onto computer intelligence, soft bodies onto hard pixels, fever dreams onto stop-motion animation.

Like his exhibitions, Kahn's apartment in Bushwick, Brooklyn, is a gallery of extremist expressionism. Every surface squirms with hand-painted color, an anarchy of material, and mixed metaphors. To talk about his work, Kahn uses such words as "chaos," "imbalance," "friction," "bacchanal," and "binge." Things come together and "go awry." If your eyes aren't clicking and whirring to make audible lens adjustments, you've surely got them shut tight.

Heavy Metal Planet object. Bronze, steel, glass, chrome. 2021.

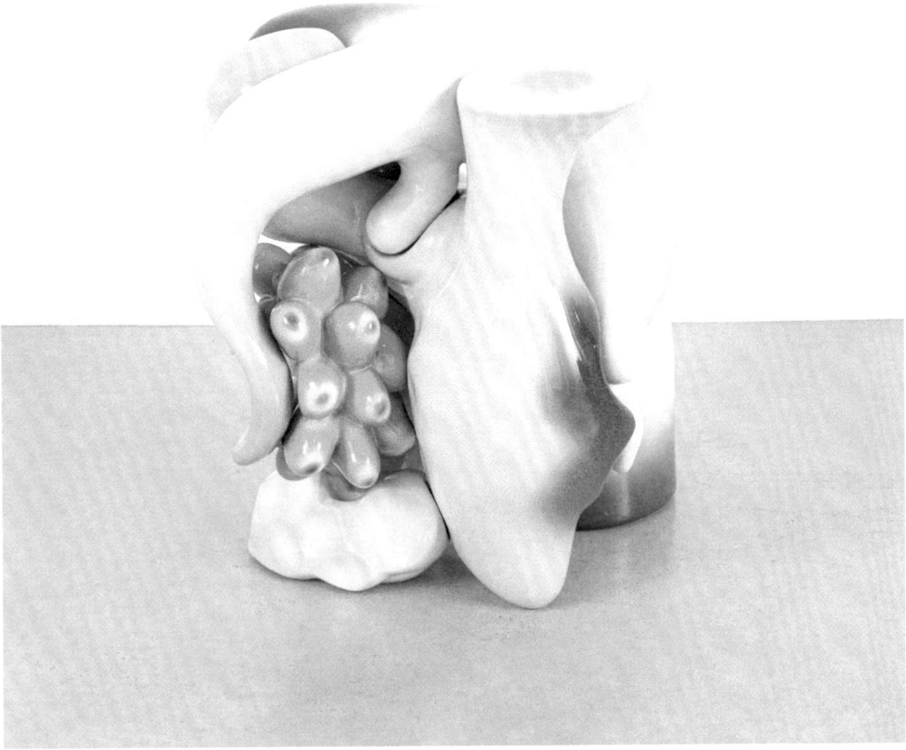

Hellenistic Vector object. Plastic, paint. 2022.

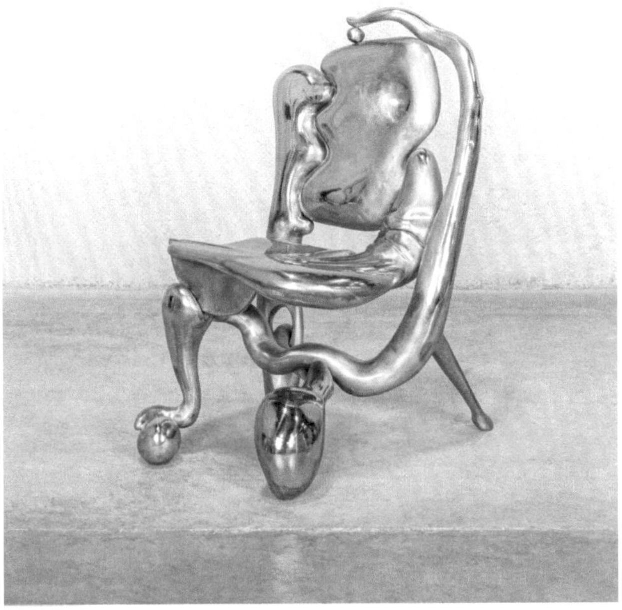

One Shoe, A Fold of Love Handle, a Rogue Dog Ball chair. Bronze. 2019.

The Ever Sessile Pupa chair. Aluminum, beaded and embroidered fabric. 2022.

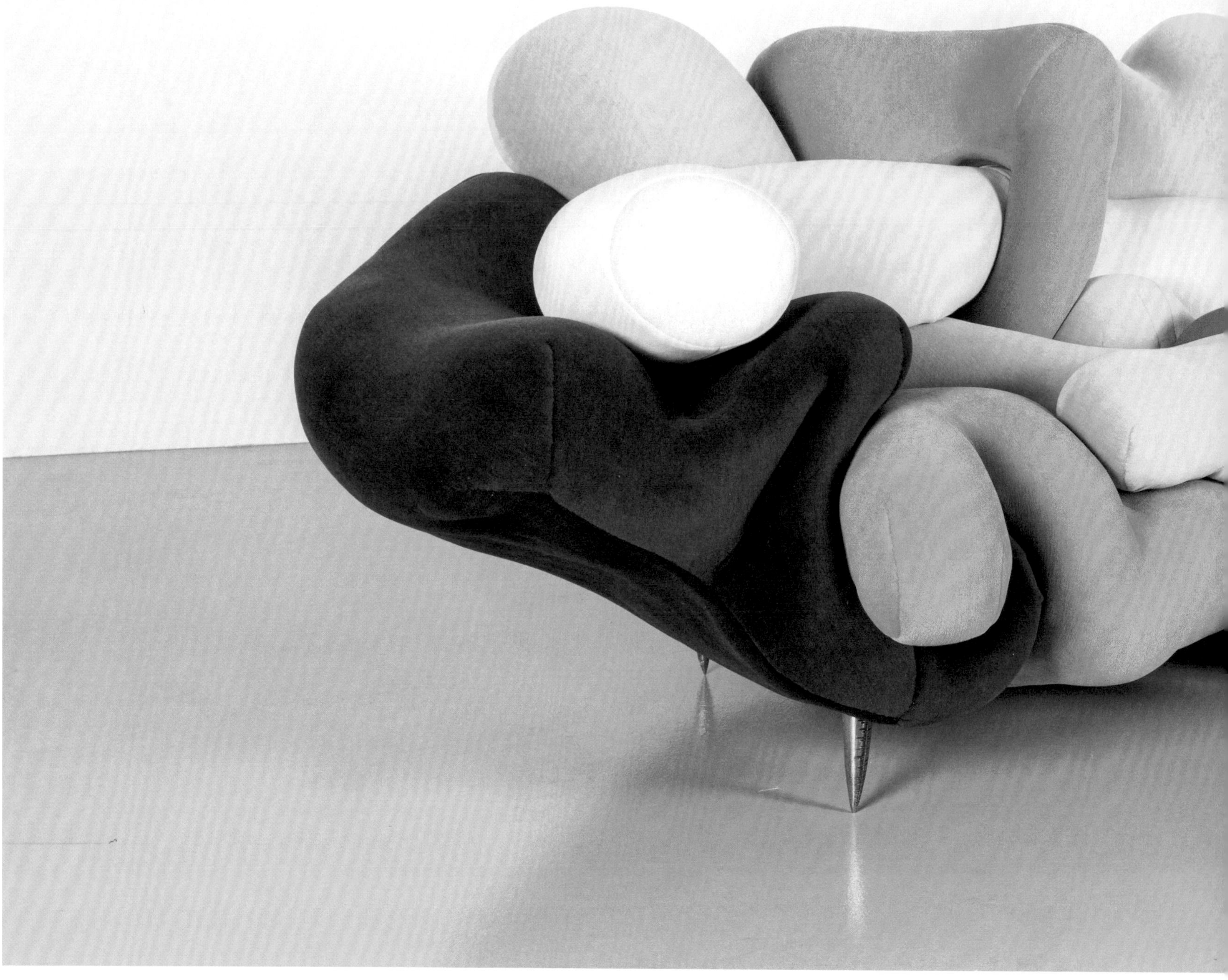

Shaped Potato, Potential, and Actual sofa. Fabric, foam, steel, white bronze. 2022.

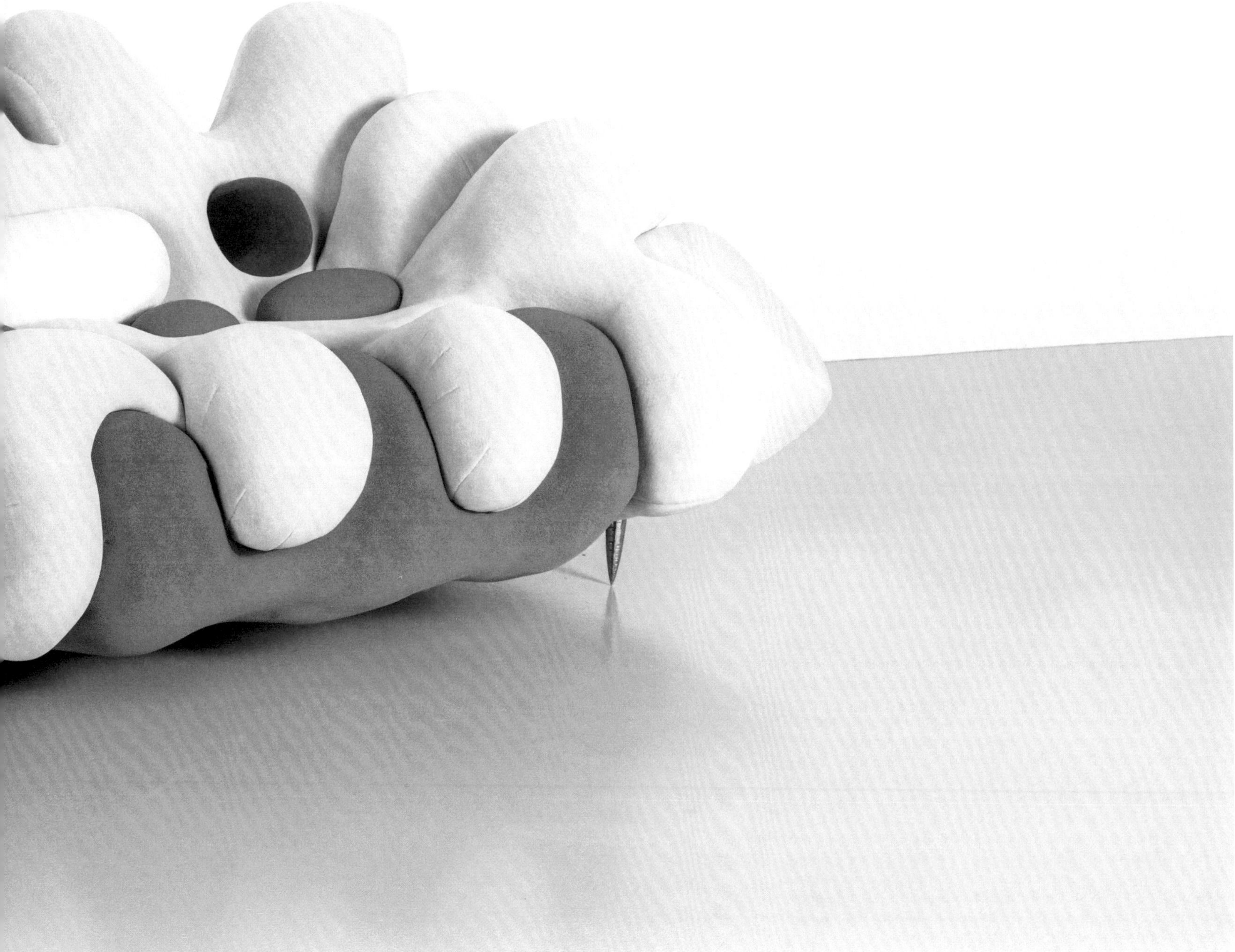

CHARLOTTE KIDGER

Browns Fashion Block Composition Purple window display. Various materials. 2020.

Informed by a desire to repurpose industrial waste, the work of Charlotte Kidger is distinctive for transforming the unwanted into the desirable through objects, furniture, and public art installations. In her hands, the dust of waste polyurethane from CNC (computer numerical control) factories is reprocessed with hand-dyed resin to become a raw material that is manipulated to form crafted industrial collectibles. The process continues to evolve with new research into waste extraction and reuse, but her ingenuity has already caught the eye of the venerable London boutique Browns Fashion. Known for identifying young talent, the store provided a platform to exhibit Kidger's 19-piece work, including side tables, a console, and a plinth, which were installed in its flagship South Molton Street store in 2020.

Kidger's unusual, saturated pieces complemented the surrounding rails of avant-garde fashion. Block Composition (2020), for example, appears as an overscaled chain fragment and brings together interlocking chunks of eggplant-colored links that are stacked to create a bold plinth. Similarly arresting is her three-part set of side tables and a plinth, marked out by their marbled green hues and porous fluted forms. Recalling the historic architectural orders, their classical perfection is interrupted by crumbling edges that suggest a process of decay and introduce a contemporary edge.

The commission for Browns drew on Kidger's "Industrial Craft" collection, a balance of design and art, for London Design Fair and Make Hauser & Wirth Somerset. In the company of other leading makers, Kidger explored her technique by producing a sustainable cantilevered side table with a smoothly cast circular top, pierced and supported by a crumbling vertical fragment.

With a further commission for Browns and exhibitions at prestigious venues, Kidger's timely work wins appeal for creating beauty through sustainability. It is this quality that also won her *Wallpaper** magazine's Best Element of Surprise for 2023.

Industrial Craft Table. Waste polyurethane foam, resin. 2018.

Browns Fashion Column and two Side Tables Green window display. Various materials. 2020.

MINJAE KIM

Helmet Lamp. Quilted fiberglass, wood, resin, acrylic paint. 2022.

A preference for creating "total environments" underpins the work of the Seoul-born, New York-based designer Minjae Kim. He is the son of the Korean painter MyoungAe Lee, and his sources of inspiration are broad and varied, circling through Sigmund Freud and Henri Matisse to Korean folklore. Alongside this sits his architectural training at Columbia GSAPP (Graduate School of Architecture, Planning and Preservation) and a period practicing interior design at Studio Giancarlo Valle in New York. The result is a holistic understanding of how spaces and surfaces can be shaped.

Since 2019, Kim's vision for an immersive environment has expanded to furniture created by hand from wood, fiberglass, and lacquer. The tactile results are both sensual and practical, his Lacquered Chairs (2020) being a case in point. Hewn from Douglas fir in simple, chunky profiles, they are almost anthropomorphic, with stocky legs and gently curved profiles of stiles and top rails. Pronounced buttock-shaped impressions on each seat bear maker's marks.

Extending Kim's repertoire is Upholstered Armoire (2022), a bespoke piece fashioned from aluminum, sapele, oak, and fabric, with upholstery by Ateliers Jouffre. Forming part of his exhibition at Matter, New York, that year, alongside Lee's paintings, the eye-catching wardrobe stands 8 ft (2.5 m) tall. Its padded teal-green doors partially cloak timber drawers and aluminum doors, which peek out from a narrow gap that exposes teardrop-shaped handles begging to be touched, with a lone knob picked out in duck-egg blue.

Soft and hard, matte and gloss, wood and metal, Kim's dexterity with contrast is a delight. No wonder that his solo debut at Marta gallery in Los Angeles in 2021 was quickly followed by exhibitions at Matter (2022) and Nina Johnson, Miami (2022–3), as well as favorable coverage in lifestyle and design journals.

Ikebana Lamp. Ceramic, brass, resin. With Natalie Weinberger and Nedda Atassi. 2019.

Various, including Lacquered Chairs. Douglas fir. 2020.

KITT.TA.KHON

BoaBoa chair. Rattan, nylon rope, canvas seat. 2023.

The Thai designer Teerapoj Teeropas founded Kitt.Ta.Khon in 2019 with the support of his mentor, Suwan Kongkhunthian. As the creative director, Teerapoj's vision is to blend ethnic language and traditions with contemporary design. From his Bangkok-based studio, he pays tributes to different cultures and pushes the idea of craft as a universal language by allowing elements to co-exist in his designs. He creates pieces that belong "everywhere, and nowhere at the same time," blurring the lines between countries and each reference's true origin. By adopting this method, Kitt.Ta.Khon is forging a reputation for translating artisanal skills into sensational furniture.

Take the BoaBoa chair (2023), a black-painted rattan structure finished with nylon rope. The chair borrows from the familiar formal reference of a classic bentwood dining chair. This piece, however, becomes a canvas for the reinterpretation of Southeast Asian wickerwork, with multicolored ropes wrapping and patterning the chair, finished with an upholstered seat in a patterned canvas or handwoven recycled fabric.

The Sukpha stool (2021) complements the chair series with a similar technique and color palette. Its name means "to wash clothes," and the Sukpha is a version of the familiar low stool typically used in Thai culture for this task. Fashioned simply from painted rattan with hand-knotted nylon rope, each seat can be customized to create a joyful cacophony of color.

Chino (2012) draws on the familiar form of a Qing dynasty console with its distinctive scrolled legs and slim proportions. Mining this rich history, Kitt.Ta.Khon reinterprets the piece as a highly decorative feature. The elaborate rattan work that weaves across the structure includes references from Africa, Morocco, and Europe. A transparent glass top frames the detailed handiwork, its simplicity setting off the heady mix of pattern and technique.

While arresting for its palettes and patterns, Kitt.Ta.Khon's range of tables, daybeds, and seating are also comfortable and familiar, drawing from the age-old and universal language of making. Through a potent collage of vernacular forms and techniques, it put forward a new approach to convey the global appeal of craft.

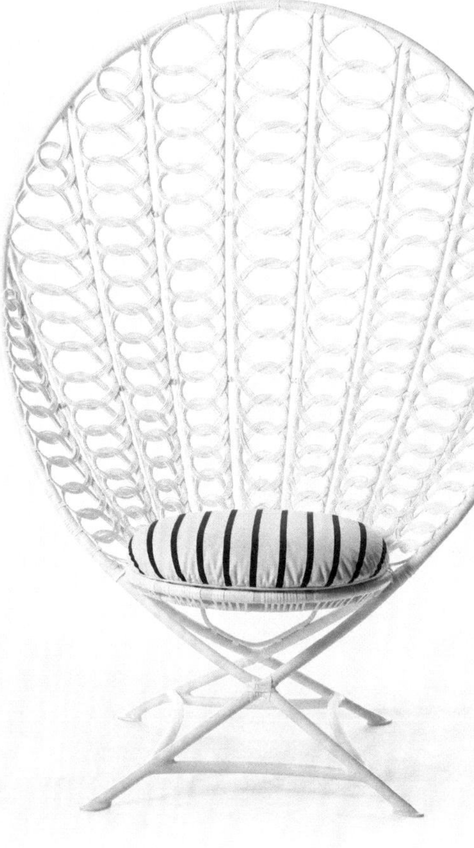

MookMook chair. Aluminum, recycled plastic. 2023.

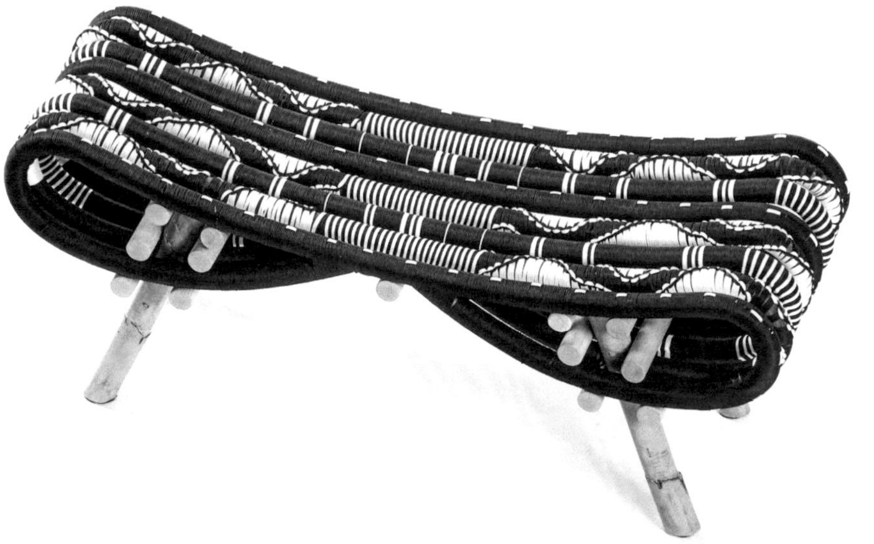

Kaanso stool. Rattan, nylon rope. 2019.

Chino console table. Rattan, nylon, tempered glass. 2012.

JORIS LAARMAN

Does Joris Laarman's furniture look pixelated or sinuous, rational, or emotional? Is it science or science fiction? As the world fast-forwards from the industrial into the digital era, Laarman's Amsterdam studio is an experimental playground where emerging technology, digital tools, and parametric processes fuel creativity and craft to create forms inspired by nature.

Laarman co-founded his eponymous Lab after graduating from the Design Academy Eindhoven in 2003. Today, he works with a multidisciplinary team of coders, engineers, and artisans, exploring artificial intelligence, digital and robotic fabrication, parametric modeling, and augmented and virtual reality to create poetic intersections with the physical world.

In 2006, Laarman's Bone Chair, for Droog and Friedman Benda, was inspired by the new human capacity not just to imitate nature stylistically, but also to tap the natural world's underlying mechanisms to generate shapes using evolutionary methods. Trees build up woody tissue where they need to increase strength; bones slough material where extra strength is not needed. With software capable of copying these processes, Laarman gave the chair maximum strength using minimal material. Simulating the application of stress to certain points on a 3D model of the seat, he used an algorithm to remove non-essential material. Bone was then cast in aluminum using a 3D-printed ceramic mold.

Since then, Laarman has continued to innovate processes, tools, and materials. To create his Aluminum Gradient Chair (2014), his team retrofitted a 3D metal printer and for their Dragon benches they even invented their own large scale robotic 3D metal printer. Experienced welders watched them tinker in disbelief, not expecting the adjustments to work. But those unconventional settings were the only way to print by connecting a welder and robot with their own software. The Symbio Benches connect all the worlds they work in: the natural, the digital, and the world of craft. Cut with the help of augmented reality, organic Turing patterns of moss wrap around geometrically shaped benches of natural stone. All Laarman's designs are based in this intense, evolutionary process of development, iteration, refinement, and re-iteration until they look like magic: impossible, effortless, and enchanting.

Forest Table XL. Aluminum, resin. 2002.

Digital Matter (Voxel Series). Neodymium magnets. 2023

Aluminum Gradient Chair. Aluminium. 2014.

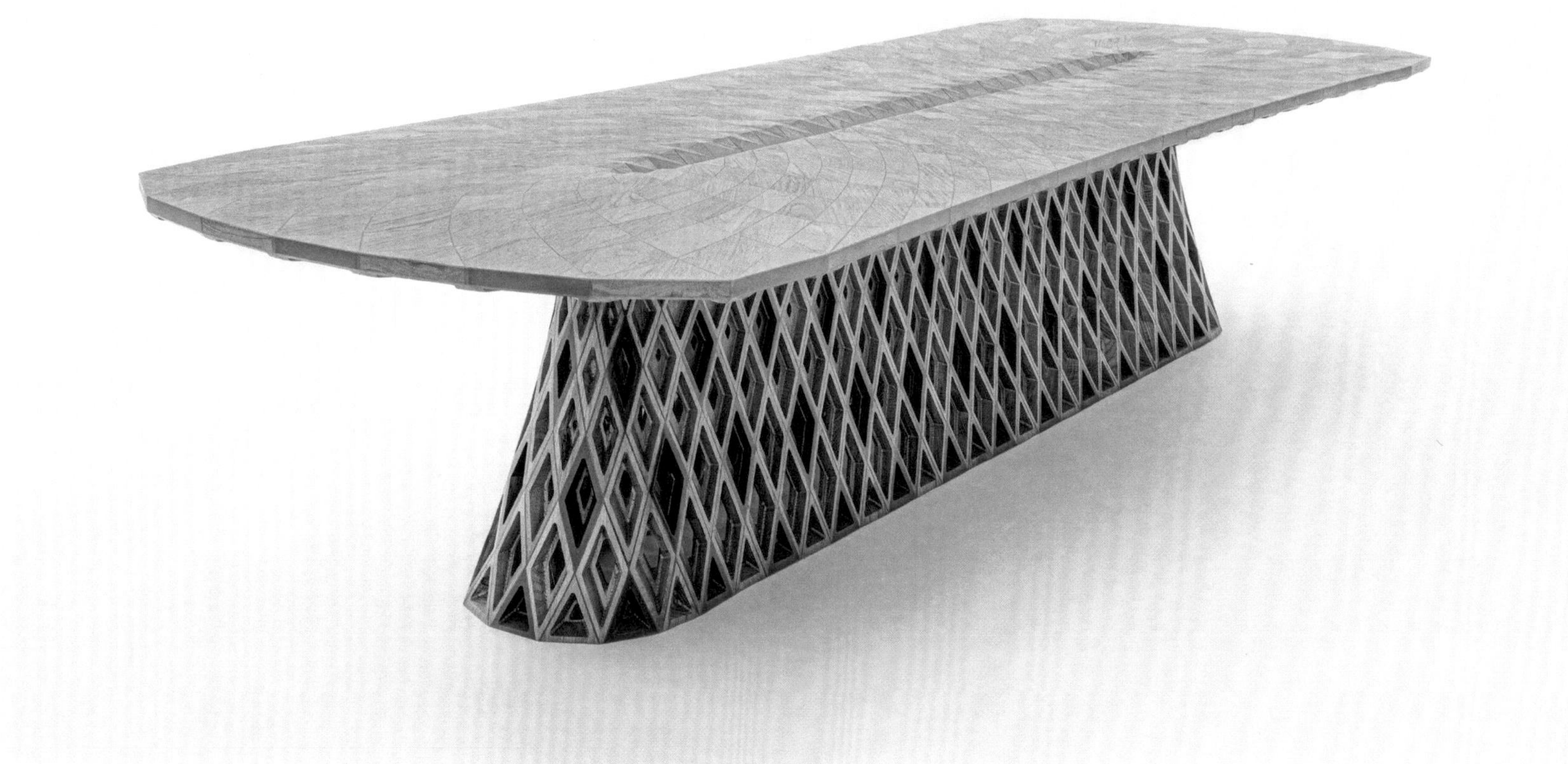

Diamond Maker Table. Wood. 2021.

Symbio Bench. Gritstone and local bryophytes.2023.

Urushi wall shelf. Cypress, *Wajima-nuri urushi* lacquer. 2019.

MAX LAMB

For the furniture designer Max Lamb, the meaning and beauty of design rest in the labor rather than the outcome. He often sets himself challenges, such as producing sixty chairs in three days, or traveling from his London studio to China, Ireland, and rural parts of the United States to work with local materials. His focus on process has yielded distinctive, arresting pieces whose sources and methods of making are foregrounded.

Perhaps the main function of a Lamb chair is to showcase its material. Consider his 6×8 Chair (2021), hand-cut from a single piece of Western red cedar and worked without jigs or other fixtures. The final product appears to be a gratifying solution to a puzzle, a new iteration in an age-old encounter between man and wood. The Cleft Chair (2016), split from one piece of sycamore, is carved then covered in gold leaf, testament to the value of perceiving the raw grain. The granite Feather + Wedge chair (2020) is named after the stonework technique of its manufacture. Ceaselessly at work, Lamb spent a year collaborating on a furniture line with craftspeople in Honshu, Japan, using *urushi*, a finishing practice that is at least 9,000 years old. The *urushi*—sap of the lacquer tree—is gradually and slowly applied to objects, over and over again, until the wood is prepared to last for generations.

Lamb studied at London's Royal College of Art—where the designer Martino Gamper (p. 96), another maestro of the chair, was one of his tutors—and came to understand himself as a designer through seeing what he had actually produced: objects that, ideally, lodge in the mind, like landscapes or old friends. Lamb may be fixated on the labor, but luckily for the rest of us, his outcomes promise permanence and are never short of memorable.

Feather + Wedge chair. Tonalite granite. 2020.

Urushi low table. Cypress, *Wajima-nuri urushi* lacquer. 2019.

6×8 Chair. Western red cedar. 2021.

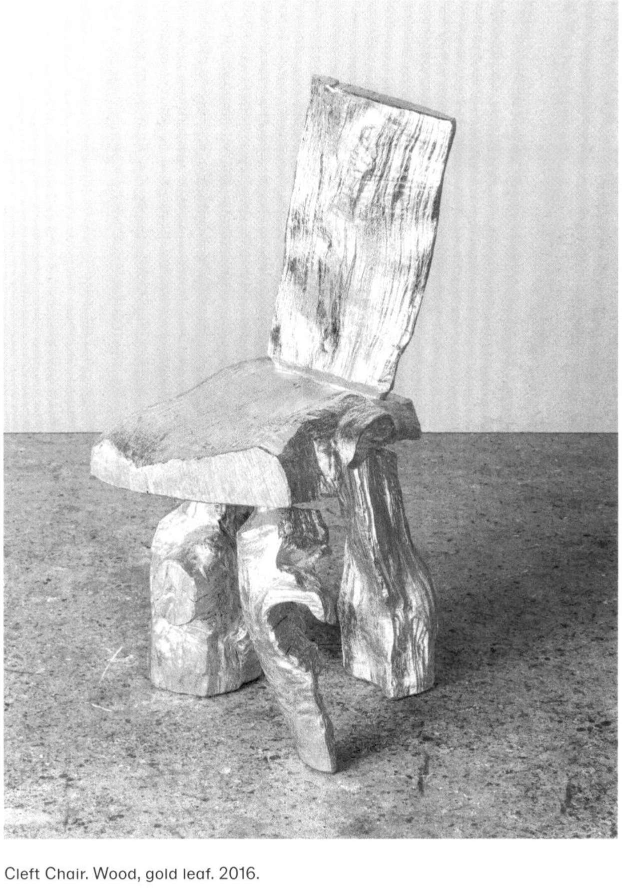

Cleft Chair. Wood, gold leaf. 2016.

FERNANDO LAPOSSE

Pink Beasts installation. Sisal, cochineal dye. With forty-five Mayan women weavers and Angela Dammon. 2019.

The transformative power of craft and design is fundamental to the work of Fernando Laposse, who calls on his Mexican origins to create pieces that are rooted in Indigenous production. He is much more than an industrial designer, showing how to harness design and speak to the urgent global issues of our age. A graduate of Central Saint Martins in London, he has earned a reputation for design logic paired with Mexican materials as a means to champion local knowledge of ecology and farming. In particular, he encourages crops of Indigenous agave, corn, and luffa, all of which were once grown widely in Mexico but are threatened by the advent of plastic and the introduction of industrial hybrid varieties. Laposse provides an incentive to grow and use these vulnerable crops by collaborating with the Mixtec farming community of Tonahuixtla in the south of the country.

Laposse's "Totomoxtle" series (2016) creates a distinctive mosaic of ecru, burgundy, umber, and lilac, sophisticated hues that belie their humble origins. Promoting a circular economy, these textural surfaces transform the husks of Indigenous Mexican corn into wall coverings, lamps, and table tops.

A comparable process is seen in the Lufa daybed (2012), which appropriates the dried gourds of *Luffa cylindrica* for an elegant daybed on a simple wooden frame. Laposse harvests and crushes the fibers of the luffa, then combs and hand-knots the ribbed material, at the same time highlighting subtle color striations in the spongy, rustic upholstery.

A project with sisal in 2019 transformed these agave fibers into a bench and, in 2021, a series of silky, hirsute stools collectively titled "The Dogs," recalling shaggy sheepdogs. As well as creating charming benches, the pieces promote discussion about biodiversity and biodegradable materials through the use of agave, a plant traditionally used for ropes and nets that is now scarce.

The Dogs bench. Sisal-covered bench. AGO Projects. 2019.

Lufa daybed. Various materials. 2012.

Totomoxtle furniture. Various materials. 2016.

White Agave Cabinet. Birch plywood, sisal, steel mesh, Canadian maple. 2021.

LAUN

The designers behind LAUN play in sunny, sophisticated fashion with color, form, material, and geometry. Rachel Bullock and Molly Purnell, who studied architecture at the University of Texas at Austin, united their skills in 2018 to collaborate on residential architecture, interiors, and furniture.

They absorb inspiration from everything around them, including the Art Deco Streamline Moderne buildings of Los Angeles, where they're based, and the nature photography of Karl Blossfeldt. LAUN's Mondos Chaise Lounge, Club Chair, Sofa, and Loveseat (2023), co-designed with Chet Architecture, reference the seawall and waves on legendary Mondos Beach, an epicenter of California's surf culture, in a materials palette that's all about that culture: fiberglass, neoprene, aluminum, and vinyl in vibrant pelagic blues to neon greens.

LAUN's color schemes are based on art by the likes of Amy Sherald, Georgia O'Keeffe, and Amy MacKay. They also take cues from the form-making, material innovation, and detail in work by such fashion designers as Alexander McQueen, Hussein Chalayan, and Issey Miyake. The "Ribbon" collection (2020) is both delicate and bold, comprised of layered aluminum tubes that can be stacked in an infinite combination of forms with increasingly dramatic curves. The cast-aluminum or fiberglass Octavia Chair and Butler Table (both 2021) were influenced by the symbolism and Surrealist imagery in Octavia E. Butler's science-fiction novel *Dawn* (1987). The chair is Laun's take on a 1950s chair prototype by the French interior designer Jean Royère.

Usually working with metal, silicone, and jasper, as well as wood, stone, and leather, Bullock and Purnell start by passing sketches and small-scale models back and forth. After making a digital model, they prototype in foam, wood, or steel, cutting and re-welding until the proportions are right. They make most pieces in-house, but it took outside ingenuity to perfect the cushions for the Octavia Chair. After some epic molding, sculpting, and tracing, Purnell says: "Our upholsterer is a genius."

"Dawn" collection, Butler Table. Aluminum, silicon. 2021.

"Dawn" collection, Octavia Chair. Aluminum, fabric. 2021.

Curved Ribbon Sofa and Bench. Aluminum. 2023.

Mondos Sofa. Neoprene, fiberglass. Designed by LAUN and Chet Architecture. 2023.

Ribbon Sofa. Aluminum. 2020.

KWANGHO LEE

Copper Shelf. Welded copper. 2022.

The inspiration of the designer Kwangho Lee ranges from childhood memories of his grandparents' farm to objects encountered on his trips to Seoul's sprawling Euljiro materials market. As a student focusing on metal art and design at Hongik University in Seoul, Lee tried his hand at furniture for his final project, and struck a rich vein of creativity. Now, working from two studio spaces in the capital, he employs traditional processes in innovative ways, building on the knowledge of generations of Korean artisans while creating unique installations, interiors, and furniture suited to the modern moment.

Some of Lee's most striking pieces are crafted from nylon and PVC, both fortuitous discoveries made at Euljiro. His black PVC chair (2022) from the "Obsession" series (2009) is a playful riposte to conventional proportions: a blocky Tetris piece-turned-real-life support. A similarly chunky blue nylon armchair from the same series, with a low back and rectangular armrest panels, is a direct descendant of his mother's crochet creations. Lee's stunning line of copper furniture, the "Shape of a River" series (2018), is a testament to his love of color and fine sense of balance, as well as his willingness to experiment. These chairs, benches, and shelves feature cherrywood frames with inlaid copper panels. The panels are covered in crushed colored glass and fired in a traditional kiln, and the melting of the glass during firing produces unpredictable waves of color that contrast gorgeously with the angularity of the pieces.

In addition to work that is now in the collections of SFMOMA, the Montreal Museum of Fine Arts, M+ museum, and Powerhouse Museum, Lee has made pieces for Tajimi custom tiles, Hem, and Vaarnii. And the drawings by Lee's young children, displayed in his studio, may well prove to be this singular designer's bridge to the future of the tradition.

Yellow Enameled Copper Bench. Welded copper and enamel on copper. 2022.

Blue Nylon Armchair. Knotted nylon rope. 2022.

SHAHAR LIVNE

"No ideas but in things," the poet William Carlos Williams famously wrote in the early twentieth century. Eindhoven-based Shahar Livne lives that line. She asks how humans can better understand and interact with the changing world and the world we are changing—through objects.

Israel-born Livne grew up enthralled with nature, biology, science, and philosophy, turning them into a creative practice through intuitive materials experimentation while studying at the Design Academy Eindhoven. Opening her studio in 2017, she makes dramatic products and original materials (including "dystopian" jewelry made from recycled ocean plastic for Balenciaga) based on deep-dive explorations of social and ecological issues. Her research starts with stories about places, cultures, and the relationship between people and resources, while her designs incorporate unusual ingredients: blood, minerals, collagen, milk, artificial "fossils."

"The Meat Factory" (2014–) is a series of experiments that highlight the wasteful and cruel treatment of animals. Livne uses abattoir offal to create new materials, employing blood and other industrially extracted animal parts to make commercially useful materials ranging from rubber to yarn. To make her Sustainable Blood Sneakers (2018–19), Livne developed a handmade "bio-leather" by using discarded fat and bones from Dutch slaughterhouses, using the blood as a colorant and plasticizer.

In 2014, scientists who found rocks on Hawaiian beaches formed from sand and waste plastic dubbed them plastiglomerates. "Metamorphism" (2017–) is a research and speculative design project that envisions a future in which plastic permeates the planet's ecosystems to the point that it melds with organic matter to become an entirely new "natural" resource and precious, extractable raw material, "lithoplast." Livne makes design objects—an urn, a stool—out of lithoplast. Without fear and with great creativity, she imagines the inevitable shift from nature being the only force of nature to humans becoming one too.

"Metamorphism" research project. Lithoplast. 2017.

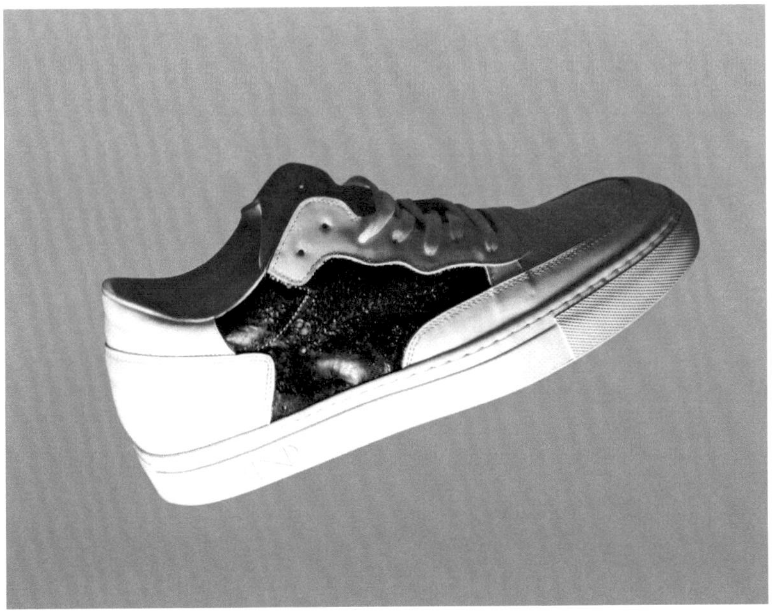

"The Meat Factory," Blood Sneakers. Blood "bio-leather", leather, glass, cork, rubber. 2014.

Memento Mori Sculptural functional objects. Ceramic, cast. 2017.

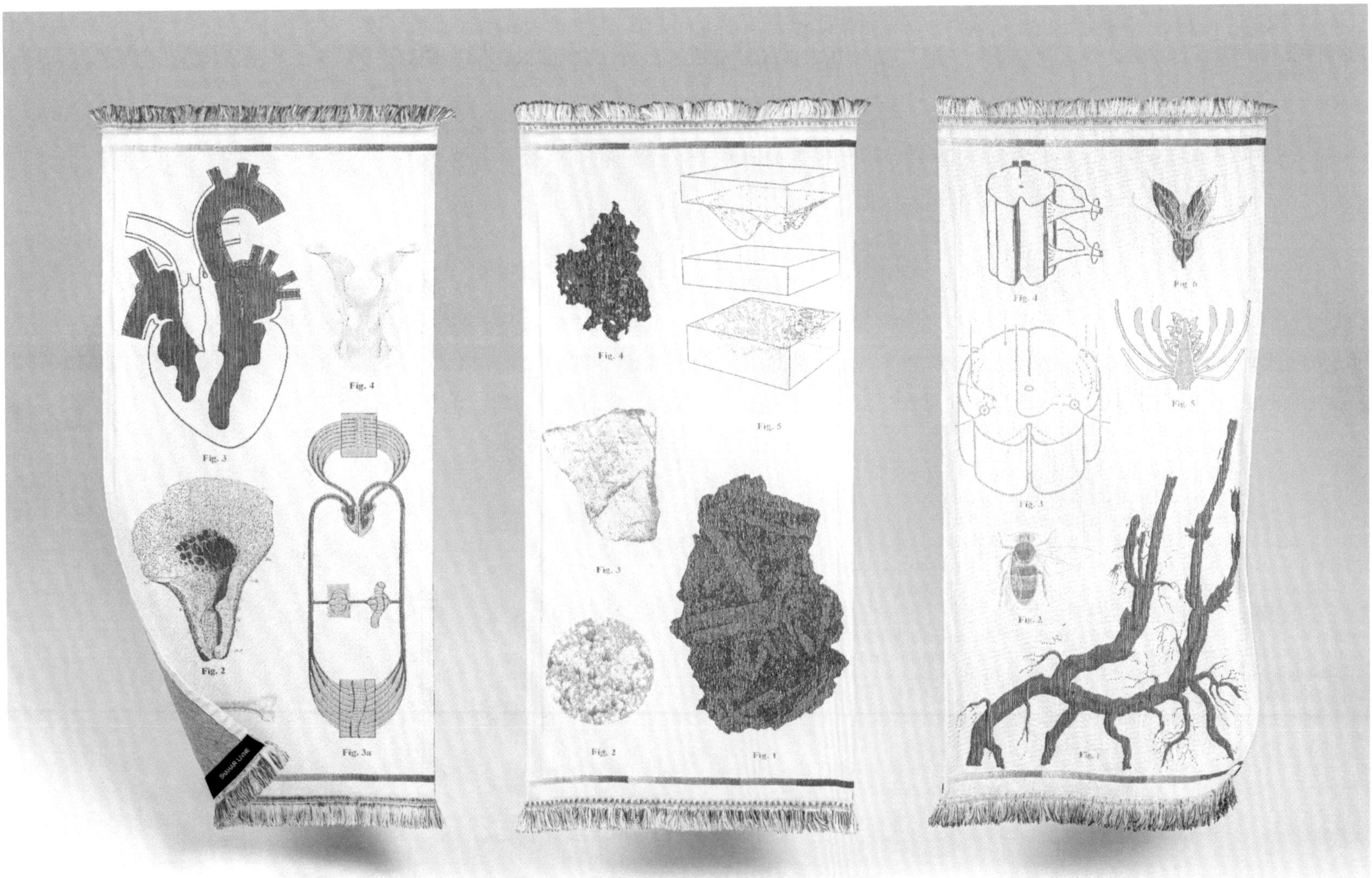

Alchimia tapestries. Collagen, milk, cotton, wool, blood, iron, and plants. 2022.

MABEO

Foro Chair, Chichira Cabinet, and EFO Stool. Various materials. Fendi Casa. 2021.

A connection to local materials and techniques is the hallmark of Peter Mabeo's work, which he has explored since establishing his studio in 1997. Based in Gaborone, Mabeo has always enjoyed working in collaboration with others, as is shown by the successful range of designs his studio has produced with leading designers and practices, including Claesson Koivisto Rune, Garth Roberts, and Patricia Urquiola (p. 252).

The Italian fashion house Fendi recognized Mabeo's singular approach and commissioned his exhibition for its 2021 Design Miami booth. The result was a ten-piece collection entitled "Kompa," a word introduced to Mabeo by a Hukuntsi villager that means "together." Doing what he does best, Mabeo collaborated with artisans across Botswana, forging connections through a search for skilled makers to help him realize the collection in wood, clay, metal, and weaving.

The theme of togetherness is seen readily in Mabeo's Shiya Seat from the exhibition, created from the durable tropical hardwood panga panga. Forming a pair of generous, scooped chairs, this piece reinterprets the traditional love seat and translates the effect of steam-molded wood through handcrafted methods created with artisans of Mmankgodi village in southern Botswana.

Mabeo's Foro Chair from the same exhibition also embraces the qualities of panga panga, with an undulating frame and simple one-piece seat. Extending the range of his artisanal collaborators, it is also available in clay, drawing on the craft of both metalsmiths, to create the original mold, and potters from the village of Molepolole, to realize and fire the form. Arresting metalwork is also evident in the Gabi-Gabi seating of galvanized steel sheeting, a silver two-pronged sculpture, and its sister, the Gabinyana brass lamp, with equally sinuous form.

Collectively, the pieces in the exhibition speak to the rich aesthetic heritage of Africa and the keen awareness of a modern entrepreneur. Both are qualities that set Mabeo's work apart.

Booth at Fendi Design Miami. 2021.

Shiya Seat. Panga panga wood. Fendi Casa. 2021.

INDIA MAHDAVI

A self-described "polyglot and polychrome," India Mahdavi has carved a reputation for design that celebrates color, pattern, and eclecticism. Born in Tehran to Egypto-Persian parents, she experienced a peripatetic background living across Cambridge Massachusetts, Germany, and in Paris, and that, along with professional training at Cooper Union and Parsons School of Design in New York and accreditation (Diplôme par le Gouvernement, DPLG) from the French government, formed the bedrock of her distinctive practice in interiors, architecture, product, and scenography.

Madhavi's pink dining room at Sketch, London, was her iconic global debut, introducing sherbet hues across walls and upholstery when the Gallery restaurant opened in 2014. She has since picked up dozens of awards and bespoke commissions for hotels, restaurants, and installations from Monaco to Mexico, Australia to Italy, where she recently refurbished the Villa Medici in Rome.

Mahdavi's work enlivens spaces, and her Bruno rotating bookcase (2020) of lacquered wood, laminate, and steel is a case in point. Instead of playing a support role, it is formed of colorful blades that stack and twist in a vibrant array of chromatic combinations.

Similarly, the Bishop stool (2000) appeals for its crisp geometry and richly colored, glossy ceramic finish. Originally designed for ubercool New York club APT, it sits as easily in modern as in traditional interiors. It includes such variations as Primadonna Bishop (2021), a special edition made with the historic factory Émaux de Longwy, that is entwined with a luxuriant honeysuckle pattern. Mahdavi's playful elegance is also expressed in the Don Giovanni and Casanova lamps that compose the "Seducers" family (2013). These effervescent globes of ribbed Bohemian glass perch atop bodies with brass detailing and cast a soft and seductive glow—a reflection of their libertine namesakes.

The vivid worlds Mahdavi creates feature regularly on Instagram feeds. However, she has also won industry and institutional gravitas with several industry accolades, works in permanent collections, and a Commander status of the French Ordre des Arts et des Lettres (2015).

Bruno revolving book case. Lacquered and laminated wood, steel. 2020.

Don Giovanni and Casanova table lamps. Bohemian glass, brass. 2013.

Primadonna Bishop stool. Ceramic (with cloisonné technique applied). Manufacture des Émaux de Longwy. 2021.

Piña Colada dining table. Rattan, fitted ceramic tiles. 2023.

PHILIPPE MALOUIN

DS-707 armchair and modular sofa. Handmade leather. De Sede. 2020.

The Canadian designer Philippe Malouin is faithful to the fundamental principles of industrial production. His designs express an attention and attachment to manufacturing methods and forms that derive from his deep understanding of the most important processes involved in the production of furniture. This knowledge has allowed him to use glass, metal, ceramic, leather, and fabric with remarkable mastery, and has brought about collaborations with some of the most important companies in Europe.

Malouin's visual language tends toward dry, essential forms that perform their functions with measured grace. His design vision is clear, with an aesthetic code that has become instantly recognizable. He aims to realize a precise idea of comfort and function through solutions that determine the formal aesthetic character of his objects. For example, the Bilboquet table lamp (2023) features a metallic sphere that serves to change the direction of the light; the orthogonal angles of Chop Chair's leg (2023) give it stability and make it stackable; and the slight inclination of the Sacha Chair's backrest (2022) enhances the postural ergonomics of the armchair.

Now based in London, Malouin studied at the University of Montreal, ENSCI-Les Ateliers (L'École nationale supérieure de création industrielle) in Paris, and the Design Academy in Eindhoven. He has won important awards, including *Wallpaper** Designer of the Year, chaired the jury of the Design Parade at Villa Noailles in Hyères, France, and taught at the Royal College of Art in London, nourishing his research with international experiences.

Malouin is not afraid to venture into the world of limited editions while maintaining the industrial aesthetic that he has come to represent. Take, for example, his Steel Works (2021) made from scrap metal found in junkyards in the UK and Greece for the Breeder gallery in Athens, where the combination of strong color and manual craftsmanship creates striking pieces that nevertheless maintain their essential nature.

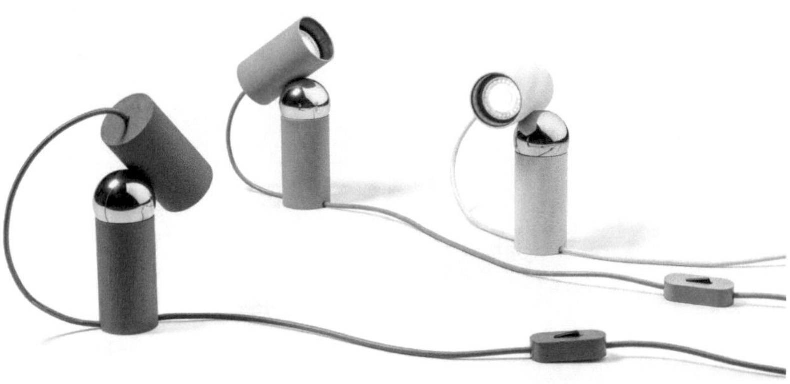

Bilboquet table lamps. Bioplastic, neodymium magnet. Flos. 2023.

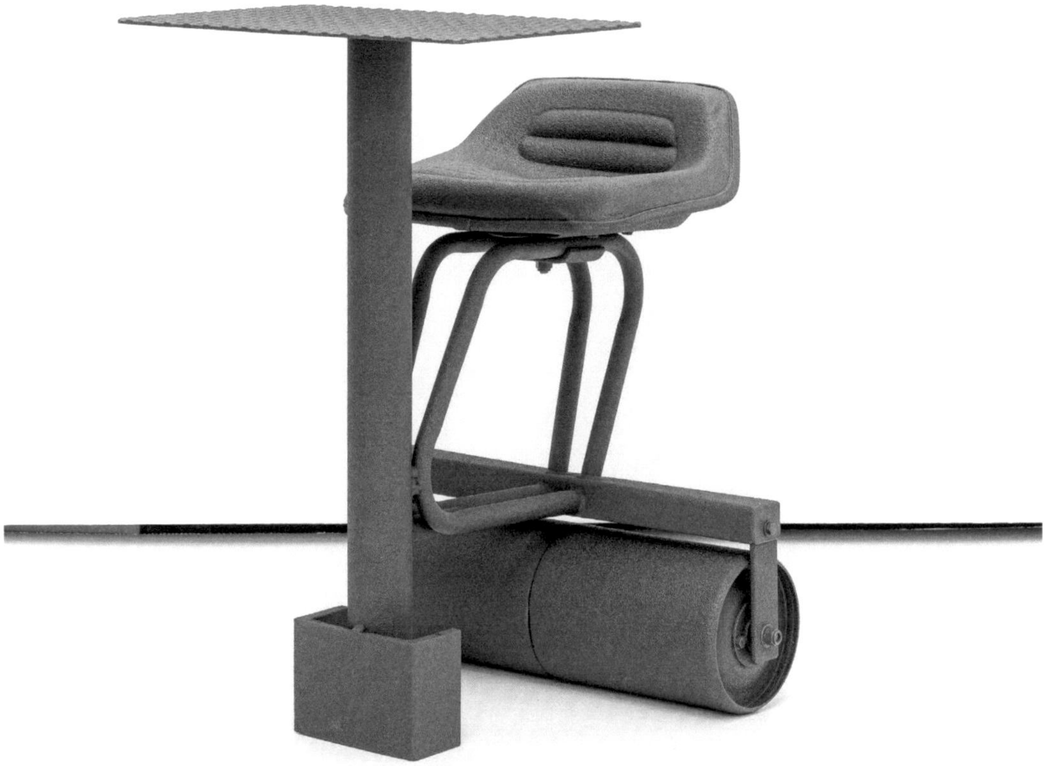

Steel Works furniture. Scrap metal. 2021.

Sacha Chairs. MDF, foam, steel. Resident. 2022.

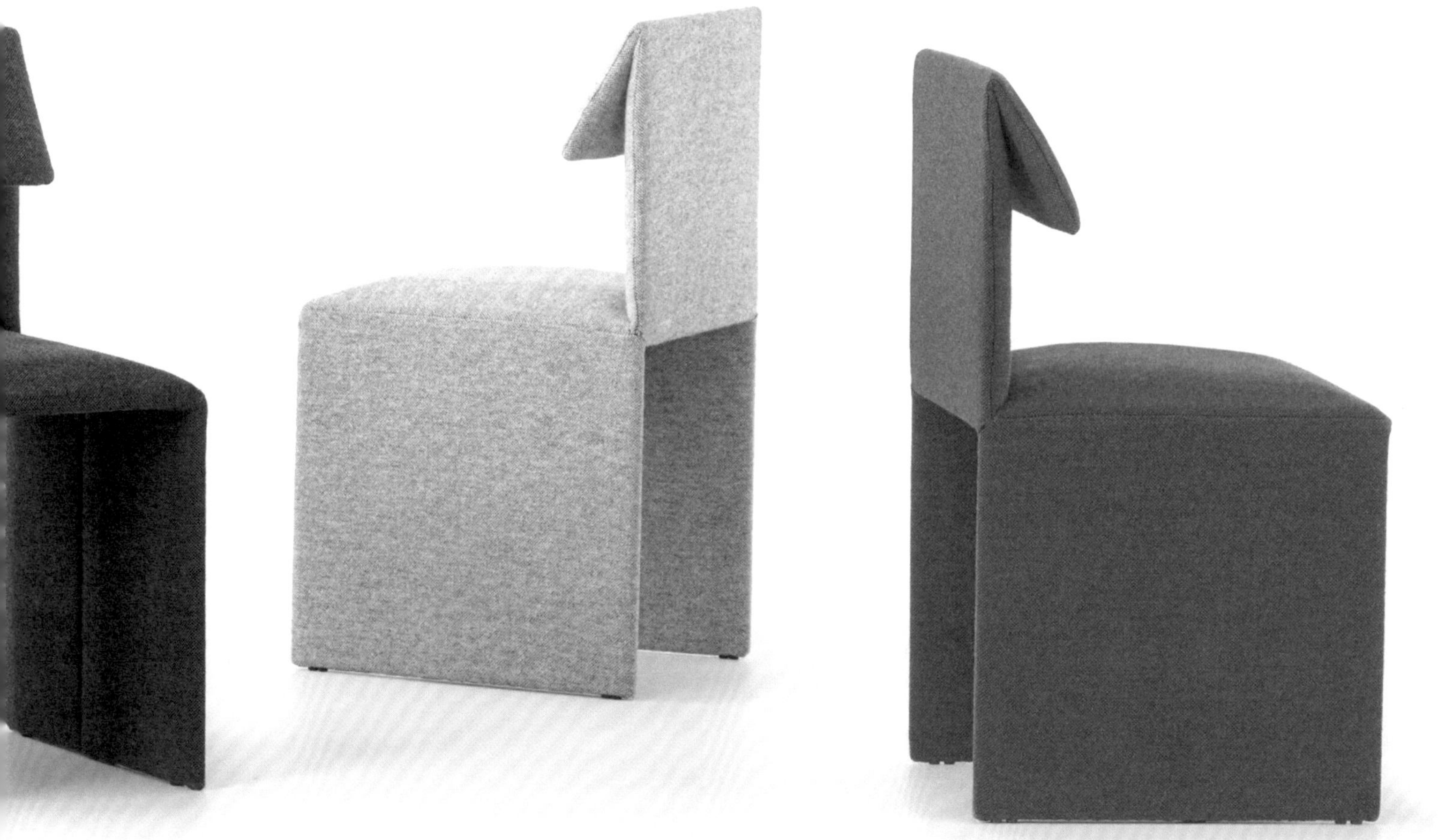

CECILIE MANZ

EN table and chair. Wood. Maruni. 2022.

For the Danish designer Cecilie Manz, every product must have a good reason to exist. Between industrial design and furniture, branded objects, and experimental one-offs, her work is as sculptural as it is rational, as serene as it is expressive. Whether it's speakers you can shove into a shoulder bag or a ladder that's also a chair, her designs have function and longevity, simplicity and purity.

Manz was born in Odsherred and studied design at the Royal Danish Academy of Fine Arts before launching her office in Copenhagen in 1998. Today she creates furniture, tableware, lighting, and electronics for clients including Duravit, Fritz Hansen, Hermès, Iittala, and Muuto. She sees each project as a "fragment" of a larger, ongoing project, a series linked by concepts, meticulously considered materials, or aesthetics. Her ideas are generated by research, drafting, and modeling, not lightning strikes of inspiration. While designing updated Bluetooth speakers for Bang & Olufsen in 2020—the Beolit 20 (robustly curved, subtly colorful, user-intuitive) and the Beosound A1 (like a water-worn stone)—she did a lot of research. Although she enjoys music, Manz isn't an audiophile. So, she asked questions and listened carefully to the engineers.

Manz's forty-seven-piece "CMA Clay" porcelain dinnerware collection for 1616/arita japan (2021) is an exquisitely balanced design uniting austere and soft, glazed and unglazed. It is the result of three years of close dialog and listening, hundreds of hand-drawn sketches, 3D files, 2D drawings, mock-ups, 3D prints, and countless prototypes. Her seating designs are balanced and minimal, but full of character. The EN chair (2022) is rich with contradictions: its loop-frame legs look modern, but its rounded backrest was inspired by an ancient Greek *klismos* chair. Modest in scale but generous in proportion, it blends crisp edges and radiused corners and is spare but welcoming. It is impossible to separate its function from its beauty.

CMA Clay dinnerware. Porcelain. 1616/arita japan. 2021.

Beolit 20 bluetooth speaker. Aluminum, leather, polymer.
Bang & Olufsen. 2020.

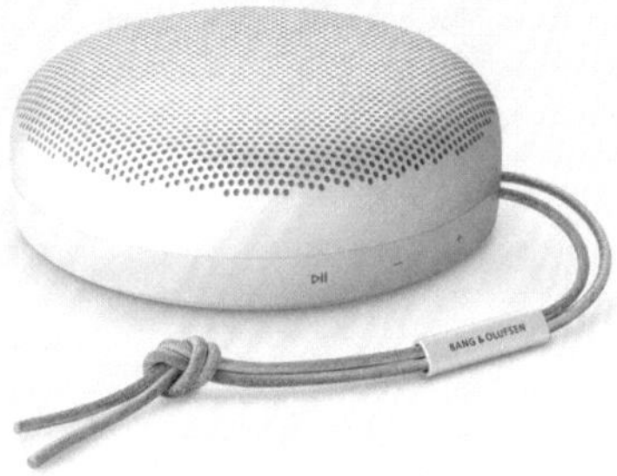

Beosound A1 bluetooth speaker. Aluminum, polymer, leather.
Bang & Olufsen. 2016/2020.

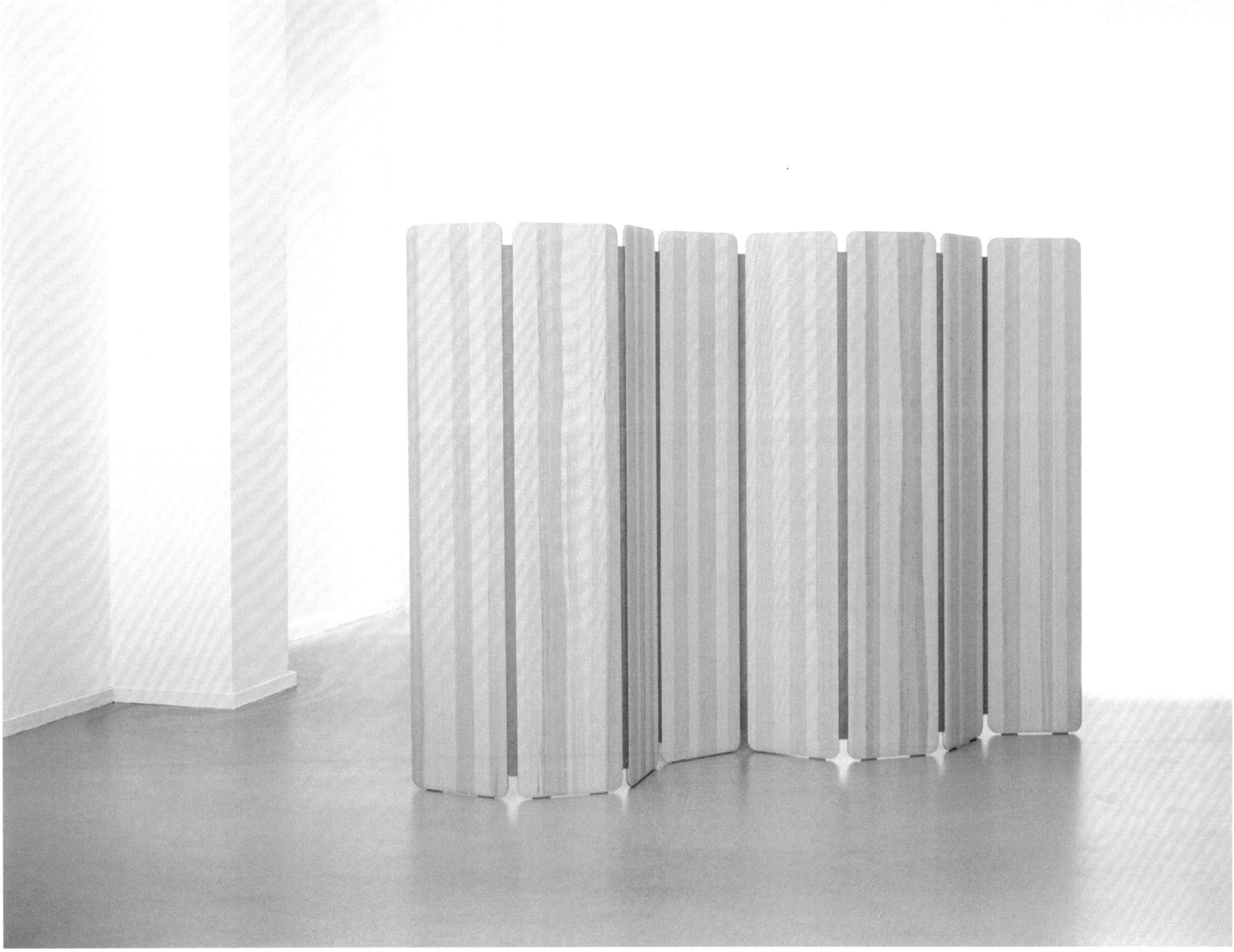

Separat room divider. Northern pine or European ash, leather. Nikari. 2018.

SABINE MARCELIS

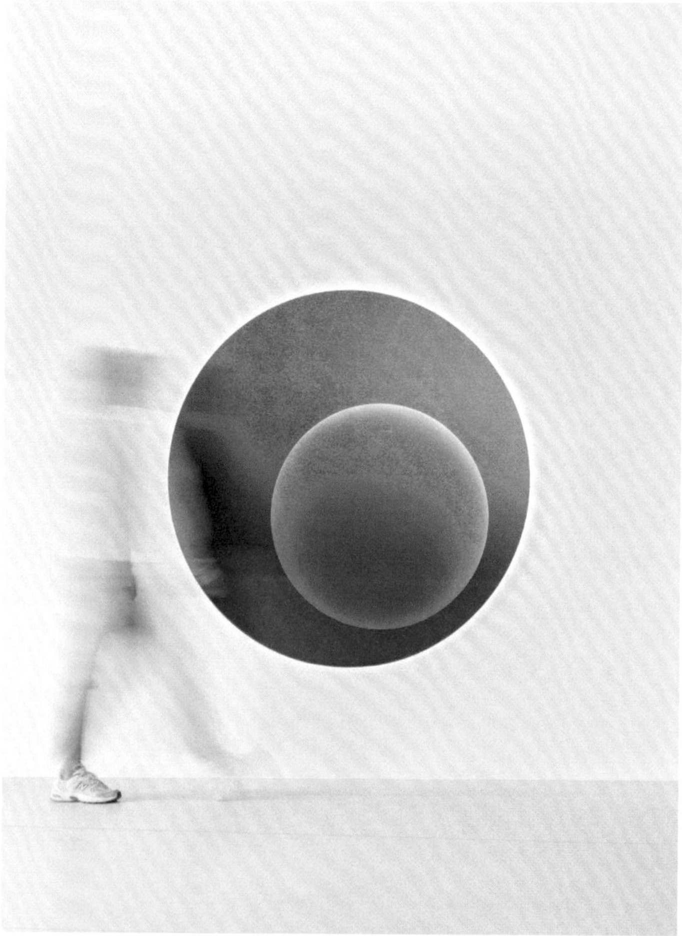

Mirage Mirrors. Layered glass, LED. 2021.

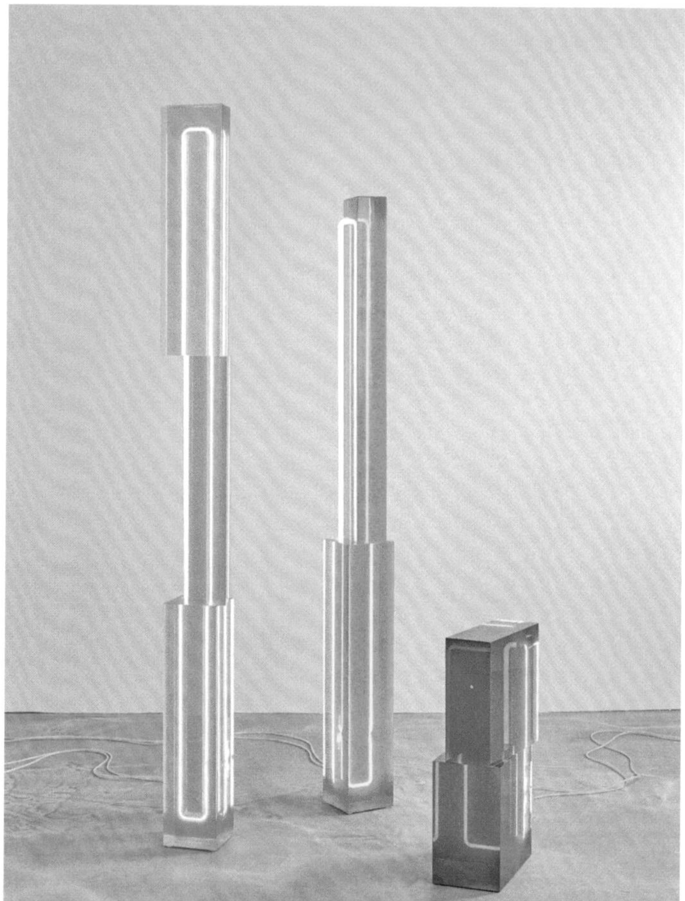

Totem Lights. Cast polyester resin, glass neon tubes. 2018.

For Sabine Marcelis, the function of a chair isn't just to provide a seat. It's to provide an experience that draws on the senses, an experience that becomes the function. Marcelis grew up in New Zealand, but was born in the Netherlands and graduated from the Design Academy Eindhoven in 2011. She opened her studio in Rotterdam to carry out product, installation, and spatial design focused on materials research and experimentation. Her work has a purity of form that highlights unconventional materiality while exploring light, color, and translucency. Today, her clients include the fashion designers Céline and Dior, the luxury watch label A. Lange & Söhne, IKEA, and Renault.

Perfectly formed, perfectly contained, and essential, Marcelis's pieces sometimes evoke places or ephemeral qualities and showcase materials in poetic ways. "Mirage" (2021) is a series of partially sand-blasted glass sculptures. Inspired by the hues and quality of light in Dubai, each layered, geometric piece reflects and diffuses ambient light, embodying the soft lines of dunes and the winking of city lights at dusk.

Likewise, Marcelis's public installations are as simple as they are sophisticated, as restrained as they are expressive. *Swivel* (2022) is a playground for passersby. Marcelis stacked thick slabs of different marbles and granites in contrasting patterns to build swiveling armchairs that sit in St. Giles Square, central London.

For *No Fear of Glass* (2019), an exhibition in the Mies van der Rohe Foundation's Barcelona Pavilion, Marcelis created sculptural but functional furnishings that seemed to emerge from the glass, travertine, and chrome of the pavilion's architecture: two pillar lights, a ribbon-like reflecting fountain, and chaise longues made of delicate slivers of ombré-tinted glass slotted into stone berms. Instead of mimicking the architecture that inspired them, they assumed their own life: sympathetic, dynamic, and rich with character.

Mirage Mirrors. Layered glass, LED. 2021.

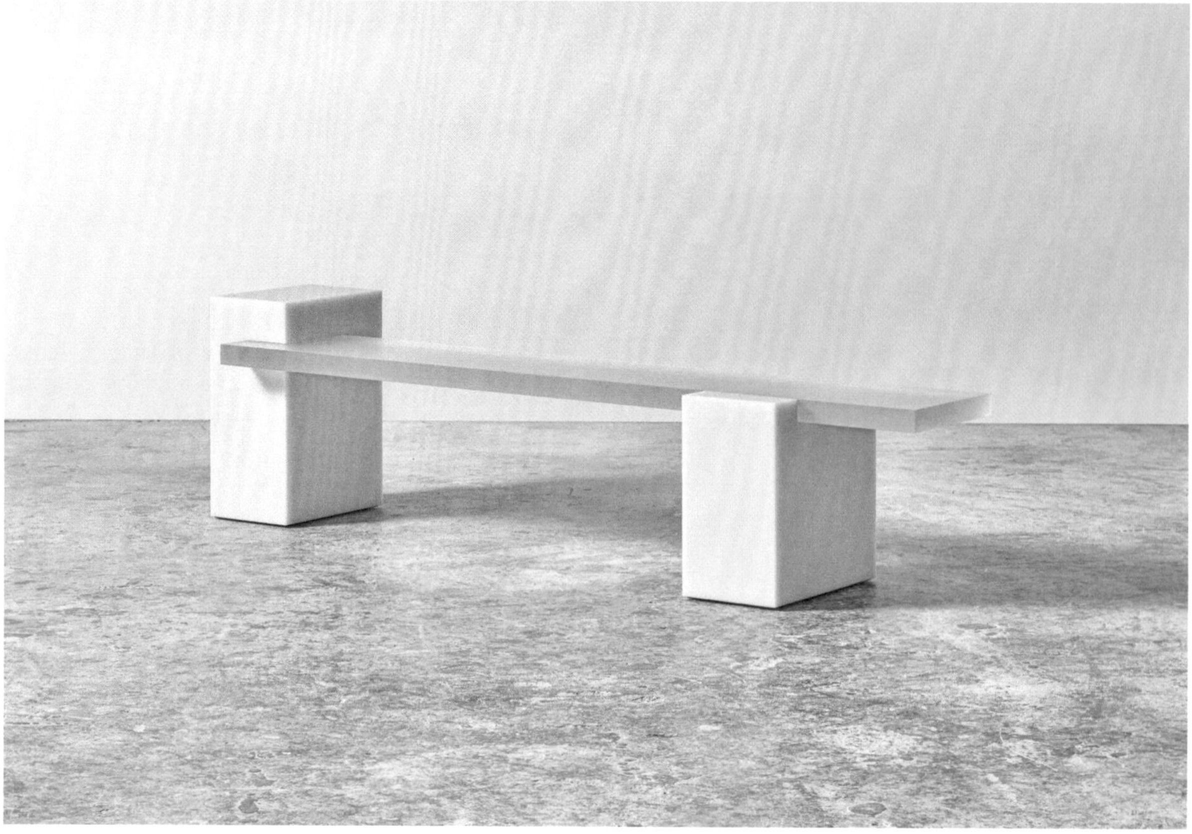

Butter Bench. Cast polyester resin. 2023.

Swivel chairs. Marble, granite. 2022.

No Fear of Glass. Stone, layered glass. 2019.

NIFEMI MARCUS-BELLO

LM Stool. Steel. Tranos. 2018.

Nifemi Marcus-Bello grew up in Lagos taking things apart. Apprenticing with a welder while still a teenager, in his spare time he peeked inside swing sets and footballs to learn how they worked. After studying product design in Leeds, UK, he worked on medical devices and furniture before returning to Lagos to establish nmbello Studio in 2017, plugging himself into the city's busy manufacturing infrastructure in order to start putting things together.

Marcus-Bello's personal spaces tend to be minimalist, but his professional interest isn't so much in streamlining as in adapting to the systems and materials already in use. Thus the multipurpose, geometric LM Stool (2018), the result of an investigation into the electrical power generators used across Nigeria. The casing of the generators is made of sheet metal, and the stool comes from the same material, with everything inessential—including legs, which are replaced with angled panels—trimmed away. Similarly, Marcus-Bello's Waf. Kiosk (2021–22), a modular set-up developed for a local skateboarding brand, came from an exploration of another popular material, the bamboo used in Benin for window blinds. An elegant hexagonal structure, its tubular-steel frame wrapped in bamboo, the kiosk can be set up in a variety of ways, evoking the stands of local merchants just as much as a Leonardo da Vinci sketch for a flying machine.

The designer's trademarks are perhaps his inquisitiveness and his light touch, both of which allow him to hew new forms from familiar materials. In the installation *Orikì (Act I): Friction Ridge* (2023), techniques of lost-wax casting once used to sculpt Benin royals in bronze have been adapted to create handsome semicircular benches. In the background, a recording plays of Marcus-Bello's mother reciting *orikì*—Yoruba praise poetry—a warm affirmation that structures all the designer's creations.

Friction Ridge seating sculptures. Bronze. With Godwin Ehizogie Eboh and Balogun Segun Joshua. 2022.

Waf. Kiosk. Steel, bamboo. With Fatai Adisa, Kofi Narh, and Jaiyeola Oduyoye. 2021–22.

MARZ DESIGNS

Bermuda Wall Light, Plum. Marble, aluminum. 2019.

Selene Uplight. FSC certified timbers, aluminum. With Timber Turner: Melbourne Table Co. 2022.

The idyllic setting of Byron Bay has been the base for Coco Reynolds's successful studio, Marz Designs, since 2019. Her work explores a connection to place through materials and makers, and for Reynolds, the design process tests this through the inherent qualities of material textures and characteristics. From clay through wood, glass through metal, her lighting compositions are especially arresting and rely on collaboration with artisans.

The Bermuda Wall Light (2019), for instance, produced by Marz, was designed as a simple yet arresting geometric wall sconce whether switched on or off. Its austere form—a triangular base with an offset circular diffuser—is a foil for the veined textures of red, Carrara, or Verde Antigua marble, detailed with three tiny pins in brass or blackened brass.

Material contrast is employed to effect in the Selene Uplight (2022), in which turned wood is set against the rigidity of metal. Formed of a quarter-sphere of ash or walnut, the smoothly hewn shade reveals growth rings that create a delicate pattern across the precise shape. Cross-grained lamp holders continue this effect, complemented by a wall plate of metal (brass or aluminum).

Reynolds also recognizes the power of collaboration. In the "Lini" lighting range (2022), each borosilicate tube is individually blown by local artists Formation Glass. With immaculate carbon-tooled details, the design exploits opaque and reeded glass to form the milky and transparent sleeves, which are suspended from woven flex cord or rigid steel and nested to create a soft, diffuse glow.

In keeping with Reynolds's vision for a sustainable design agency built on collaboration—the "many hands" that built each light—every design is custom-made to avoid waste. This timely outlook, paired with her raw modern aesthetic, continues to win her a loyal following.

Lini Pendant Light. Glass, aluminum. With Formation Glass. 2022.

MASH.T DESIGN STUDIO

Bright Light. Timber and beads. 2021.

Hlabisa bench. Ilala palm. Houtlander. 2019.

The first product Thabisa Mjo designed was a sculptural pendant light with boldly curved lines that match bright beads, yarn, and cord, inspired by South Africa's colorful pleated Xibelani skirts. She dreamed up the idea in 2015 after deciding, on a whim, to enter Nando's Hot Young Designer Talent Search competition. To her surprise, her design won, marking the start of a whirlwind creative trajectory. The light was later released as the Tutu 2.0 (2016) and is now in the permanent collection of the Musée des Arts Décoratifs in Paris.

Mjo, founder of Mash.T Design Studio in Sandton, South Africa, has emerged as a leading light in South Africa's contemporary design scene, fusing a rich collision of technology and traditional crafts with the texture, colors, and stories of her homeland. For Mjo, luxury equates to the crafted and the handmade, fueling socially conscious collaborations with traditional artisans across the country.

Mjo's work is also flavored with the stories, rituals, and narratives that define her homeland's DNA, as reflected in the Hlabisa bench (2019). The undulating back evokes childhood memories of visits to the hills of Kwazulu-Natal, while the angled legs were inspired by the cast-iron *potjie* cooking pots in her grandmother's home. The patterned textile required more than 1,300 hours of craftsmanship, using natural and dyed ilala palm tightly coiled. The bench is reportedly the first South African object to have entered the Design Section of the Centre Pompidou, Paris.

Mjo's Bright Light (2021) is a pendant lamp as bold in form as it is painstakingly handcrafted. Its strong, tiered form is wrapped in vivid patterns brought to life from thousands of glass and wood beads, expertly arranged on a turned timber carcass at Qaqambile Bead Studio in Cape Town. This formula of balancing the crafted with a distinctly modern South African design voice is threaded through her creative output—from lighting and furniture to ceramics and collectibles.

The Act of Measuring table. American red oak, ebony slow stain. With Always Welcome, Houtlander and BOS Timbers. 2022.

Bright Side tables. Ilala palm. With Bambizulu. 2021.

MATERRA-MATANG

Pleyel Interior, sofa, bookshelf. Birch, earth lime plaster. 2021.

Integrating design, architecture, and research, the forward-looking work of Materra-Matang is marked out by its focus on experimenting with natural materials to create contemporary work with a strong connection to place. Formed in 2022 of three architects and carpenters—Ophélie Dozat, Lucien Dumas, and Lou-Poko Savadogo—the atelier is young, but its approach is imbued with the age-old wisdom of the natural world.

At once spare and arresting, the Rassoï bench S.04.F (2020) is expertly crafted from a frame of ash, its stripped construction forming a frame across which Danish paper rope is tautly woven. Dyed in gradated hues of rust, ocher, and lemon created from turmeric and the roots of madder and alkanet, the string seating enlivens the spartan form, while two white keys honed from Makrana marble secure the frame.

Natural dyes and ancient techniques also mark out the Burnt Cabinet R.03.Cb.01. (2021), which recalls the weight and presence of an eighteenth-century commode. Its deeply burnished cedar body draws on the Japanese art of *shou sugi ban*, preserving wood through a flamed finish, while its hinges, handles, and fixtures are picked out in Danish paper cord dyed vibrant yellow with turmeric.

Materra-Matang's interior and architectural projects demonstrate a deep respect for place and context at a larger scale. A commission in 2021 for a 1930s apartment in the Batignolles district of Paris called for a comfortable yet functional living and workspace. On closer inspection the walls were found to carry the remnants of frescoes, so the studio worked with these layers of history by delicately inserting a "library" and sofa into the space, complemented by lime-plastered walls. Crafted without ironmongery, the expressed ash and oak connections of the bookcase speak of traditional joinery methods, while the sofa revisits burned timber finishes, set atop cork feet fixed together with paper cord and marble keys.

Burnt Cabinet R.03.Cb.01. Burnt cedar, paper rope. 2021.

Rassoï bench S.04.F. Ash, weaving, paper rope. 2020.

CASEY MCCAFFERTY

Sculptural Coffee Table in Oxidized Walnut and Stone. 2022.

Sculptural Console in Oiled Walnut and Chlorite. 2022.

A sculptor working with wood, stone, and metal, McCafferty blends images from nature, history, myth, and science fiction to create anything from unique furniture, lighting, and objects to wall-hung and freestanding artworks. He has no formal training. Descended from bricklayers and stonemasons, he is familiar with masonry, but he studied business and went to work for a bank. By 2016, however, he'd found his sculptural footing and opened a workshop in Los Angeles.

Today, McCafferty's studio in Fair Lawn, New Jersey, is kitted out with chainsaws, grinders, hundreds of hand tools (such as mallets and gouges), and classic woodworking equipment for milling and gluing up. He rarely limits himself by sketching ideas by hand or on the computer. Instead, starting with a block of material and a cutting tool, he gives his pieces such elaborate, intuitive forms that it's hard to believe they're functional. They usually are.

McCafferty's *Totem Vignette* (2020) demonstrates his movement along the spectrum from traditional woodworking to freer expression and greater complexity. At first his pieces were classical and vertical. Later objects, such as his *Sculptural Wall-Hung Totemic Light* (2022), are weightier, grander in scale, and latent with a powerful feeling of captured motion. He's also stopped perching flat tabletops over his sculptures, instead creating monolithic, seamless, uncompromising pieces, such as *Sculptural Console in Oiled Walnut and Chlorite* (2022).

McCafferty now grafts stone sculptures onto the wood, as he did with one of the feet of his *Cairn Series Chair* (2023). Other pieces have elements that can come apart. For the *Sculptural Coffee Table in Oxidized Walnut and Stone* (2022), he carved a hole in the tabletop into which a carved stone can nest. Clients have the choice to take it out or leave it in, allowing them to interact more fully with the finished piece.

Cairn Series Chair. Ash, stone. 2023.

CHRISTIEN MEINDERTSMA

Pigeon Service. Woven and tufted linen. With Jos Vanneste, volunteers of museum Texture, and Stoffenhuis Langhorst. 2015.

The Dutch designer Christien Meindertsma investigates provenance and process, raw materials and resources, the life of a product and the impact it has on human life. At times, the result of her research is the record of a production process or a memento of a place or event; often, it also becomes a designed product, itself the product of the investigation of a product. Through deft inquiry, documentation, and rational artistry, Meindertsma's projects detail industrial processes from which consumers have become increasingly alienated. Her designs identify a problem, then suggest an invariably elegant solution, sometimes delivering good news and bad in a single object.

Meindertsma was born in Utrecht and graduated from Design Academy Eindhoven in 2003. Since then, her work has explored forestry in the Flevopolder region of the Netherlands, the relationship between Japanese porcelain and Dutch linen, and ways to reincarnate old linoleum floors. Her book *PIG 05049* (2007) connects raw materials and everyday belongings. For three years she traced and photographed 185 commercial products to which the body of one slaughtered pig had contributed material. The book exposes the links between consumer and consumed.

When commissioned in 2014 to design a tapestry for Kortrijk's new flax-centric Texture Museum, Meindertsma created a lyrical memorial. During the First World War, the former warehouse had housed thousands of captured pigeons believed by occupying Germans to be used for spying. She bridged the histories of material and place by creating (with the tufter and linens expert Jos Vanneste) more than 300 textile birds tufted and hand-sewn by volunteers using diverse linen yarns. *Pigeon Service* (2014) was picked up by Thomas Eyck, a visionary curator and champion of designers, materials, and craft, for his "t.e." collection. Eyck also commissioned *Acoustic Poster* (2020), for which Meindertsma rescued upholstery offcuts and remnants, layering and felting them to make collage-like wall hangings.

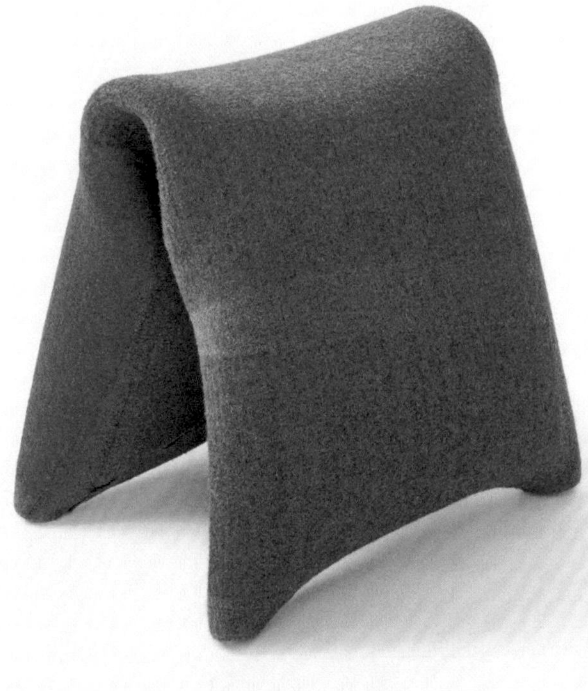

Saddle Blanket stool. Beechwood base, fabric offcuts, felted. With Gelderland for t.e. and Kuperus & Gardenier. 2020.

Renoleum material research project. Reused linoleum floors. With Blauw crushing, Forbo Proeffabriek, and Dalton College Alkmaar for Forbo Flooring. 2019.

Acoustic Poster wall hanging (back). Fabric offcuts, needle felted. With Gelderland for t.e. and Kuperus & Gardenier. 2020.

Acoustic Poster wall hanging (front). Fabric offcuts, needle felted. With Gelderland for t.e. and Kuperus & Gardenier. 2020.

MIMINAT DESIGNS

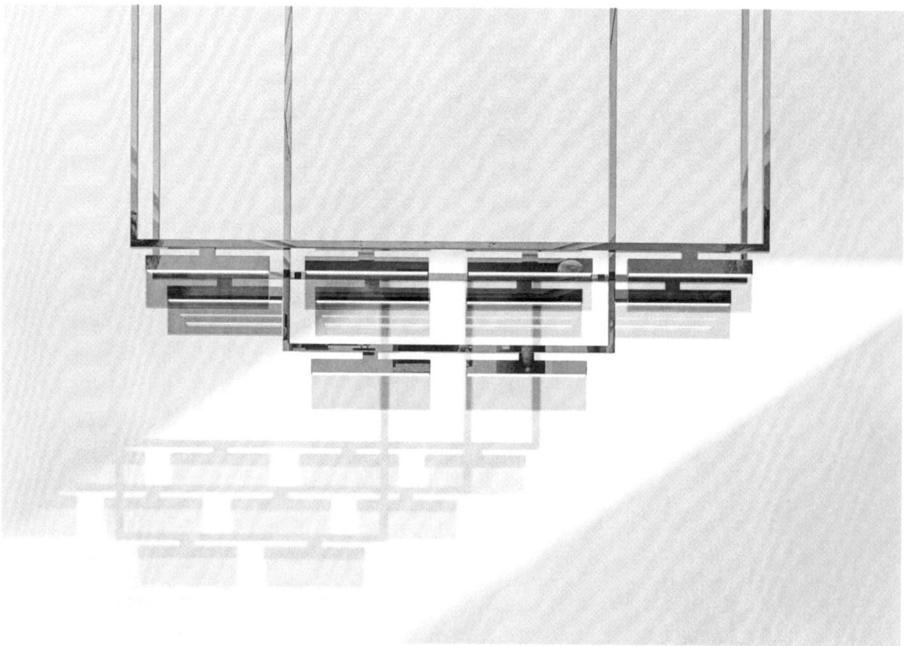

Jude Pendant light. Brass, polycarbonate glass, LED. 2021.

NRIN Vessels. Ash, aluminum. 2023.

Form precedes function in the flowing, graceful pieces of Miminat Shodeinde, a young designer who founded her studio, Miminat Designs, in 2015, while still a student in Edinburgh. Miminat Designs produces both products and interiors, and also markets its own creations, but perhaps the most significant of the studio's offerings is the sense of disciplined possibility inherent in each object and composition. Influenced by the greatest Modernist architects of the twentieth century—Ludwig Mies van der Rohe, Oscar Niemeyer, Lina Bo Bardi, and Carlo Scarpa—Shodeinde designs art objects for a future that seems just about to arrive.

In her attention to line and her careful selection of textures and materials, the British-Nigerian designer leans minimalist, and aims to merge traditional European and African approaches to craft. Her geometric Howard Daybed (2022), part of a collection inspired by the iconic reclusive pilot Howard Hughes, is handmade in London from titanium travertine, oil-stained ash, aluminum, and nubuck leather. The result is sleek and solemn, implying ritual as much as relaxation. The Rina Cabinet (2021), a structure of Cor-Ten steel, mahogany, brass, and oxblood aniline leather fronts, looks both ancient and futuristic, like storage for space travel. The Jude Pendant lights (2021), designed for a client in Kuwait, seem to multiply as one looks at them. Formed of panels of smoked polycarbonate glass suspended beneath horizontal bars of polished brass, the lights are a fixture for earthly use but seem equally suited for a cosmic voyage.

Shodeinde paints in her spare time, but her other true love is music, which might seem paradoxical for a creator of objects with such emphatically physical presence. But the tension is perhaps key to her work: concepts that she sets to paper and that her studio works rigorously to produce, manifesting these solid embodiments of ethereal thought.

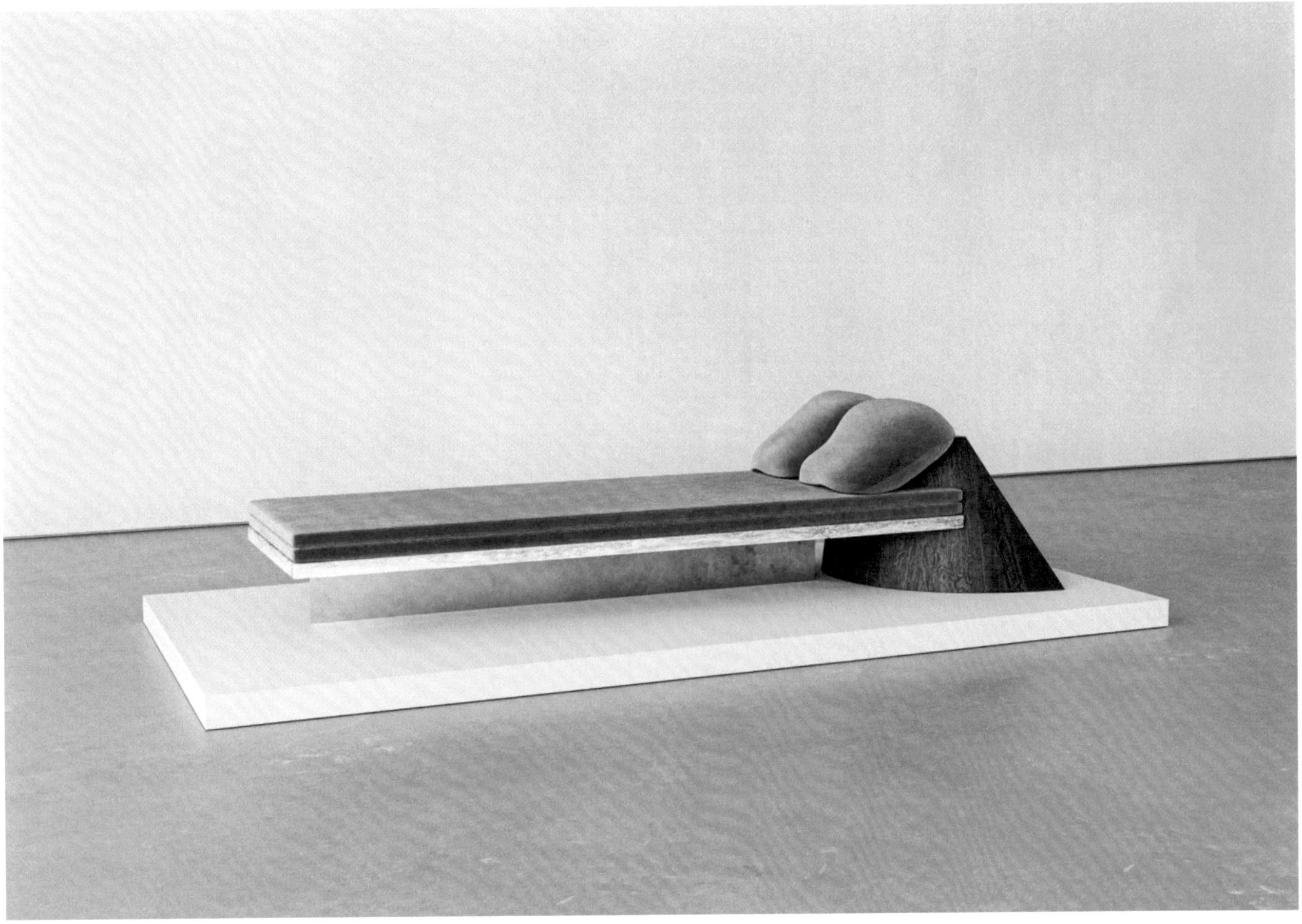

Howard Daybed. Aluminum, titanium travertine, ash, nubuck leather. 2022.

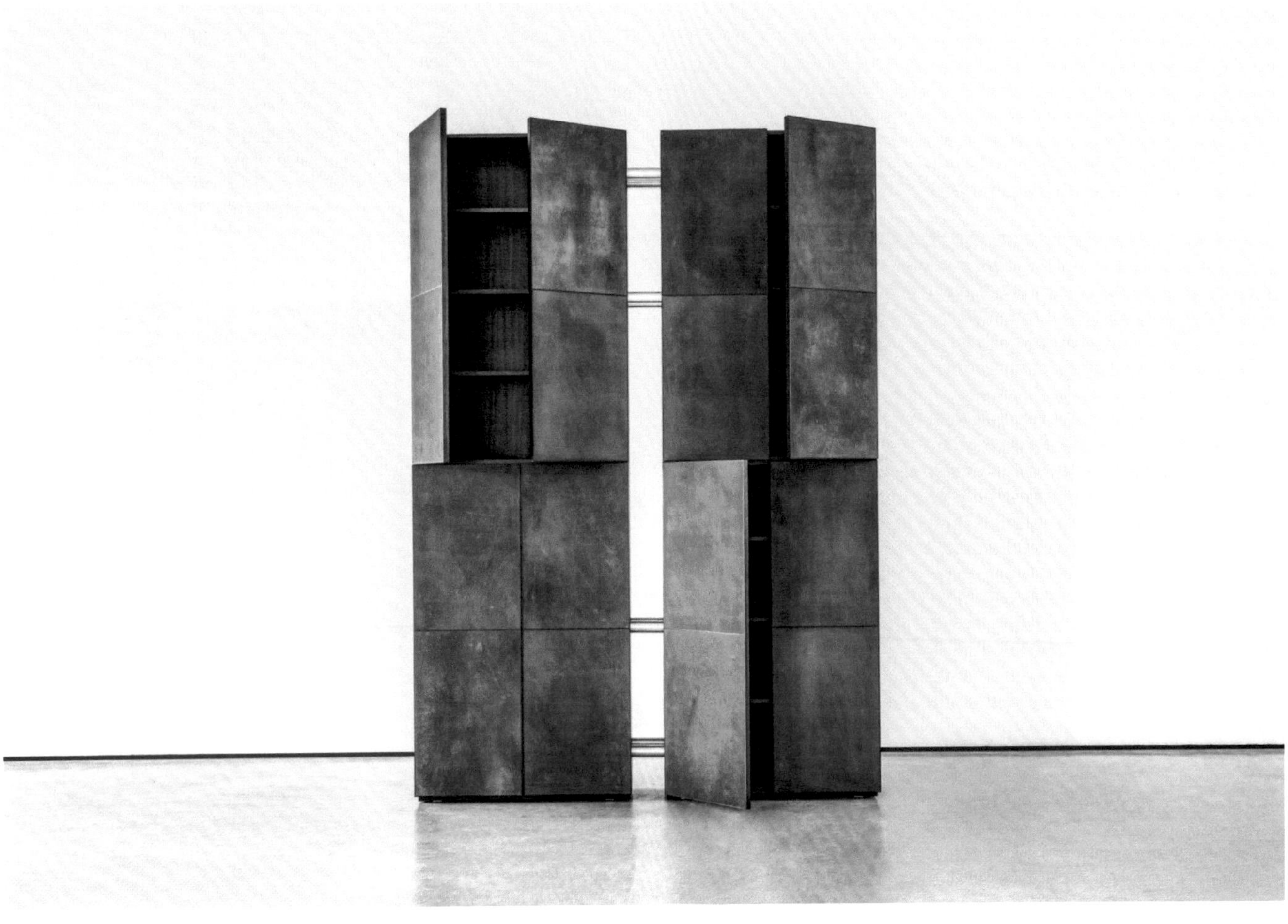

Rina Cabinet. Cor-Ten, brass, mahogany, oxblood aniline leather. 2021.

MISCHER'TRAXLER STUDIO

Breathing Chandeliers. Aluminum, fabric, Velcro, linear motors. Bruckschwaiger. 2022.

The studio that Katharina Mischer and Thomas Traxler founded in Vienna in 2009 is a research hub with the mission to seek out design solutions that span kinetic art, industrial design, and the study of materials. Mischer'traxler's approach is experimental; they assess the conditions of each context and examine the conceptual importance of every decision made in each phase of the project. One of the commandments the studio lives by is to create work with a unique element. This attitude gives its projects a revolutionary edge, as they challenge the user, causing unexpected reactions that result in a sense of wonder.

A constant theme in mischer'traxler's work is the creation of scenarios that generate spaces for relationships, places of interaction, and corners for reflection: in essence, artifacts that are rich in meaning and layers of interpretation. Their idea of design includes and embraces function as an opportunity to explore consciousness, not simply as a response to a need. The Access glassware (2022), for example, invites contemplation of the global distribution of clean drinking water. Each of the six glasses reflects the percentage of safely accessible clean drinking water (represented by the transparent part of the glass) in a specific region of the world.

Mischer'traxler's signature style is based on light, as well as an evolved and hyperbolic fascination with chandeliers. So, hotel lobbies, public spaces, and private interiors are the privileged contexts that have welcomed the studio's elaborate, colorful, and intricate lighting installations. These works bring the topics of nature and endangered species into a visual and conceptual conversation with the user, who—thanks to the entertainingly decorative aspect of the installations combined with the function of the illuminations—can ponder the themes that resonate with them the most. Mischer'traxler measures the world with products designed to arouse awareness and incite intellectual curiosity.

Entomarium Extinct lighting installation. Various materials. 2020.

Access glasses. Glass, engraved. 2022.

Reversed Volumes bowls. Food-safe resin. 2013.

"Ratio" collection. Zinc, stainless steel, copper, brass, aluminum, metal ores, lacquer. 2020.

Zn
8
1000
CuZn 37
Fe

NICOLE MONKS

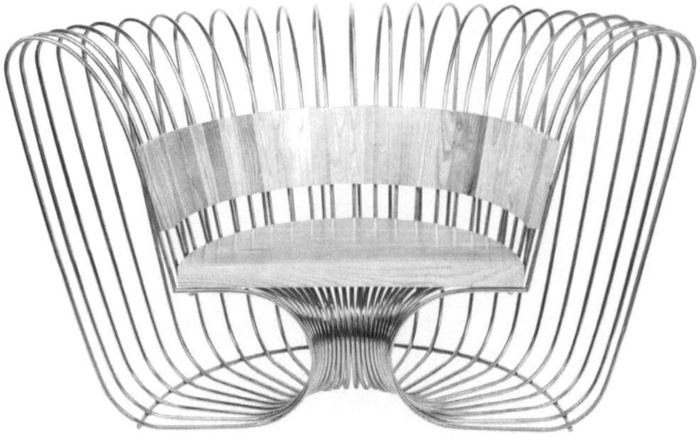

"Marlu" collection, Walarnu (boomerang). 24-carat-gold-plated steel, Tasmanian oak. 2016.

Connection to Country is integral to the artist and designer Nicole Monks, given her rich Dutch, English, and Yamaji Wajarri (Western Australia) heritage. Now living and working in Worimi and Awabakal Country (Newcastle), she produces work that discusses Indigenous understandings of Country, often through collaboration and by using materials sourced from the lands in which she works.

Time spent with family in Yamaji Wajarri inspired the three-part "Marlu" collection (2016) for the Australian Design Centre. Drawing on family stories, the pieces interpret memories of gatherings and of Monks's great-grandmother's kangaroo-tail stew. From this deeply personal source, Monks created the Walarnu (boomerang) chair, a composition of twenty-five hooped-steel bands united centrally to form the seat and back of a springy chair, unholstered in kangaroo skin. Another work from the collection, Wabarn-Wabarn (bounce), recalls a decadent, inviting robe of stitched furs draped over the circular frame and secured with native timber and kangaroo leather details. Each is custom-made, with editions produced to order so as to avoid waste.

Monks's understanding of collective power is conveyed in Miyarnu*wimanha* (2020), a commission for the Lock-Up arts space in Newcastle. The title, meaning "learning; becoming knowledgeable," was an opportunity for her to create site-specific installations that brought together work by Yamaji Wajarri and other First Nations artists across Australia. Natural materials feature heavily in the works, which range from floor installations of sand, sea fern, and eucalyptus bark through bags carefully crafted from animal skin. The collaboration encouraged learning from other Indigenous groups, and introduced layers of meaning that it would be impossible to create solo. The collective produced a rich, complex story of rivers, land, resources, and Indigenous practices.

Forging an important path to integrate design with Indigenous knowledge, Monks has received several national awards. Her works are also held in private and public Australian collections.

"Marlu" collection, Wabarn-Wabarn (bounce). Hemp canvas, 24-carat-gold-plated steel, recycled Tasmanian blackwood, kangaroo leather, fur. 2016.

Miyarnu*wimanha* exhibition at the Lock-Up. Kangaroo pelts, various materials. With Yamaji artists Jenine Boeree, Elvie Dann, Charmaine Green, Barbara Merritt, Yarra Monks, Donna Ronan, Chloe Sims, Michelle Sims, and Margaret Whitehurst. 2020.

"Marlu" collection, Nyinajimanha (sitting together). 24-carat gold plated steel, Tasmanian blackwood, kangaroo fur. 2016.

JASPER MORRISON

Oplight. Aluminum, polycarbonate, LED. Flos. 2021.

Jasper Morrison's dictum that "objects should never shout" guides all of the legendary designer's output, from industrial design through books through curation. Born in London, Morrison opened his studio there in 1986, and as a young designer fashioned objects from existing parts, absorbing the need for economy into his practice. Now, with designs in the collections of the Cooper Hewitt and the Museum of Modern Art, New York, and with numberless industry awards and collaborations with brands including Emeco, Hermès, Olivetti, Samsung, and Punkt under his belt, Morrison continues to dream up objects in the "super normal" style. These streamlined pieces approach the platonic ideal as nearly as extant objects can, and have become ubiquitous parts of the contemporary visual landscape.

The breadth of Morrison's work hasn't prevented him from spending years developing and testing prototypes, and his collaborations have been equally long-lived. To follow the Glo-Ball lights (1998–9) for Flos, he designed the Oplight (2021), a wall light in powder-coated die-cast aluminum, with a panel that reflects the LED light away from the wall: a sleek, perfectly self-sufficient, fully realized object. Likewise, Morrison's APC chair (2016) for Vitra, made from recyclable polypropylene and polyamide, appears—and is—simple. Yet two steel pins, allowing the back to pivot, subtly set the chair apart from other plastic models.

In interviews, Morrison has spoken about his interest in atmospheres and the inspiration he finds in objects with no designer attached—pieces whose great achievement has been to serve their purpose reliably over time. These, he finds, are often the most important objects in a space. By virtue of their long service, they acquire an aura, coming to define the place where they're situated. By this logic Morrison himself may be the echt designer—a definitive figure, entirely dedicated to the task at hand, and with remarkable aesthetic gifts that are perfectly suited to his work.

EVO-C chairs. Polypropylene. Vitra. 2020.

Wall Clock. Aluminum, acrylic. HAY. 2023.

Zampa chair. Ash. Mattiazzi. 2020.

JONATHAN MUECKE

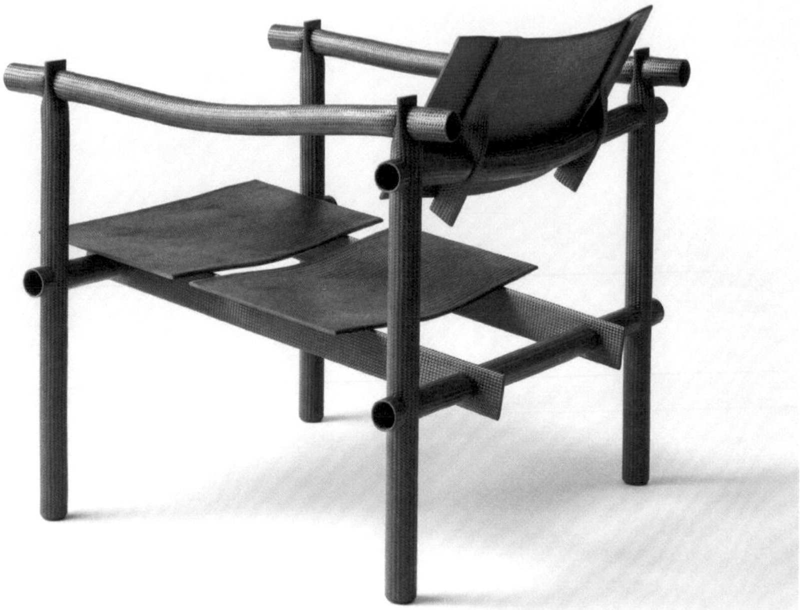

Jonathan Muecke's work is like the answer to a Zen *koan*. Rational and clarifying but experimental, hard to define, and with details unexpectedly full of meaning, his design resists pigeonholing and thrives on contradiction. Trained as an architect and a designer, he nonetheless has, as he puts it, "a general disinterest in objects." As he works, he scrutinizes the scale, proportion, spatial qualities, and material of an object "without addressing the sum of these qualities."

Stripping narrative and meaning away from his objects, Muecke is himself a man of few words. He simplifies and reduces and even names his products by describing their constituent parts and construction, not what they do—Fiberglass Stack 1 (2019, for MANIERA gallery, Brussels), instead of Fiberglass Shelf—then abbreviates that title further: FS1.

Today, Muecke's work feels architectural, partly because he tends to test material properties rigorously and, in the process, refines forms over and over, examining how they generate positive and negative space. WFB, created in 2022 for the Volume Gallery in Chicago, is a wooden box that rests on the floor. Large, uniform holes cut into it describe a grid, turning the box into an expressive, even decorative, coffee table.

Muecke describes his work in broad, simple terms, leaving out the reasons and revelations. His products have an intentional, often repetitious, straightforwardness, which he feels "frees the object from any kind of narrative." In the simplest terms, he works assiduously to explore what makes a specific object that object and not another object, then experiments to make it more and more itself and less and less not itself. His process often begins with an intensive period of research, during which he tests a material "in the abstract" before beginning to transform it into an object. The object, itself, is almost superfluous.

CTL (Carbon Tube Lounge) chair. Carbon fiber. 2022.

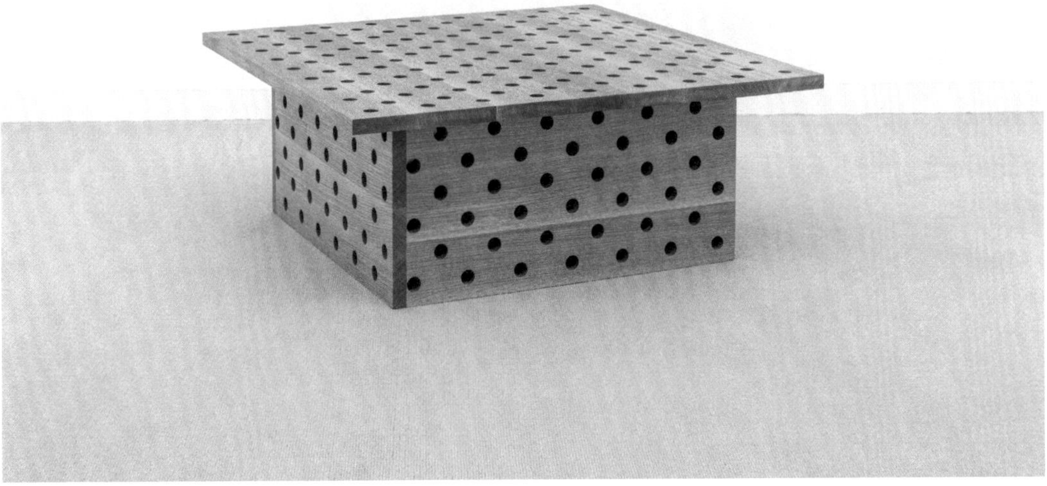

WFB (Wood Floor Box) table. White oak. 2022.

WS (Wood Stack) shelf. Douglas fir. 2022.

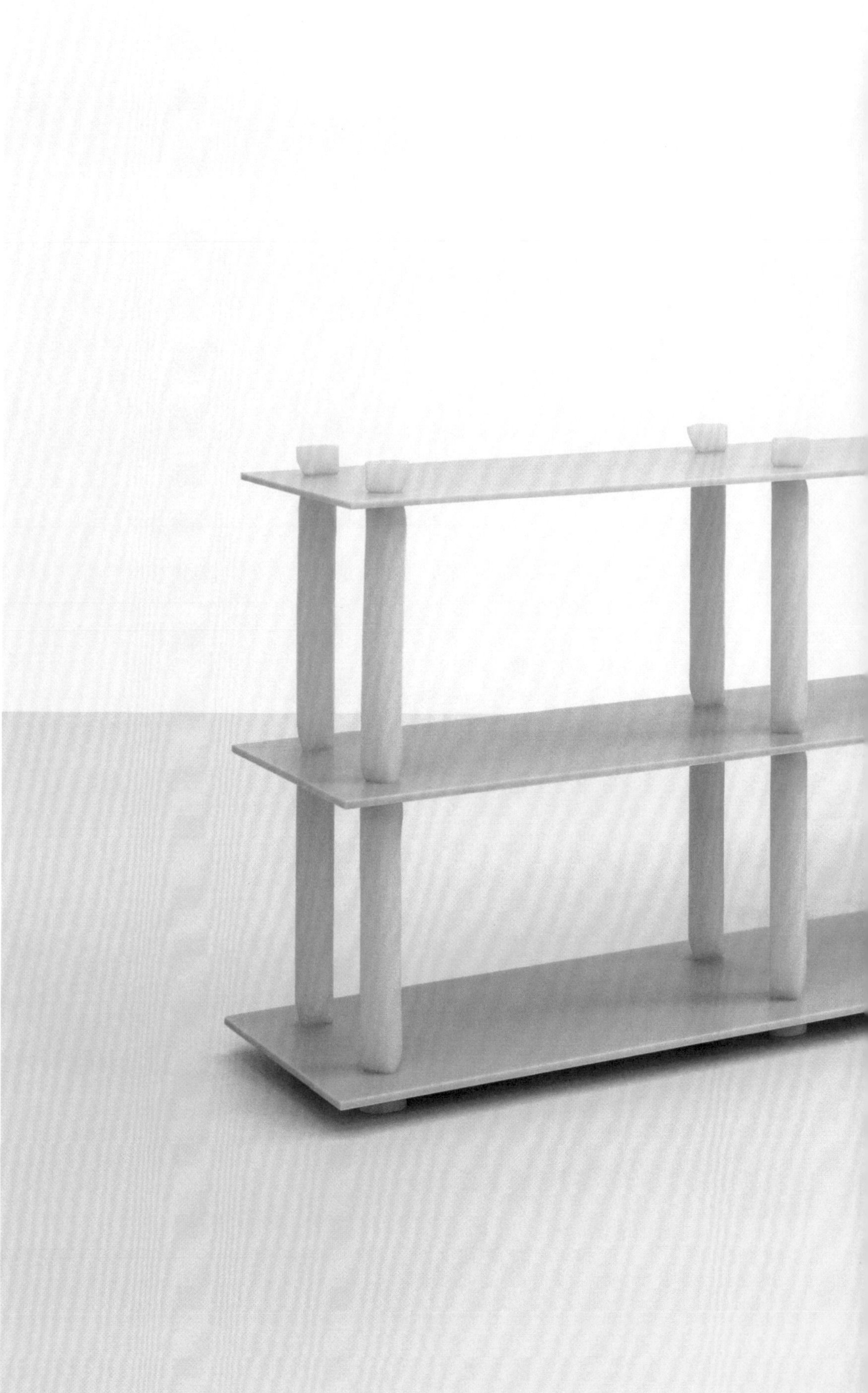

FS (Fiberglass Stack) shelf. Fiberglass. 2019.

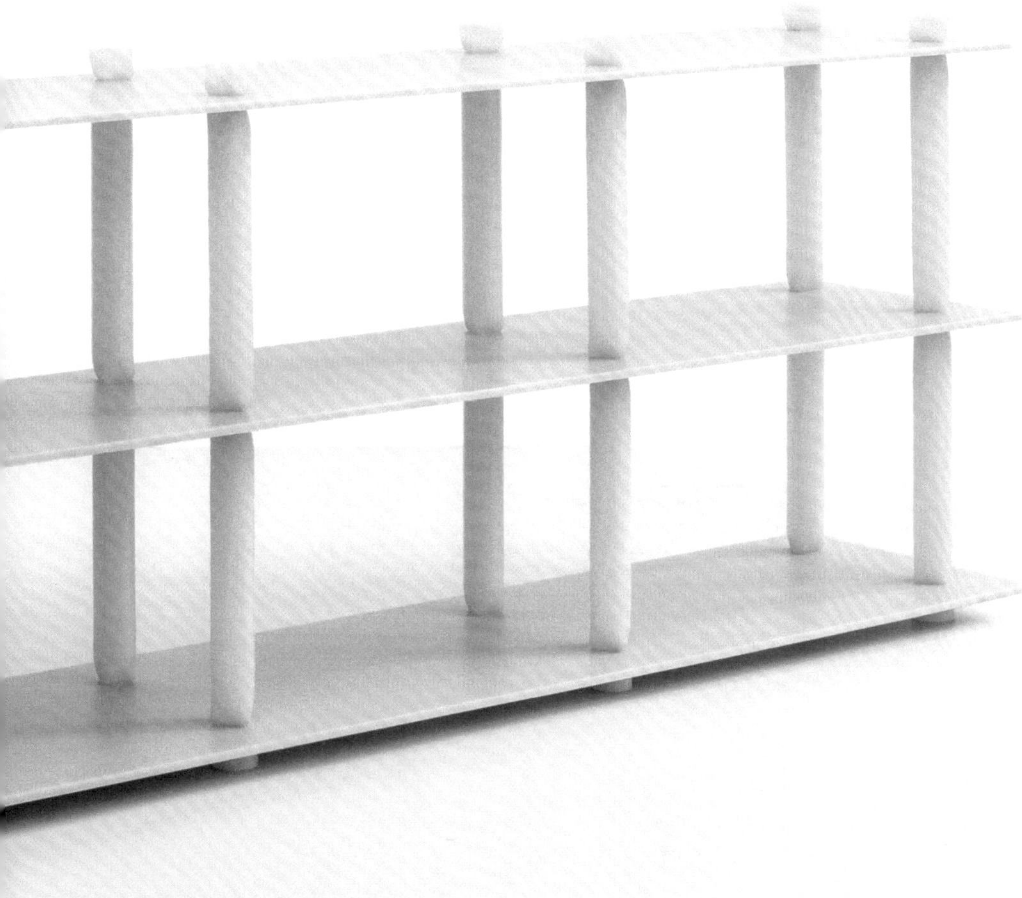

MULLER VAN SEVEREN

Future Primitives furniture. Steel, polyethylene, leather. 2012.

Chromatic color schemes, sculptural forms, material explorations... such elemental qualities make the unique creations of the Belgian design studio Muller Van Severen instantly recognizable. The studio, launched by artists Fien Muller and Hannes Van Severen in 2011, possesses a distinctive visual language that consistently shines through in its furniture, lighting, and objects for daily life. The founders' backgrounds in sculpture and photography have left a creative imprint on their work, which often floats between design and art.

An early defining moment was its participation in the exhibition *Future Primitives* (2012) at Belgium's Biennale Interieur in Kortrijk, for which the studio dreamed up furniture for the future. The result was innovative structures combining basic functions into a single object, structured cleanly from configurations of steel bars, with color-burst inserts of polyethylene shelving and natural leather seating. The pieces not only tapped into a functional sensitivity to the limitations of domestic space, but also explored how design can juxtapose experiences for the user (as is the case with Rack + Seat, which provides a chair for the reader right next to their bookshelf).

A love of material, in all its raw and irregular beauty, has also been a continuum throughout the studio's creations, and the designers have long been drawn to a spectrum of textures: leather, polyethylene, brass, marble, and steel. Testimony to this is the "Alltubes" collection (2020), which taps into aluminum, repeated tubes of which form a family of contemporary seating and cabinets. The mundanity of cutting boards has also been transformed into abstract artworks, with four organically shaped polyethylene boards (2011) in typically playful colors hanging from a brass peg.

A distinctive creative voice in European contemporary design, the studio has long collaborated with a raft of institutions, from the Vitra Design Museum and Centre Pompidou, Paris, to HAY and Galerie kreo.

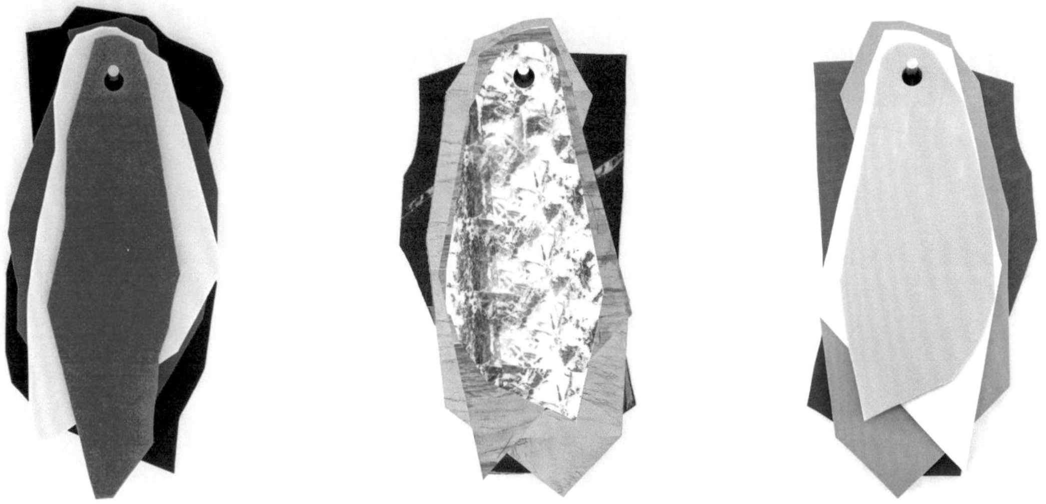

Cutting Boards. Polyethylene, brass. valerie_objects. 2022.

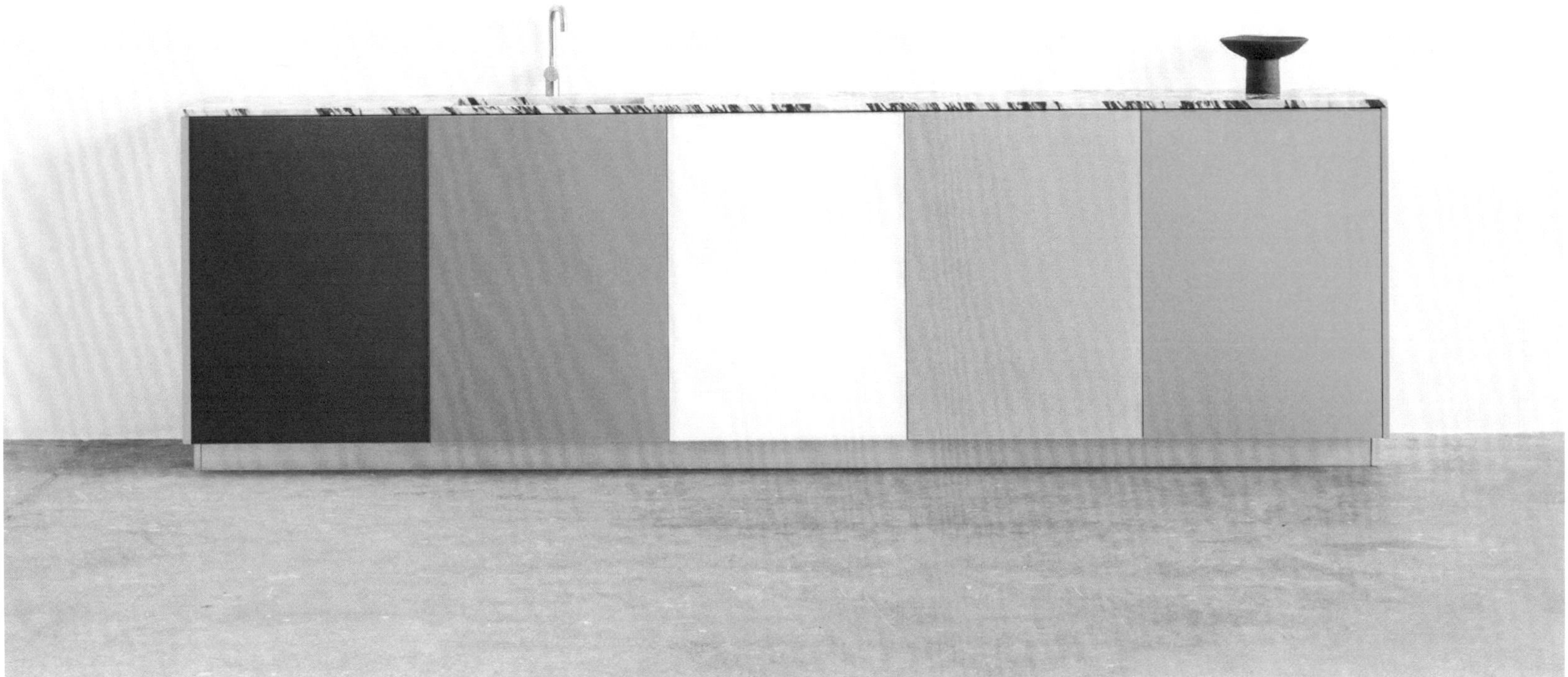

Match kitchen. Polyethylene, brass. Reform. 2018.

Future Primitives furniture. Steel, polyethylene, leather. 2012.

Alltubes cabinet, bench, and chair. Aluminum. 2020.

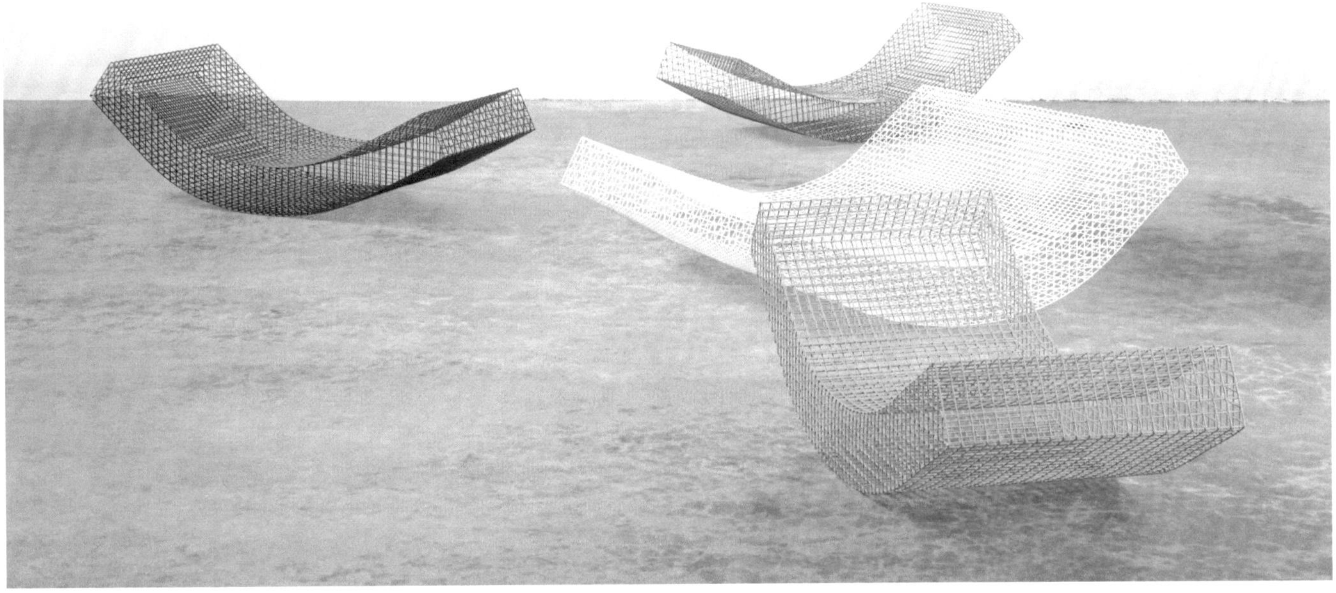

Wire s seats. Stainless steel. 2016.

Wire s shelving. Stainless steel. 2016.

NENDO

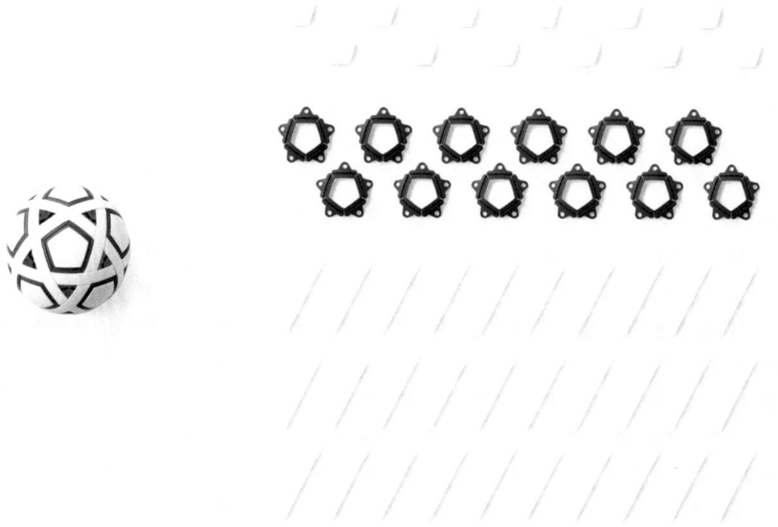

My Football Kit. Polypropylene, elastomeric synthetic resin. Molten. 2021.

It was in 2002 that Oki Sato set up nendo with five friends in his parents' garage in Tokyo. It is today one of the most distinctive design voices in Japan. Playfully functional, minimalist, and modern, its prolific output is instantly recognizable and complements every element of the quotidian, from houses to paperclips.

A clue to the studio's shapeshifting vision lies in its name—"clay" in Japanese—and it embraces a malleable mix of forms, including architecture, interiors, graphic design, and daily objects. Also key is a fluidly international outlook, no doubt a legacy of Sato spending part of his childhood in Canada, fueling an unusual clarity in unraveling and translating Japan's complex cultural layers for the outside world.

The studio turned heads early with the Cabbage Chair (2008) for an exhibition curated by Issey Miyake, crafted from rolls of paper left over from the iconic brand's pleated textile-making process and now part of the permanent collection of the Museum of Modern Art in New York. The studio's fast-paced trajectory hit a high in 2021 with the Olympic Cauldron for the summer Games in Tokyo: a white sphere inspired by the sun, with panels opening like petals.

The Chaise Medaillon 3.0 (2021), meanwhile, filters the classic medallion chair beloved of Christian Dior through a minimalist modern prism, resulting in a barely there transparent structural imprint. Its simplicity of form belies a complex exploration of high-tech innovation.

More often than not, daily life is center stage for nendo. My Football Kit (2021) aims to increase the accessibility and popularity of soccer among children around the world. Inspired by woven Japanese bamboo balls, nendo designed a modular soccer ball with fifty-four interlocking pieces, to make it more durable, portable, and easily maintainable than its conventional inflatable counterparts. For nendo, it's not about big gestures; it's about dreaming up simple, playful ideas that improve people's lives.

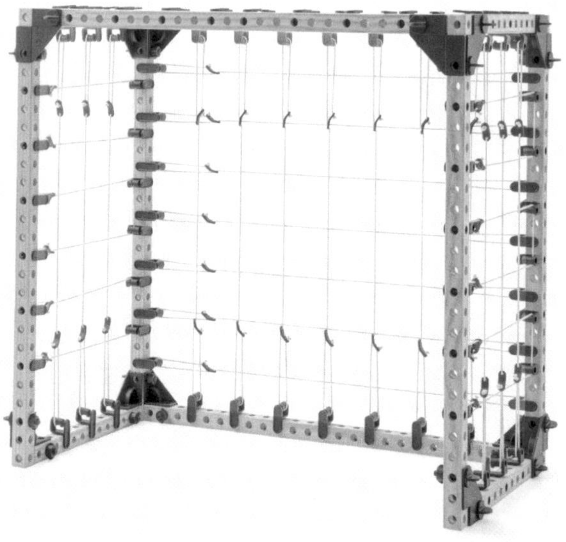

My Football Kit, Goal Kit. 2×2 lumber, synthetic resin mixture. Molten. 2023.

Jellyfish vase installation. Silicone vases in aquarium. 2017.

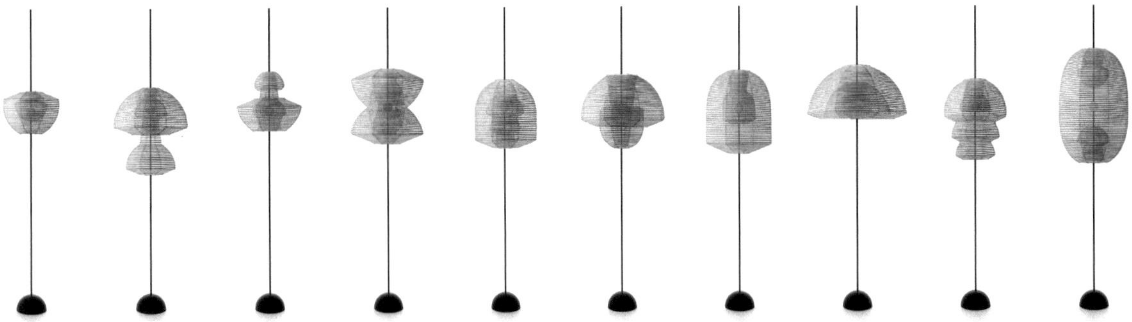

Hyouri lanterns. Bamboo, silk lining. 2021.

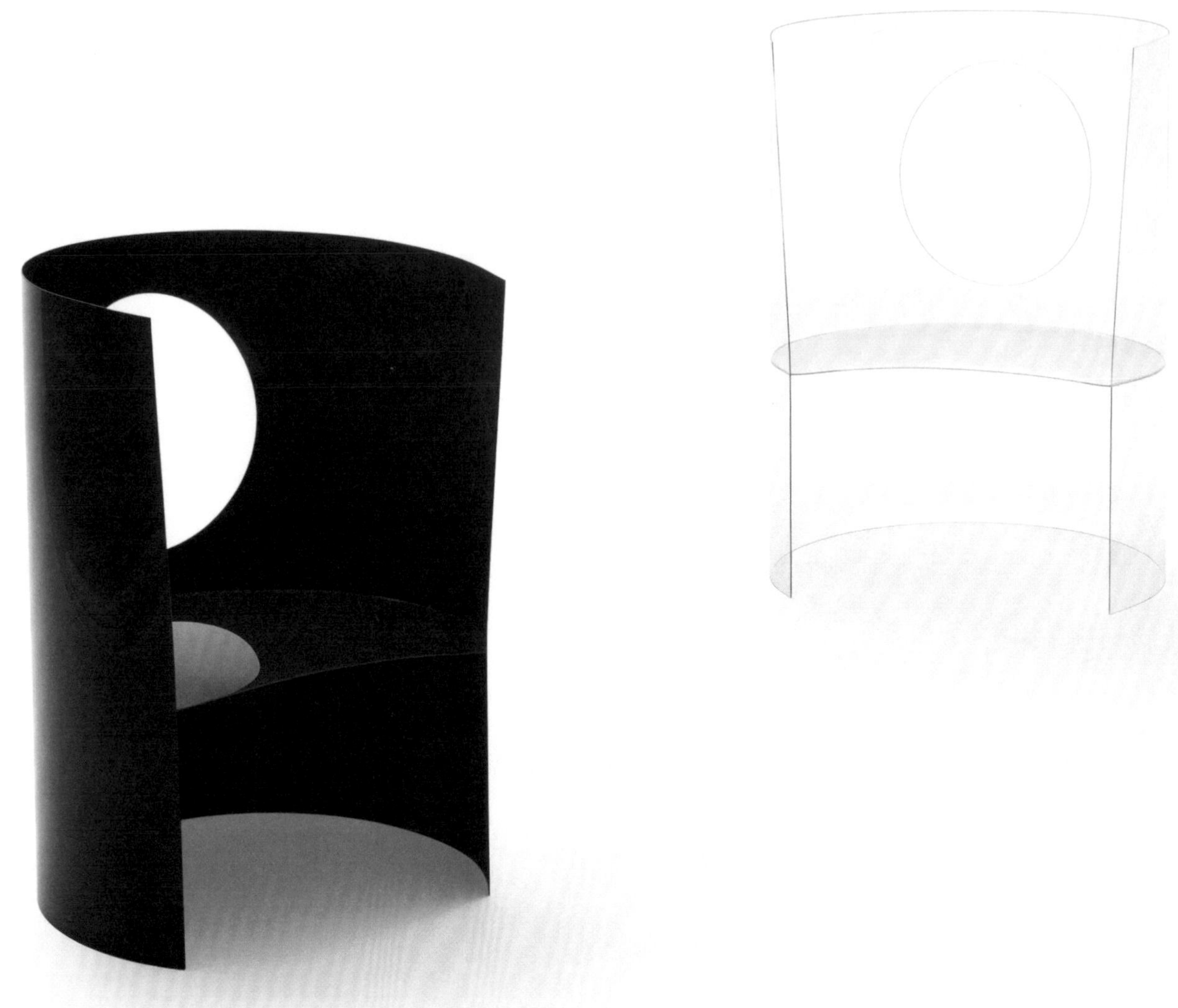

Chaise Medaillon 3.0 chairs. Glass. 2021.

EREZ NEVI PANA

Bleached material experimentation. Recycled wood, locally sourced luffa. 2018.

The astonishing work of Erez Nevi Pana evokes the possibilities of the natural world. In the twenty-first century, these possibilities include rapid and tumultuous change, the outcome of mass industrialization. For Nevi Pana, who grew up among the plants in his parents' nursery, design has meant creating a blueprint for a responsible relationship with the environment. His ethics are inextricable from his aesthetics, and his research has yielded objects that are prized by galleries and museums from Holon through Hauts-de-France.

Nevi Pana is perhaps best known for his work with salt. As a master's student, he began to explore the Dead Sea region, where the effects of local industry have brought about evaporation, sinkholes, and an excess of salt. By heating the salt, Nevi Pana caused it to recrystallize at a much higher rate than normal, creating tiles of built-up organic matter that resembles marble, an uncanny alternative to excavated materials. And by submerging luffa-wrapped furniture frames in the sea for his "Bleached" series (2018), he created pearlescent pieces that look as though coral has organized itself into seating—a sea creature's dream of a chair or a glimpse of a possible future.

By extracting materials from their usual contexts and introducing them into new uses, Nevi Pana activates a sense of wonder in those who see his works; he also hopes to provide models of ethical engagement. On a trip to India, he worked with artisans to transform all the trash he generated on his travels into baskets, coated with a glaze made from by-products of local cashew processing. Currently at work on a doctorate at the University of Art and Design Linz, Austria, Nevi Pana is concentrating on vegan approaches to design. His designs promise to continue being as innovative as they are uncompromising.

Wasted Baskets. Waste, 'glazed' in a liquid derivative of the Indian cashew-nut industry. 2018.

Salts stool. Recycled wood, vegan glue, Dead Sea salt. 2014.

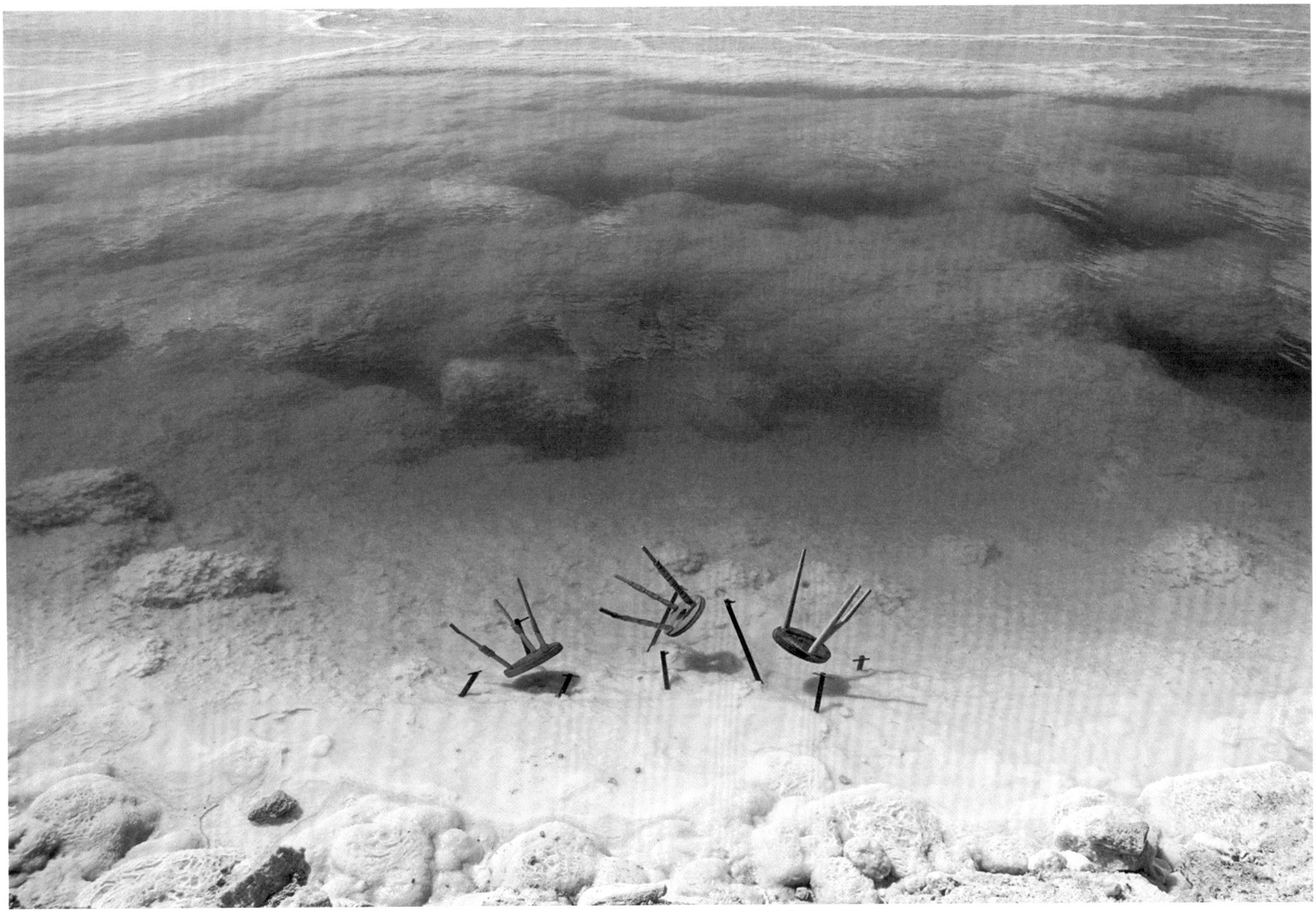

Salts material experimentation. Recycled wood, vegan glue, Dead Sea salt. 2014.

CAROLIEN NIEBLING

The Sausage of the Future. Mortadella with Vegetables. 2017

The Zürich-based Dutch designer Carolien Niebling thinks the day is dawning when we'll all be eating sausages. The food futurist was studying product design at ECAL (École cantonale d'art de Lausanne) when she began to delve into the design concept of the seemingly humble sausage—a familiar food staple that was due for reinvention. As Niebling researched its history and considered sustainable alternatives to meat, she realized that the path toward reduced meat consumption was best traced with the involvement of the existing industry. The imaginative revisions that appear in her book *The Sausage of the Future* (2017) contain updates on classics as well as playful but practical interventions, including fruit salami and a pâté made from insect flour and tonka beans. The blood sausage of the future contains not just blood but also chocolate.

Niebling's design portfolio extends to research, consulting, teaching, and strategy, and since the publication of the book, which won the Design Prize Switzerland among other prizes, she has continued to dream up new options for our diets. In the installation *Future-Proof Plating* at the Museum für Kunst und Gewerbe Hamburg (2022) and later Museum Für Gestaltung Zürich (2023), she returned to foods that aren't currently on the menu, but perhaps should be. The plates in the installation bear images of wild plants, mainly water plants like seaweed, either as casts or as etchings, and hanging textiles depict enticing, enlarged entanglements of other edible plants. In a trunk designed in 2021 for the 200th birthday of Louis Vuitton, founder of the eponymous fashion house, Niebling zooms in again on the weird and beguiling textures of the plants we consume. Continuing to work at the intersection of food and dietary science, Niebling—who once ate a dehydrated ant leg as part of her research—imagines the daring and delectable possibilities for times to come.

The Sausage of the Future. Insect Pâté. 2017.

The Beauty of Water Plants vases. Glass. With CIRVA. 2018.

The Beauty of Water Plants vases. Glass. With CIRVA. 2018.

Future-Proof Plating installation. Ceramic, algae, edible plants. 2022.

Future-Proof Plating installation. Ceramic, algae, edible plants. 2022.

OBJECTS OF COMMON INTEREST

Minimum chair. Silicon, metal. 2022.

Softness. Abstraction. Fluidity. Volume. Geometrics. These are all words that play a role in the creative vernacular of Objects of Common Interest (OoCI), a design unit created by Eleni Petaloti and Leonidas Trampoukis. OoCI, based in New York and Athens, came to life in 2016 as an extension of their architectural studio LoT, founded a few years earlier. A key idea is the notion of transforming the abstract into experimental objects for everyday living, created at a different rhythm, tempo, and scale from the longer-term architectural projects.

The studio has since increasingly turned heads with work that melds functionality with simplicity and abstraction of form, from furniture (recently for Kvadrat, Nilufar gallery in Milan, and Etage Projects) to lighting. Tube Lights (2019), a trio of simple, sculptural, geometric arcs, is one example. These flowing fragments of a circle appear to pour from walls, floors, or ceilings, their glowing form reflected on a stainless-steel-plate base. Light through the prism of transparency also takes center stage in the amorphous biodegradable PVC forms of Atmosphere (2021), while the patterns of natural materials are explored through textile in Moiré (2023), a rug collection for cc-tapis.

OoCI is also innovating with resin. In 2022 the studio opened an 8,600 ft² (800 m²) studio in Piraeus, an industrial district of Athens. It's home to a raft of manufacturing equipment donated by a Long Island-based craftsman friend, and it led to *Poikilos* (2023), an exhibition of thirteen poetically nuanced objects from furniture to tableware, created using a secret inherited formula for a milky iridescent resin. It is a redefinition of material that is sculptural and amorphous, simple and complex, scientific and poetic—embodying the dialogue of creative polarity that is woven into the DNA of OoCI's work.

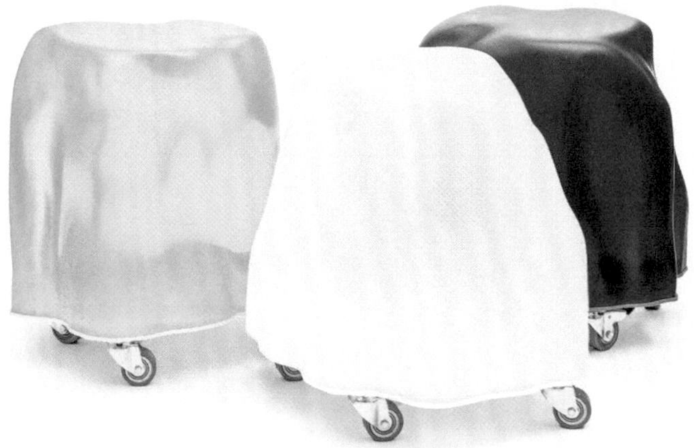

Metamorphic Rock stool. Gel, metal. 2021.

“Moiré” collection rugs. Wool, Tencel. cc-tapis. 2023.

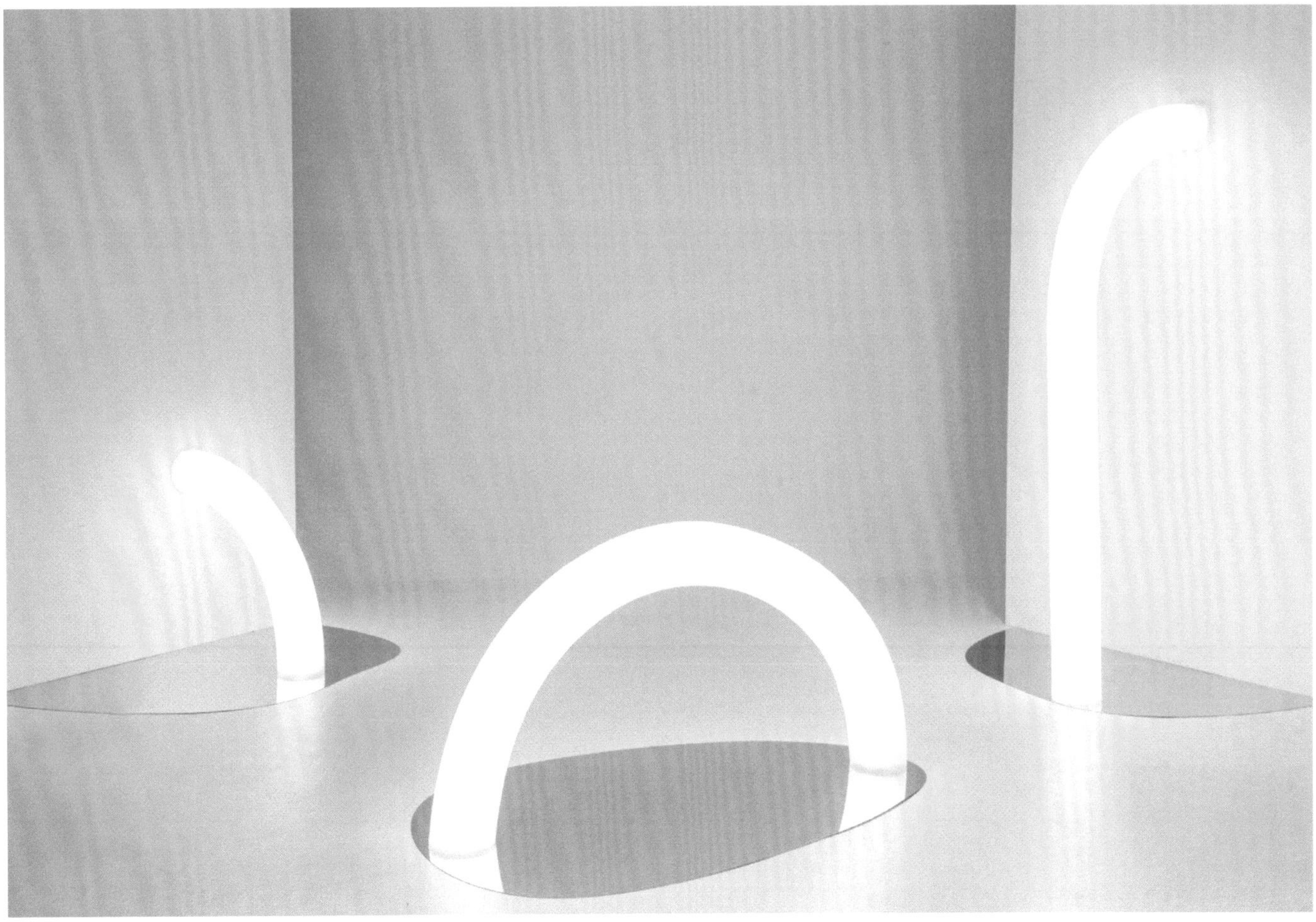

Tube Lights. Acrylic. 2019.

JONATHAN OLIVARES

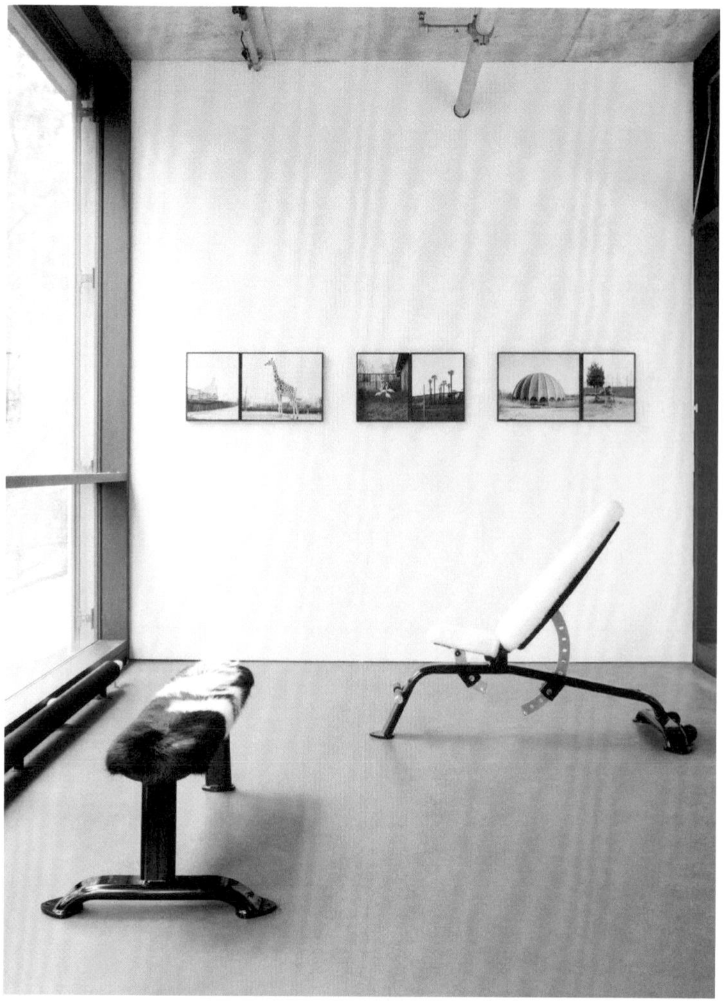

Exercise Furniture. Animal-hide upholstery, exercise equipment. 2018.

Jonathan Olivares is a design thinker, essayist, and researcher. But he's also a designer's designer, making intelligent, clarified, warm work, from showrooms and shelving through exhibitions and chairs. Designs, he says, that "ask to be used rather than observed."

Born in Boston, Olivares studied at the Pratt Institute in New York, interned with Konstantin Grcic (p. 100), and, in 2006, established his industrial design practice, Jonathan Olivares Design Research, in Boston and then Los Angeles. He designs and pursues knowledge with enterprising immediacy. For two years, he traveled the globe for Knoll to plumb the depths of the office chair, resulting in the book *A Taxonomy of Office Chairs* (2011). His projects have included a New York store for Camper (2019), the Vitra Workspace, an office furniture showroom and learning environment (2015), and the Olivares Aluminum Chair (2013)—plain, contoured, curvaceous, colorful—for Knoll. In fact, in 2022 Olivares was tapped to oversee all of Knoll's product design.

Olivares often imagines his environments and furniture in relation to the architectural context they will inhabit (and sometimes vice versa). His 46 ft (14 m) Aluminum Bench (2017) for the Victoria and Albert Museum in London guides visitors through the new Sainsbury Gallery. His shelving for the Blum & Poe bookstore (2020) in Los Angeles completes the white-box architecture with wood-grained display grids that powerfully foreground books and magazines.

An architect of color fields, Olivares designed a New York flagship for Kvadrat (2022) that plucks its formal language from the gridded paper used by textile designers. He peopled it with his Square Chair, also inspired by the basic unit that makes up the warp and weft of a woven textile. Enlarged and abstracted, the seat's form embodies the textile from which it is constructed. From macro to micro—chubby, colorful, comfortable, Cartesian—it's a thinking person's chair.

Square Chair. Polyurethane foam, polyester fiberfill, wood, steel. Kvadrat. 2022.

Solid Textile Screen. Solid Textile Board, zipped textile hinges. Kvadrat. 2018.

Aluminum Bench. Aluminum. 2017.

HUGO PASSOS

Cork Trivet. Cork. Crane Cookware. 2021.

An acute observer, avid traveler, food and wine connoisseur, and keen music enthusiast, Hugo Passos is one of the most cultured designers of his generation. He is not the disciple of any one designer; his path has rather been paved by a series of fortunate encounters, such as that with the Japanese designer Toshiyuki Kita. Yet Passos is not a designer who grew up hidden away in a workshop. With one studio in Porto, Portugal, and another in Copenhagen, he divides his time between the two cities, constantly commuting back and forth in order to conduct research that has led him to form significant partnerships with key companies of European design.

Passos's style is strongly influenced by his long association with London, although his roots are in the traditional Portuguese craftsmanship that taught him about the nature of materials and how to shape them into archetypal forms. This is complemented by his strong ties to the outstanding manufacturing capabilities of northern Europe. A great believer in the fundamental essence of being a designer, he works to redefine aesthetics and the beauty of everyday objects without neglecting the functional aspect of their design. This attitude means that he neither compromises the personality of his creations nor indulges in artistic extravagance.

A perfect example of this approach is the Piloti Table (2016), the legs of which are inserted into the top in such a way that, although highly functional, they hide the mechanics of the piece and create the rounded corners and invisible joints that characterize it aesthetically. Passos uses joints, seams, and attachments as marks that identify the elements of a piece without losing sight of the whole picture. He employs them to punctuate a rich language that aims for vital purity while refusing to take what he considers to be the shortcuts of minimalism.

Cork Trivet. Cork. Crane Cookware. 2021.

Piloti Alu tables. Aluminium frames and tops in stone, wood, and nano laminate. Fredericia. 2022.

Banco Bench Double. Solid teak. Fritz Hansen. 2022.

PEDRO PAULØ-VENZON

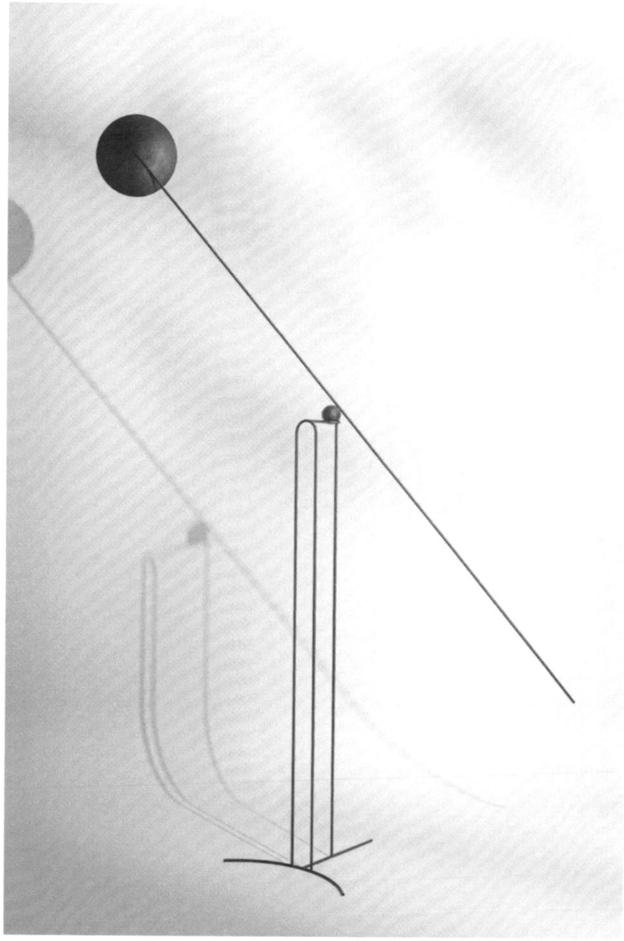

Profana lamp. Steel, aluminum, glass. 2017–18.

It all begins with the steel Moça side table (2013). Poised between material rigidity and a light silhouette, a simple circle sits atop a minimalist flow of curved lines—an abstract riff on women's crinoline skirts. The table was the Brazilian designer Pedro Paulø-Venzon's first licensed product, and it cleanly embodies his signature aesthetic, rooted in strong, minimalist lines, craftsmanship, and conceptual layers that hint at the colonial heritage of his homeland.

The designer, who set up his studio in Florianópolis in 2011, is dedicated to creating objects and artifacts that synthesize present-day dichotomies, balancing the local and the global, the crafted and the industrial, the rigid and the light. His modern creations are often minimalist in form while subtly hinting at the sensitive layers of Brazil's cultural identity and colonial heritage.

A similar dialog is threaded through the DNA of "Tríptico Infame" (Infamous Triptych), a trio of objects that explore "colonial devices" and "technologies of confession," according to the designer. Among them is Anca (Hips; 2018), a side table hovering somewhere between sculpture and furniture, consisting of three minimalist pieces of wood with a clean medley of lines and curves that evoke an abstract riff on feminine curves.

A different narrative underpins the Avoa chair (2013). Inspired by the idea of an autotelic or autonomous design discourse, its light form is reduced to elemental essentials: a small circular seat, with a simple stroke of a curve for a backrest. Each chair is handcrafted in steel without the use of computers, its form lying at the nodal point between precision and deconstruction. The designer explains: "The challenge was to think of an object as a quotation."

Avoa chair. Carbon steel, brass. 2013.

Solteira bench. Carbon steel, wood. Driade. 2017.

Uma Virtude Deitada Fica Intumescida bench. Tropical hardwood. 2020.

JULIE RICHOZ

Pipaio side tables. Beech. Mattiazzi. 2023.

Equally at home determining the logic of a hand-blown glass vase or the proportions of a precisely balanced porcelain bowl, the Swiss-French designer Julie Richoz embraces in her work a diverse catalog of references, honed by her rigorous approach. Study at the demanding ECAL (École cantonale d'art de Lausanne), from which she graduated in 2012, and time spent working in the office of the French designer Pierre Charpin (p. 64) sharpened her crisp, enquiring approach. Although a project or idea may draw on a rich variety of visual and physical references, she carefully whittles down the impact of each element to achieve essential, unfettered forms.

Take the "Pipaio" commission, a machine-milled bowl and side table of beech for the Italian wooden seating specialists Mattiazzi. The pieces all follow the same logic: three-part construction with the seat/bowl resting on three slim tubular legs, in turn supported by a tapered conical base. However, such simple elements belie the precisely shaped, invisible joinery that is central to the almost floating effect of each piece. Richoz makes an apt comparison with the image of a waiter deftly balancing a serving tray on his fingers—a sleight of hand achieved through her light, meticulous touch.

The designer also delights in the tension between manufactured precision and hand-hewn artisanal making. Richoz's "Binaire" pieces (2018) for La Manufacture Cogolin, France, capture this relationship well. Drawing on the tradition of Moroccan flat-woven rugs, Richoz brings together a careful palette of colored warp threads paired with a raffia weft produced through the automated technique of jacquard weaving. The effect creates five variations of rhythmic yet irregular patterns, their mechanical behavior tempered by the naturally rough, fibrous palm base.

Richoz already has a string of high-profile clients and accolades. Her work conveys a notable sensitivity to the balance of color, scale, and light, paired with a characteristic material experimentation.

O'Step ladder. Bamboo. Galerie kreo. 2022.

Isla vases. Glass. Nouvel. 2018.

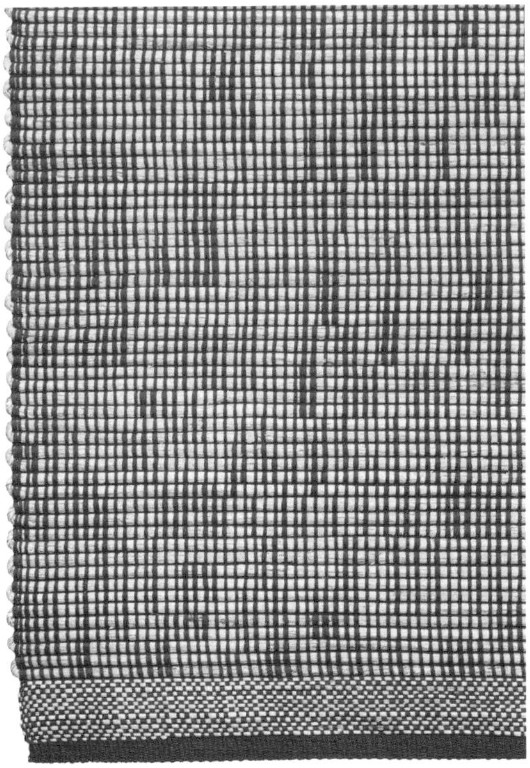

Binaire rug. Raffia, endurance fibers. La Manufacture Cogolin. 2018.

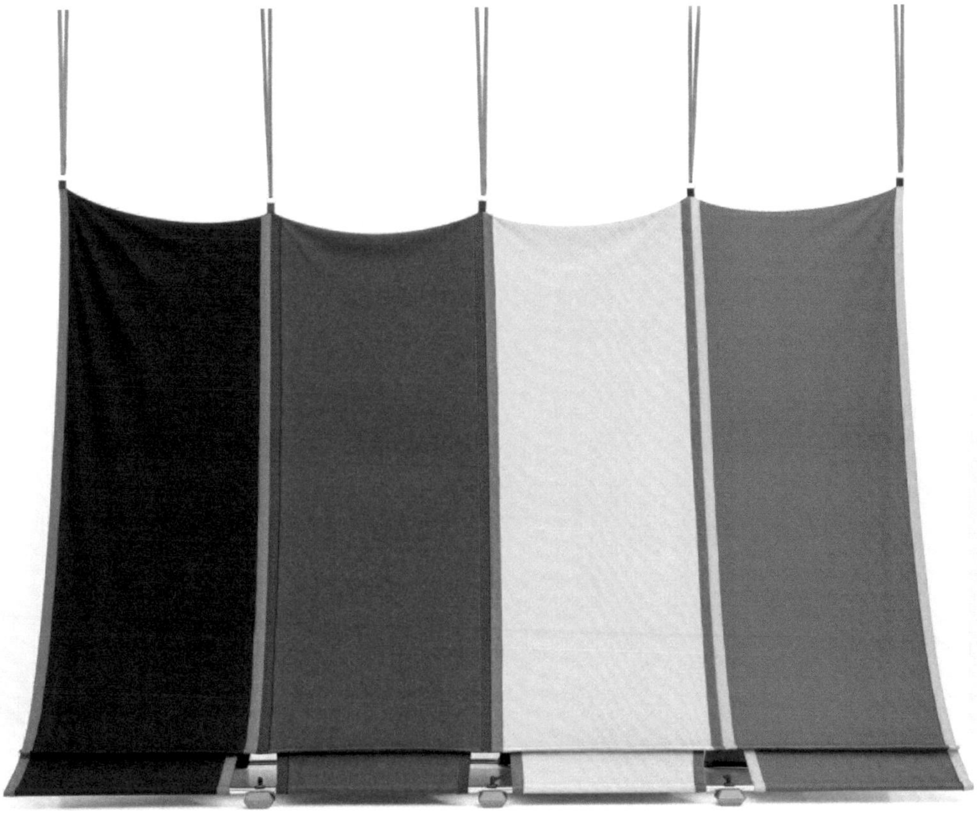

Shed compact textile shelter. Plecto textile, cords, supporting structures, weights. Kvadrat/Febrik. 2020.

DANIEL RYBAKKEN

No matter how simple it may look, a lamp is never just a lamp for Daniel Rybakken. He evokes the ephemerality and emotional impact of light through a respectful use of color, reflection, projection, and shadow. He takes what is ordinary and reveals, in one effortless gesture, that it's made of some magic that we have overlooked.

Colour (2010) is the exploded concept of a lamp, a collaboration with the Norwegian designer Andreas Engesvik. Overlapping sheets of tinted glass in various geometric forms and sizes lean from floor to wall as if merely resting temporarily. When presented in Milan that year, the prototype felt minimal and emotional, architectural and scenographic, poetic and impractical. With individual components that stack loosely against the wall and beveled glass with no edge protection, it seemed unlikely to become a commercial product, but today, after a relaunch, it's still sold by e15.

After studying art and industrial design in Norway and Sweden, Rybakken opened his practice in Gothenburg, Sweden, in 2008. Since then, he's worked with the likes of Luceplan, Vitra, Karimoku, HAY, and Givenchy. Rybakken is versatile. His work, which includes furniture for the likes of Artek, can be pragmatic, but even his most practical lighting has a gratifying emotional intelligence. Barn-shaped Fienile (2019) offers a well-lit stage for mementos or objects. Wall-mounted Counterbalance (2012) projects its 6½ ft (2 m) arm into the room, using oversized cogwheels that also give it a graphical look.

The installation *Shelter* (2022) in a Stockholm bay is Rybakken's largest—and most moving—lighting design to date. Atop steel posts, a gabled aluminum roof reflects 150,000 lumens of LED light shining from the water below. Inspired by the Norwegian explorer, scientist, and humanitarian Fridtjof Nansen, it is a reminder of the plight of millions of refugees forced to flee their homes today, and of the responsibility to protect them.

Shelter light installation. Steel, aluminum, LED. 2022.

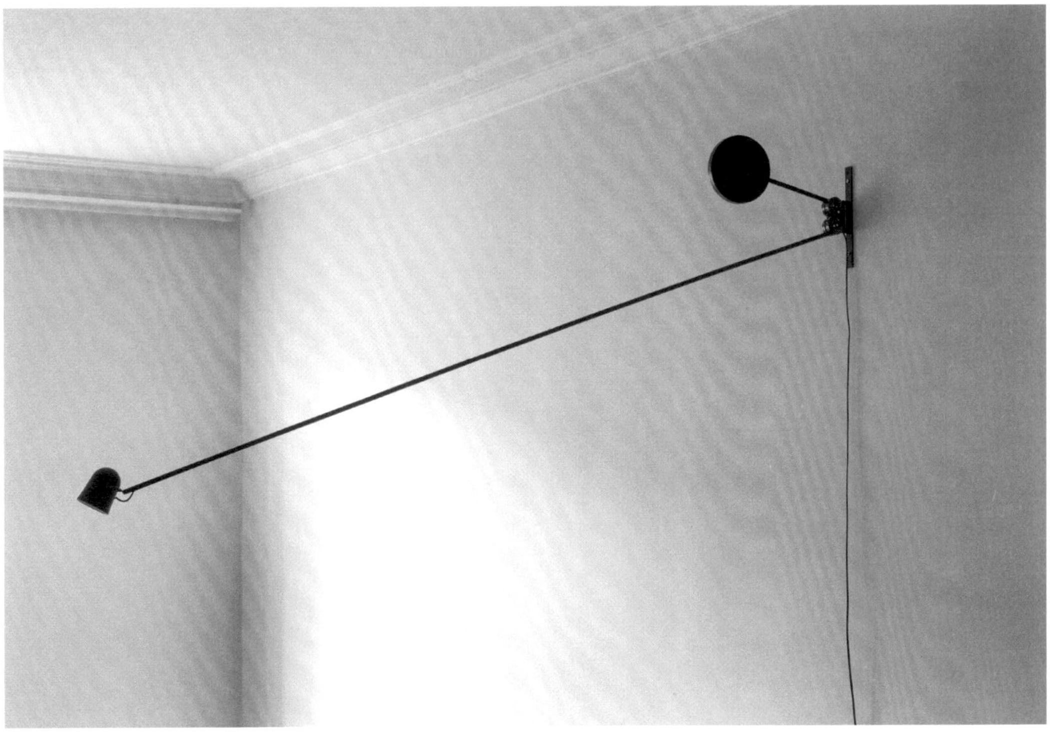

Counterbalance lighting. Steel, aluminum, LED. Luceplan. 2012.

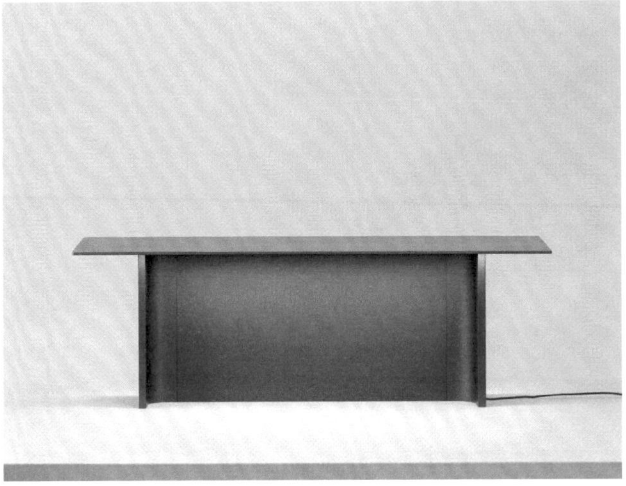

Fienile table light. Extruded aluminum, LED. Luceplan. 2019.

Petit Standard stackable chair. Steel, aluminum, plywood. HAY. 2020.

INGA SEMPÉ

Mousqueton lamps. Stainless steel, zinc. HAY. 2023.

Paris-born Inga Sempé has forged a career as a leading designer with a flair for creating furniture and lighting that bring together practicality and playfulness. She explores her design process and refines her options through prolific, animated hand drawings, a skill undoubtedly informed by the fact that she is the daughter of the Danish artist Mette Ivers and the French illustrator Jean-Jacques Sempé. Alongside this creative home environment, Sempé has described weekends wandering with her mother through Le Marché aux Puces, feasting her eyes on the antiques and curiosities of this sprawling Parisian market.

Sempé graduated from ENSCI–Les Ateliers (L'École nationale supérieure de création industrielle) in Paris in 1993 and subsequently worked with Marc Newson and Andrée Putman. Her creative output drew early commissions from Cappellini and Edra before she established her own studio in 2000, and since then her work has won admiration for its deceptively simple yet charming approach.

One of Sempé's best-loved pieces is the Matin lamp (2019), commissioned by HAY. Its appeal lies in its simplicity: a shallow pleated cone of laminated cotton fabric in a number of elegant hues, set atop a folding base of polished brass with black polymer accents. Secured with a single screw, it can be simply hung on the wall or perched on a table, and its everyday character blends with classic and modern interiors alike. The elegant Mousqueton portable lamp was also commissioned by HAY and is an indoor and outdoor lamp that can be suspended over a branch or rope when out in nature.

This sprightly reinterpretation of traditional forms for a contemporary age echo across Sempé's work. Her "Filigraani" series (2022), commissioned by Iittala, for example, appropriates the celebrated art of hand-blown Murano glass for a modern set of three delicate displays for fruit and sweets. The nostalgia of the famous little cake carries through to Sempé's "Madeleine" suite of playful door hardware (2018) for DND, with delicate shell-like impressions rendered in polished nickel, black, and gold.

Filigraani bowls and platter. Glass. Iittala. 2022.

Madeleine door handles. Brass. DND. 2018.

Matin lamps. Cotton, steel wire, brass. HAY. 2019–23.

SOFT BAROQUE

Soft Metal bench. Aluminum. 2022.

Soft Baroque makes objects for an imagined future—a vision that these startling, unorthodox creations render very convincing. The artists behind the company, Australian Nicholas Gardner and Slovenian Saša Štucin, met as students at London's Royal College of Art, and their sometimes complementary, sometimes conflicting sensibilities have led to an exciting partnership, sustained by their ongoing interrogation of design shibboleths. Their output, informed by an impish sense of humor, straddles the line between art and functional object and their projects have appeared in museums and galleries throughout Asia, Europe, and North America.

Gardner and Štucin approach today's design-saturated lived environment with ironic distance but no lack of investment. Their handmade pieces index the tidal shifts in contemporary culture: analog to digital, corporeal to conceptual. A Photographic Furniture series (2023) turns high-resolution images into panels that make up tables and chairs, materializing the virtual worlds that already house us so much of the time. These tongue-in-cheek pieces also reverse the popular practice of printing wood grain on synthetic materials. Even their more traditional-seeming objects, such as the Carved Aluminum coffee table and chair (2022), introduce asymmetric cutouts and curlicues to familiar shapes. The pieces can still be used as their names imply, but serve foremost to provoke questions about the ultimate purpose and possibilities of common objects and concepts.

The name "Soft Baroque" was initially a joke, referencing an imaginary style, but it has proved prescient and elastic, allowing an eclectic variety of experiments and attempts. In an era when dozens of styles and schools of design exist simultaneously, competing for attention, Gardner and Štucin excel at turning our consciousness back to ourselves and our expectations. Their objects defamiliarize and enchant, and Soft Baroque may well turn out to be the ruling aesthetic of the near future.

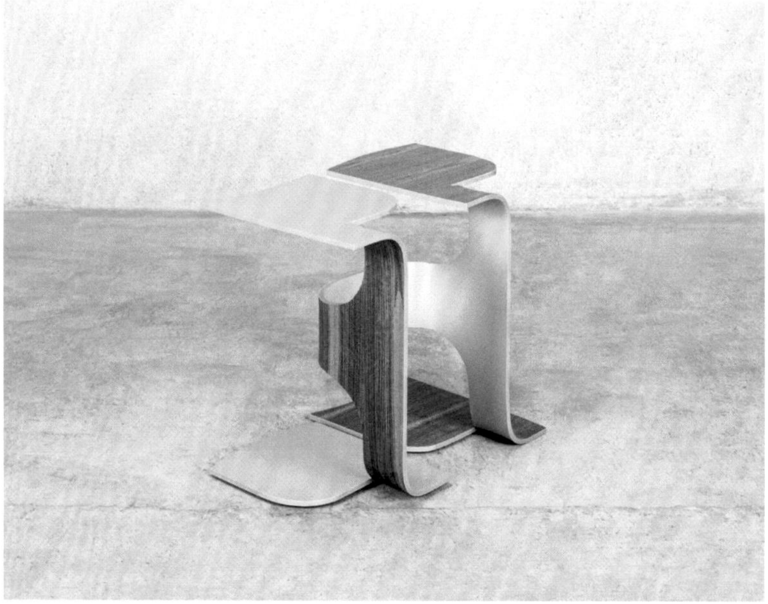

Soft Metal table. Aluminum and veneer. 2020.

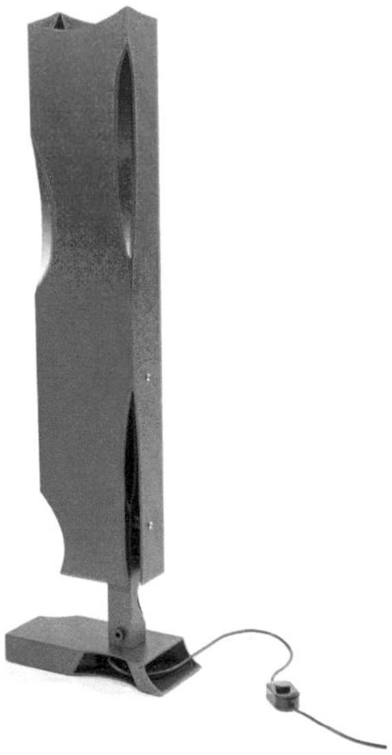

Carved Aluminum lamp. Aluminum. 2022.

Carved Aluminum chair. Aluminum. 2022.

Carved Aluminum table. Aluminum. 2022.

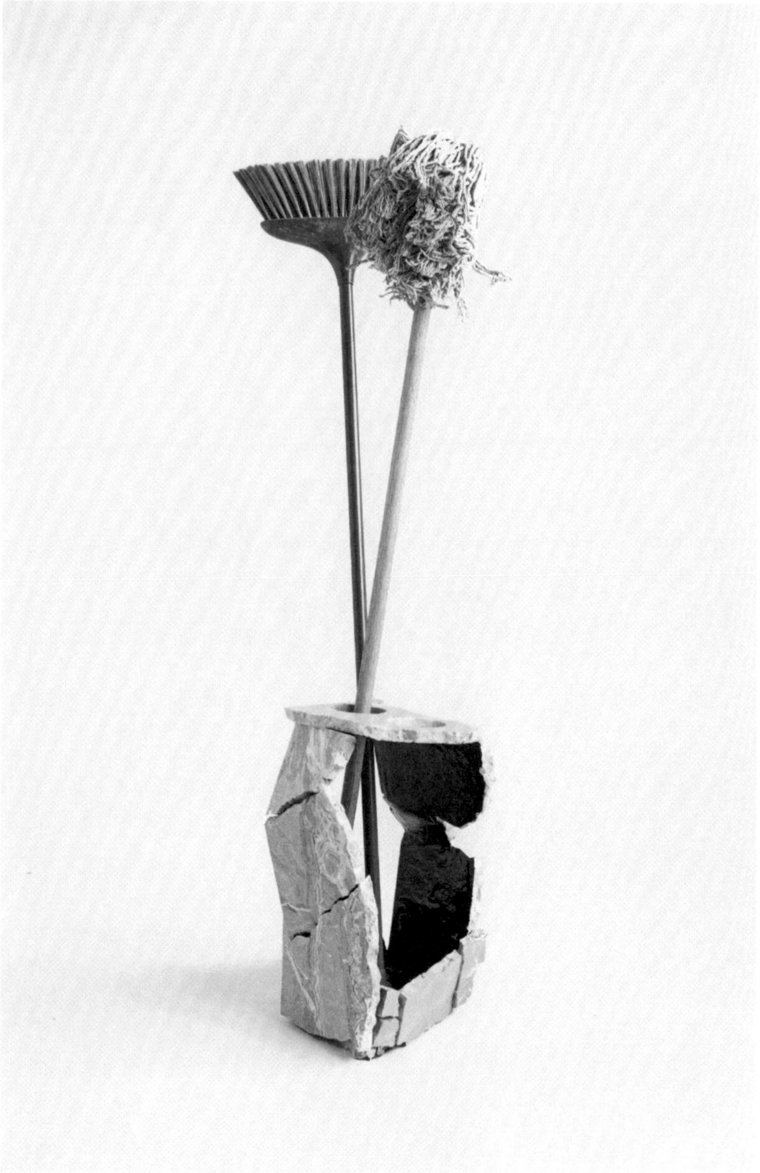

Corporate Marble stand. Marble, carbon Kevlar, resin. 2013.

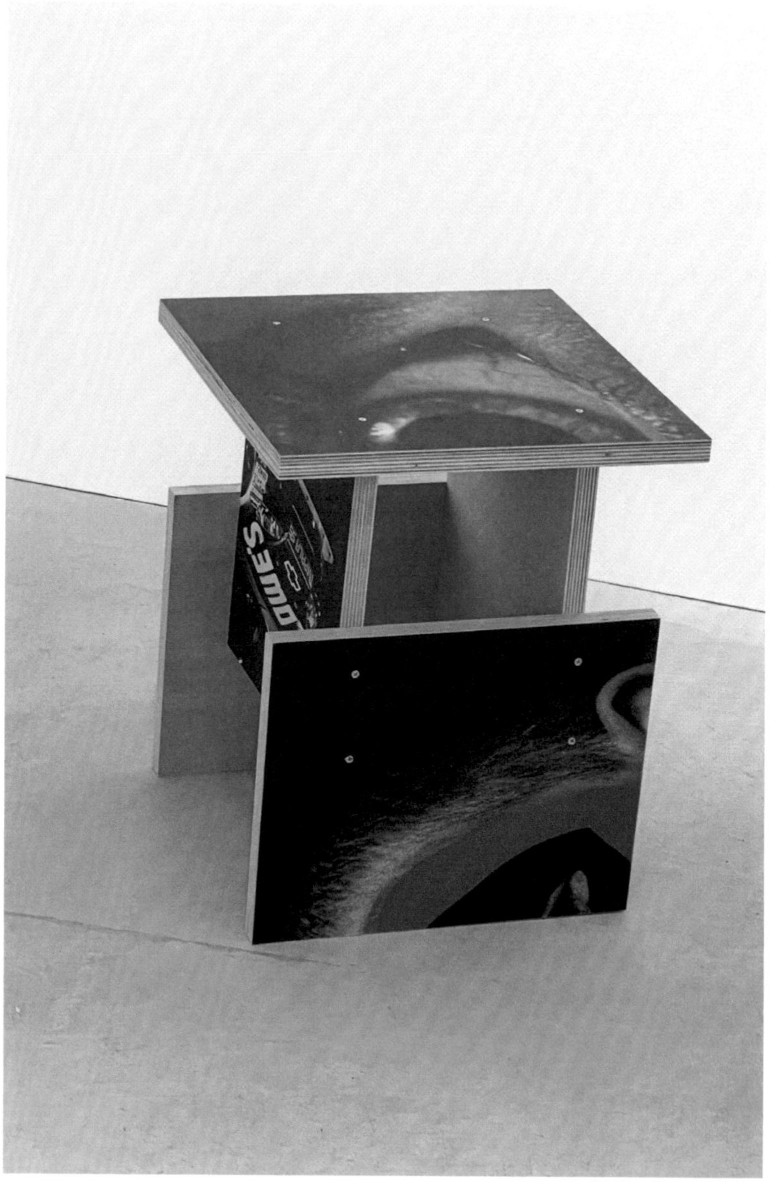

Photographic Furniture. Plywood, direct-to-media print. With Ill-Studio. 2023.

Hard Round shelf. Walnut. Zebrano. 2019.

SINA SOHRAB

Beam washbasin. Cristalplant Biobase, ash. With Joseph Guerra for Zucchetti.Kos. 2021.

A fascination with the idiosyncrasies of everyday life and the reasons for humans' connection to certain objects informs much of the work of the Iranian American designer Sina Sohrab, whose eponymous design research office is now based in Madrid. Honed through study at the Rhode Island School of Design and a subsequent partnership with the industrial designer Joseph Guerra through their New York-based practice Visibility, Sohrab's acclaimed works reconsider daily rituals. From the Barbican Trolley he designed for Dims (2018) to the Shapes Bundle of yoga equipment (2016), Sohrab's work carefully balances color, form, line, and performance and, recognized by significant international prizes and exhibitions across the globe, continues to inspire for its cerebral and tactile approach.

The Beam washbasin (2021) for Zucchetti.Kos showcases this logic in a thoughtful piece that reconsiders the everyday bathroom sink by revisiting domestic archetypes and architectural materials. Its curving basin borrows from the shape of a classic soup bowl, with an integrated shelf to hold soap or bathing accessories, or to mount faucets. Its gentle porcelain form rests on a console that is shaped like a structural steel I-beam yet fashioned from silky solid ash. This unexpected contrast of sensual materials and industrial outlines forms a design that is both familiar and contemporary.

For Kvadrat's "Knit!" commission, Sohrab focused on the potential of knitted fabric. Reinterpreting a dining table, Living Room (2020) is reread through the culturally astute lens of the Middle East. The circular piece is scaled close to the ground and set around a small pedestal table, recalling Persian traditions according to which family and friends gather on rugs or pillows. The upholstered form creates a comforting place to nestle, sparking delight with its rich, warm palette of burgundy, orange, and yellow, accented by pink and white.

Bird Pavilions "Chickadee Pavilion". Beech, steel wire, paper, found bowl, found hook. 2022.

Bird Pavilions "Purple Martin Pavilion". Beech, paper, found hook. 2022.

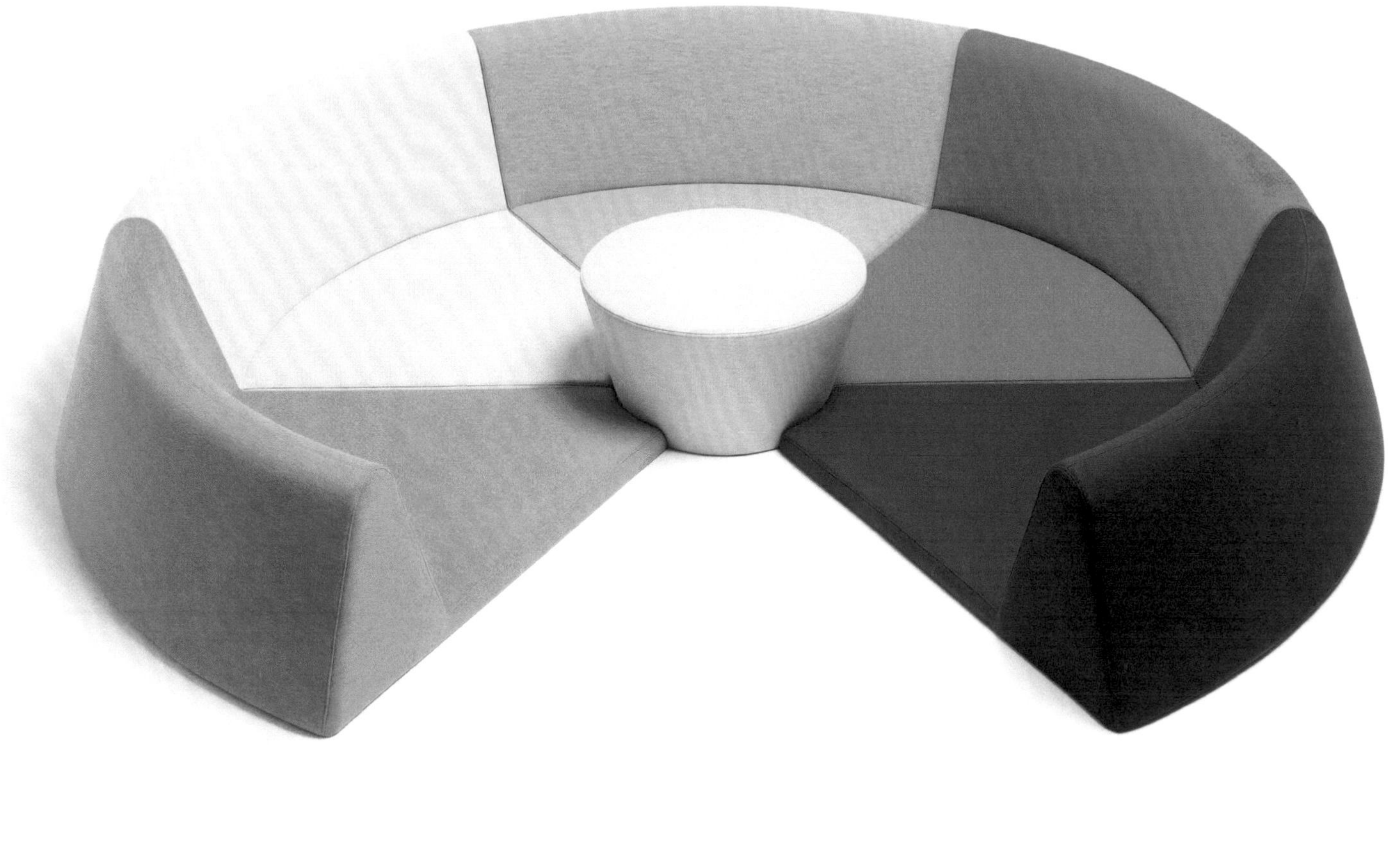

Living Room table and seating. Various materials. With Joseph Guerra for Kvadrat. 2020.

SOMIAN DESIGN

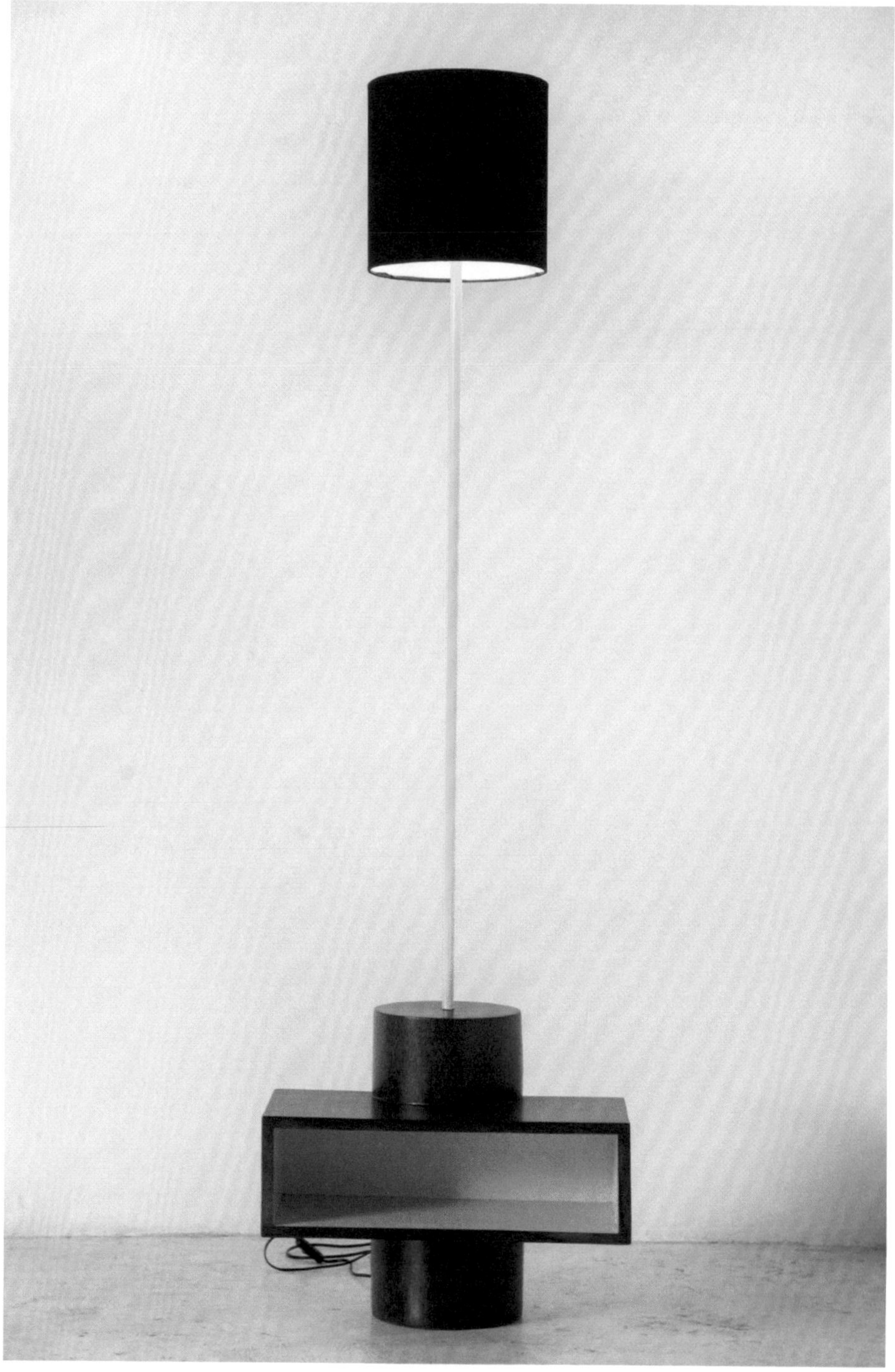

SAMO Lamp. Coconut wood, Amazakoue wood, metal, lacquer. 2022.

Jean Servais Somian's sculptural pieces combine traditional West African materials and totemic silhouettes with mid-century furniture's generous geometry and a contemporary love of the remix. Somian was born in Côte d'Ivoire and trained in carpentry and cabinetmaking in the city of Grand-Bassam, later taking a furniture internship in Lausanne and then moving to France (where he spent five years as a competitive boxer). Although he now moves between France and Côte d'Ivoire, his design practice—he established his studio in 2002—remains rooted in materials local to West Africa's southern coast. Many of his consoles and cabinets are made from coconut palms, and other local hardwood trees, such as iroko, mahogany, and amazakoué, also find their way into his designs.

Somian's process involves using wood that would otherwise go to waste. He sources his coconut palms from construction sites, choosing trunks whose shapes interest him from among trees that will be cut down. The trees are carved in his workshop in Grand-Bassam, and detailing is done in a workshop in the capital, Abidjan. What emerge after the trees have been hollowed, carved, painted, and outfitted with legs, drawers, or decorations are slim, vertical structures featuring bright lacquer and grounding swaths of black. Some become straightforward bookshelves or lamps, while others, such as *Hibiscus Mon Amour* (2022), are decorative objects. Consoles and desks may be studded with wooden beads, and leather and stone add texture. Somian makes sketches for many objects, but when it comes to the palms, he lets the tree decide: "It's almost like the coco knows what it wants to be and whispers it to me. It's strange. I love it." His understanding of the material, and his love of dynamism—shared with one of his favorite artists, Piet Mondrian—endows each piece with a buzzy sense of life.

The Drum, beaded trunk. Coconut wood, ebony pearls. Crafted in collaboration with cabinetmaker Alfred Kouassi. 2022.

Box sideboard, after Mondrian. Amazakoue wood, lacquer. 2022.

Sowden Kettle. Stainless steel, polypropylene. HAY. 2021.

GEORGE SOWDEN

George Sowden's search for creative freedom has taken him from Leeds to London to Italy. The renowned designer arrived in Milan in 1970 and stayed there, spending twenty years as a consultant at Olivetti, where he worked on the first computers, and also helped to found the influential Memphis Group in 1980. Memphis injected a shockingly anarchic post-modernism into design at a time when decoration was verboten, but the freedom of Sowden's creations belies the fact that they are actually the terminus of a meticulous production cycle, overseen by him from beginning to end. His omnivorous interest in the process has taken him to factories around the world and continues to propel him to new discoveries.

Sowden opened his studio in 1981, though his eponymous brand didn't appear until 2011. The Tulipano chest of drawers (2018), a tall creation in lacquered wood resting on white cylindrical feet, is a continuation of Sowden's approach to designing over a 50-year career. It is obviously a character, its ten rows of twenty-one differently sized drawers offering undeniable if slightly exaggerated, practicality. His other recent work also invites personification. The "Shades" lamp collection, presented at Milan Design Week in 2022, came about when Sowden's team noted the quality of light diffused through soft silicone while working on another project. The collection is now a colorful family with multiple characters, comprising pendant, table, floor, and battery lamps for indoor and outdoor use, which during use spread a warm, comfortable light.

For Sowden, whose wide-ranging work has included patterns for such brands as Uniqlo and Valentino, it is a given that objects have unique personalities. The pieces he creates have much of his personality and preferences in them, too. Take the Sowden kettle for HAY (2021), a cousin of his beloved coffee pot (2010). Sleek and multi-colored, friendly and eye-catching, the kettle offers comfort —and hot water—while unobtrusively making itself known.

Tulipano chest of 21 drawers. Lacquered wood. Memphis Milano. 2018.

“Shades” collection. Various materials. SOWDEN. 2022.

STEPHEN BURKS MAN MADE

Stephen Burks: Shelter in Place, Spirit House (memorializing bell hooks). PLA, household paint. 2022.

The studio name, Stephen Burks Man Made, says it all. Brooklyn designer Stephen Burks's workshop-based practice collaborates with artisans around the globe to create high-end furniture, lighting, interiors, exhibitions, and products, and to prove the virtuous and innovative influence the human hand can exert on the creation of industrial objects.

Born in Chicago in 1969, Burks studied architecture and then product design at the Illinois Institute of Technology, doing graduate work in architecture at Columbia University. Tapped by Missoni in 2004, he first drew craft into his practice with his handmade Patchwork vases (2004). But since a trip to South Africa in 2005, he has been crisscrossing the planet, working in ceramics, macramé, crochet, papier-mâché, basket-weaving, and more. In 2011, the exhibition *Stephen Burks: Man Made* at the Studio Museum of Harlem showcased baskets made from Senegalese sweetgrass stitched together with colorful recycled plastic. The artisans inject new life into commercial products for such brands as Dedon and Roche Bobois, while Burks's ability to find new expression for traditional materials, forms, and methods can drive local economic development and extend craft practices into the future.

Burks's work continues to expand the boundaries of contemporary design. His exhibition *Stephen Burks: Shelter in Place* (2022) comprised radical design prototypes that reconsider how we use domestic space. For everyone during the COVID-19 crisis, the dining table double- and triple-tasked as school, office, and town square, making home feel newly crowded. *Private Seat* (2022) is a micro-architectural place apart. Inspired by the Finnish designer Alvar Aalto's room divider Screen 100 (1936), it fans out to offer solo sanctuary. *The Ancestors* builds on African statuary forms to create "busts and bodies" that also function as shelving or storage. *Woven TV* is a basket-like armature used to wrap a flatscreen television. Its open "weave" can hold magazines, shopping totes, and other objects, inviting customization by the whole family.

Stephen Burks: Shelter in Place, Woven TV. Foam core, resin, household paint. 2022.

Stephen Burks: Shelter in Place, The Ancestors. Various materials. 2022.

Stephen Burks: Shelter in Place, Private Seat. Foam core, silk ribbon. 2022.

noguchi
S,M,L,XL
DESIGN
TECHNO
MOROSO
JAPANESE FOR BUSY PEOPLE
DUCHAMP
Archi-Lab
THE NEW TEXTILES
JAPANESE STYLE
SOL LEWITT
THE WAY OF THE SUPERIOR MAN
1000 chairs
THE ART OF PACKAGE DESIGN
marc newson
Katachi
Collapsible
SuperDesign
MAKING AFRICA
ECAL
BUILDING SEAGRAM
ALICE NEEL
AFTERPARTIES
EAST
MEERA SODHA

STUDIO BRYNJAR & VERONIKA

4Rooms light. Metal. La Società delle Api. 2022.

Tiro light. Aluminum, glass, LED. From Lighting. 2023.

Nature. Rituals. Light. Rocks. Myths. And the raw power of the Icelandic landscape. An otherworldly labyrinth of narratives and visual layers infuses the vision of Studio Brynjar & Veronika. Defying easy categorization, the studio leaps lightly between art and design, often pushing the edges of the real and the imagined, through an array of media: drawings, video, photography, sound, objects.

The Bavaria-based studio was set up by the Icelandic creator Brynjar Sigurðarson in 2011, joined three years later by the German designer Veronika Sedlmair. Since then, they have crafted a singular creative journey through products, performances, installations, and research, all tackling a challenge they describe as "translating transient experience into objects."

The creative medium is lighting in Tiro (2023), an adjustable pendant lamp for From Lighting. An anodized lampshade is combined with a glass rod, which allows the light to be pulled up and down. The wild energy and abstract geology of Iceland—and the way humans elementally interact with nature—is another key creative spark. "The Silent Village," an abstract furniture collection for Galerie kreo in Paris, was born out of an immersive stay in a tiny village in northeastern Iceland. Traditional knotting techniques for fishing and for hunting sharks leave a primordial imprint on the raw form and material of the collection.

A similarly otherworldly ambiance fills the Circle Flute (2016). Inspired by Iceland's atmosphere, the circular instrument is played by four flautists at once for a single listener standing in the center. Crafted in collaboration with a Parisian flute-maker and a musician, the unusual circular form results in new sonic dimensions and complex overtones to impactful effect when played in Iceland's rural landscape. It's one more example of how the duo shine when attempting to harness the "transient" and make it real—whether through geology or anthropology, music, or lighting.

Circle Flute. Silver-plated brass. Built by Jean-Yves Roosen. Lafayette Anticipations—Fonds de dotation Famille Moulin. 2016

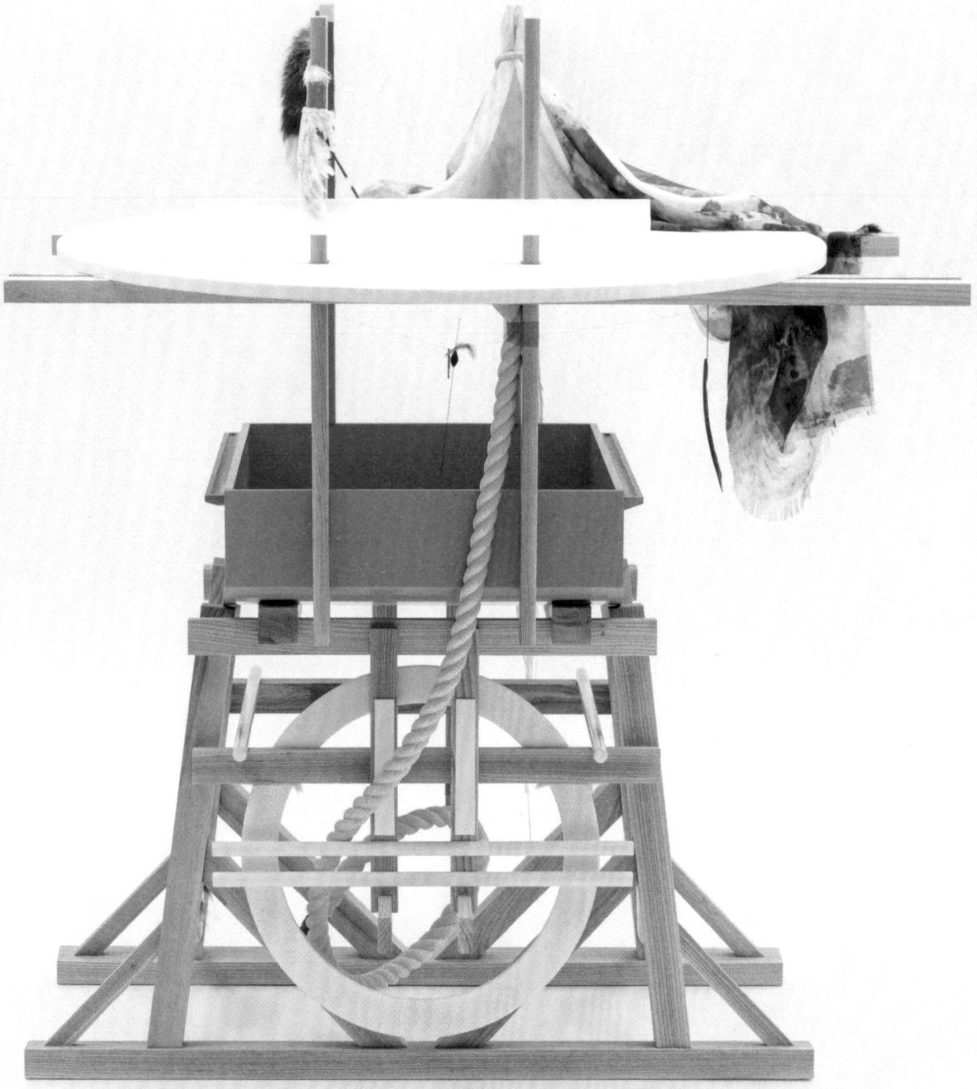

“Silent Village” collection. Wood, lacquered iron, Corian. Galerie kreo. 2014.

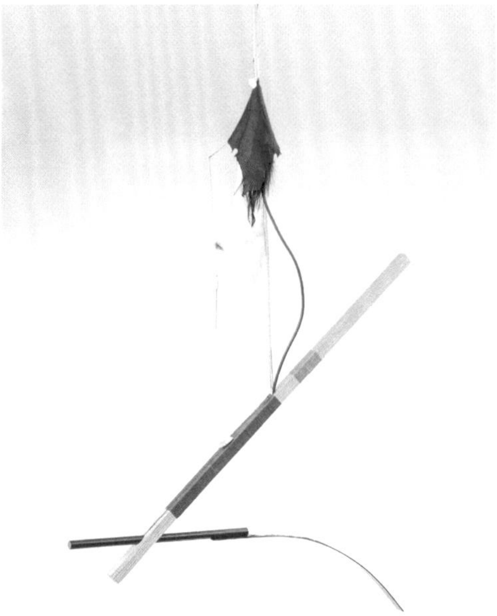

“Silent Village” collection. Wood, lacquered iron, Corian. Galerie kreo. 2014.

Rooms stool. Oak. La Societá delle Api. 2022.

4Rooms chair. Walnut. La Societá delle Api. 2022.

STUDIO JUJU

Playful, optimistic, engaging, and emotional, Studio Juju's designs include furniture and products, experiential interiors for homes and offices, public design installations, and sculpture. Timo Wong and Priscilla Lui opened their practice in Singapore in 2009. Since then, they've been creating everything from lighting shaped like birds to seating shaped like chocolates, "floating" catch-all vessels, and a sculptural washbasin in welcoming geometries.

Everything they imagine has a fresh sophistication. Their versatile coat stand (2019) looks hand-drawn, a scribble of loose coils outlining the embrace of three friends. For Living Divani, the duo created a fluid series of tables (2012) in different shapes and heights that encourages people to use each spontaneously, in a variety of ways.

Even the studio's office designs feel human: welcoming, warm, and sunny. Their space for Thoughtworks (2017) features yellow awning-stripe chairs and sea-blue sofas, as if staff have clocked in to go on vacation. Functionally, it spurs social interaction and flexibility of use.

For Studio Juju, materials are not just shaped into playful, meaningful objects; they are a source of play and meaning in and of themselves. The purposely unfinished Rope chandelier (2021) combined individual expression with a tangled technical beauty, using familiar materials—rope, metal scaffolding—in unfamiliar ways.

The studio's Duck and Crane lighting (2010) suggested that everything we live with is alive, if not biologically, at least in the character and companionship with which objects enrich our lives. Abstracting the birds, the designers put the distinctive shape and proportions of each to use as a table and floor lamp, respectively. Although never put into production, they pointed in the direction the studio would take: toward products that move us, that are simple but full of utility, that are refined and wisely naive. Studio Juju understands that objects embody ideas, experience, imagination, and memory, and that we live with, not beside them.

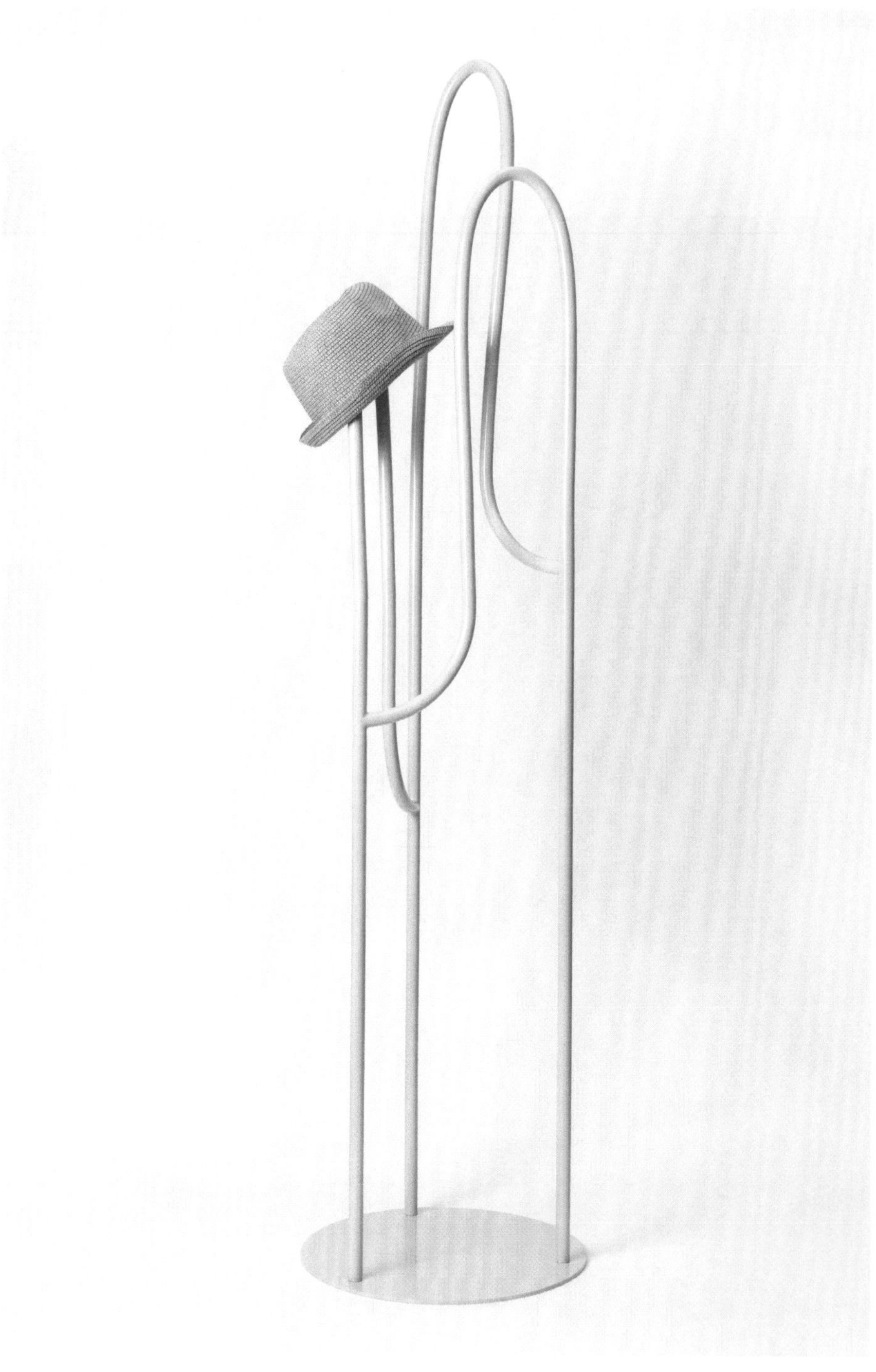

Friends coat stand. Powder-coated steel. 2019.

Duck Lamps. ABS plastic, aluminum. 2010.

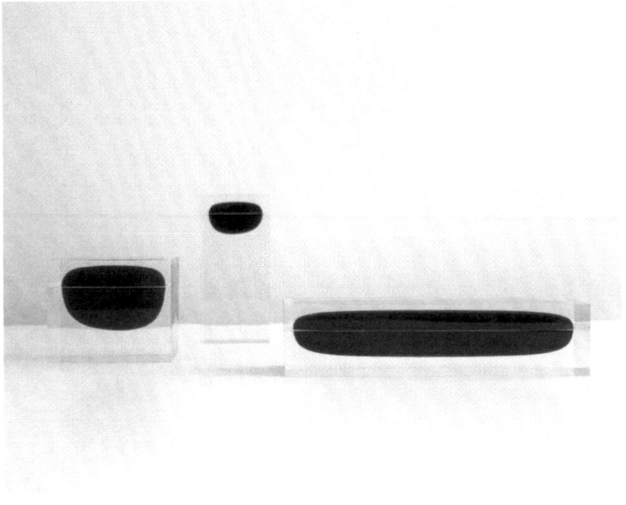

Luxury Towers jewelry vessels. Acrylic. industry+. 2016.

Crane Lamps. ABS plastic, aluminum. 2010.

Rabbit & Tortoise tables. Powder-coated steel. Living Divani. 2012.

STUDIO LANI

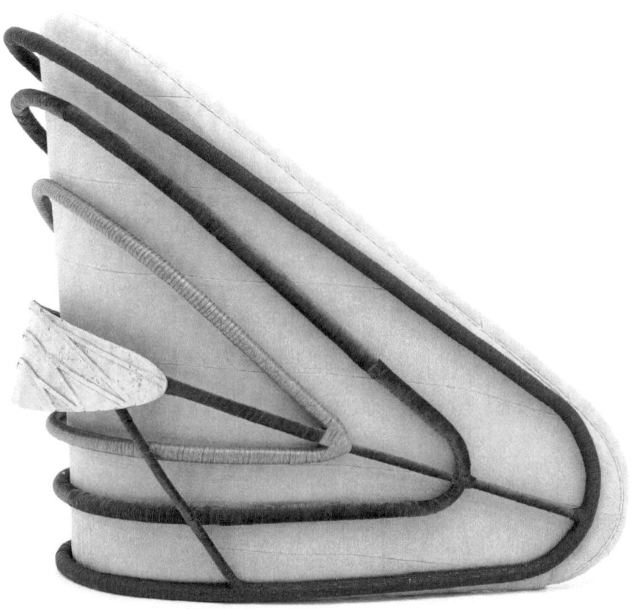

Oba Chair. Indigenous Yoruba Aso-oke, Benin bronze plate, velvet. 2022.

When Lani Adeoye left behind a career as a Fortune 500 management consultant in order to design furniture, she was channeling a creative impulse she'd had since childhood. She quickly hit her stride, and in 2022, five years after founding Studio Lani, she received the SaloneSatellite Award for the RemX, an elegant, asymmetrical walking assistance device with a wrapping of water hyacinth. The RemX shares with Adeoye's furniture, wearables, and other projects a sinuous, sculptural profile and a conceptual basis in the foundational materials and ideas of Nigerian culture.

To introduce traditional methods and materials to contemporary furniture design, Adeoye has sought the advice and collaboration of expert practitioners of all trades, from hairdressers to shoemakers. Her furniture collection "EKAABO" (2022) includes Oba, a soft beige armchair that's as solid as it is elegant, echoing the shape of the *agbada*, a Yoruba garment. The chair is upholstered in hand-loomed Aso-oke fabric, while the back is braced with world-famous Benin bronze. The Komole chair, on the other hand, is inspired by Lagosian parties, and the elegant swirl of its metal rods is reminiscent of a body in graceful motion. Overhead, the twirling EKAABO LED pendant lights display a unique clay finish.

Adeoye's works have entered museum collections and earned her accolades from design publications including *Architectural Digest* and *Elle Décor*, but they remain grounded in the West African tradition of warm hospitality. One of her most iconic items is the Hadin lounger (also in the "EKAABO" collection), woven by master artisans from recycled leather. Its sensuous stretch immediately invites admiration as well as use. Adeoye's pieces are known to radiate a sense of "rhythm, warmth, and connection" conveying the the designer's love of dance, keen eye for form, and tireless ingenuity.

Komole Chair. Metal, Yoruba Aso-oke, velvet. 2022.

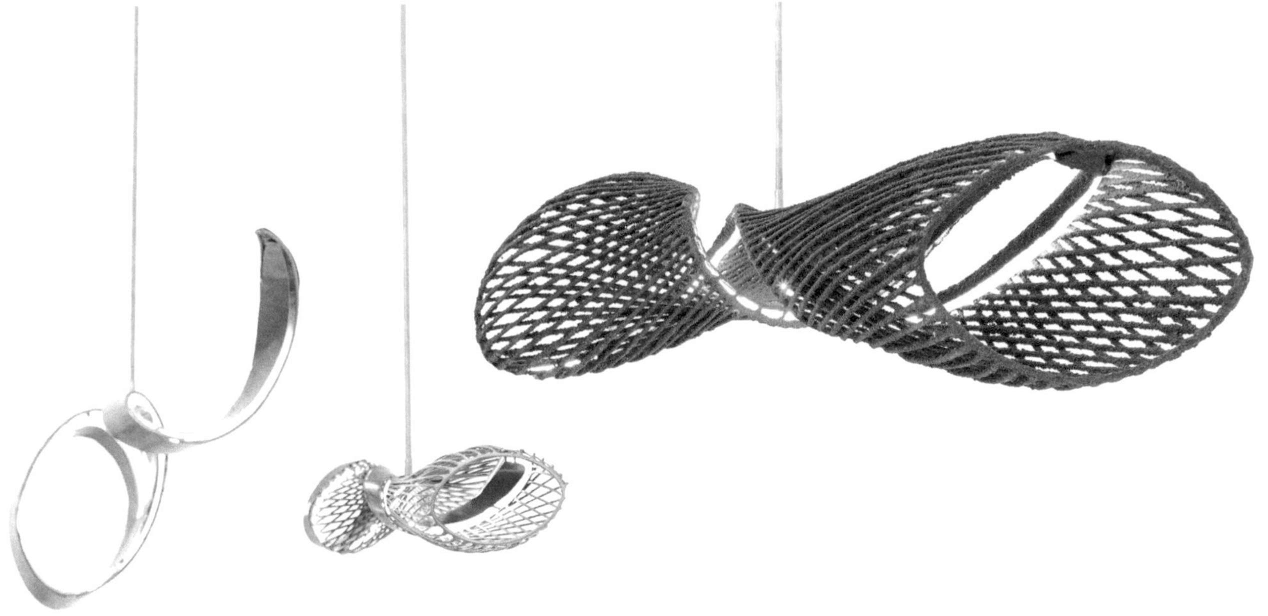

EKAABO lights. Steel, antique brass color, clay. 2022.

Hadin Lounger. Upcyled leather. 2022.

STUDIO URQUIOLA

"Pipeline" collection Freeform 1 rug. Himalayan wool. cc-tapis. 2023.

The portfolio of Spain-born, Italy-based Patricia Urquiola spans products, architecture, art-direction, and strategy, and her thoughts and approach have touched countless projects over more than twenty years of practice. She is known for her skill in finding the "fundamental element" of a project, guided by advice from her venerable mentors, Achille Castiglioni, Vico Magistretti, and Maddalena de Padova. Moving easily from designing objects to examining future living practices, she also champions heritage and innovation, bringing together seemingly disparate approaches, such as craft and industrial production.

"Pipeline" Freeform 1 and Wallhanging 2 (2023) are examples. A continuation of her collaboration with cc-tapis, they test the translation of digital drawings into the different scale and materiality of Himalayan wool. Designed as works to enliven and soften interior spaces, they present energetic circular traces that interweave and spiral, recalling the path of an animated computer game frozen in time. Woven from an enthusiastic palette of pink, red, oranges, lilac, ivory, and sage, the finishing also varies, with shorn, rounded surfaces bumping up against fringed detailing to create an unruly woven work that disobeys the traditional linear boundaries of a rug.

An altogether more sedate aesthetic is found in "Rows" (2023), Urquiola's collection of tables, consoles, and desks for Moroso. Named for the ribbed detail of oak-veneered MDF that forms the base and faces of the furniture, this graphic, textural finish reinterprets the language of a fluted column. Translated into subdued tones of gray, green, cinnamon, or taupe wood, the classical reference is shored up by marble or glass table-top finishes, which offer both literal and allegorical weight.

A doyenne of design, Urquiola is celebrated as both creator and mentor. She continues to work energetically from her own studio and since 2015 has also led creative direction at Cassina.

"Rows" collection cabinet. MDF, oak, marble. Moroso. 2023.

"Rows" collection console table. MDF, oak, marble. Moroso. 2023.

Moncloud sofa. Various materials. Cassina. 2023.

TAF STUDIO

Balk pedestal. Oregon pine. 2023. Wood Lamp. Muuto. 2009.

Mattias Ståhlbom and Gabriella Lenke, the founders of TAF Studio, conceive of their work as "spatial design," a field located somewhere between interior design and architecture. It has been a fertile field indeed for the Stockholm-based studio, earning TAF the Elle Deco Swedish Design Award, among other industry accolades. Since meeting at the Konstfack (University of Arts, Crafts, and Design) in Stockholm and establishing their studio in 2002, the pair have conceived of each project as an occasion to practice their commitment to pragmatism and to continue exploring the processes of production.

Ståhlbom and Lenke's superbly sensible designs foreground the designers' preference for making the structure and purpose of an object visible. Their Atelier chair (2018), manufactured by Artek for Sweden's Nationalmuseum, is a sleek, stackable marvel. And what the Atelier does to make a public space welcoming, the Bleck easy chair does for the home. Launched in 2017, it comprises cushions comfortably stuffed with down and foam, cradled by a beams-and-braces beech frame inspired by the frames of oil paintings: turn a painting around, and the canvas stretchers become visible. TAF's Ambit wall lamp, with a spun aluminum shade and rotating arm and head, is infinitely adaptable and human-scale—undaunting, appealing, reliable.

Abidingly curious about traditional Nordic design and local possibilities for manufacture, the designers have also worked with artisans in Japan. The two often spend time in the studio before taking their designs into the wider world. Their working space contains an "idea shelf," where they keep objects that inspire them, and a workshop, in which they can experiment with small-scale versions of products and spaces. But no matter the scale, they imbue the spaces they design with a sense of structure and ease, each object a material manifestation of their gift for inspiring confidence.

Bleck easy chair. Beech, duck-feather padding, polyether, leather. Gärsnäs. 2017.

Atelier Chair. Beech. Artek. 2018.

Famna sofa. Birch, upholstery. Svenskt Tenn. 2020.

NAO TAMURA

Meno water bottle. Borosilicate glass, wood. Iittala. 2023.

Nao Tamura's design is a harmony of opposites: East and West, art and design, nature and technology, purity and emotion. From a transparent cell phone and public restroom to fragrance bottles, she has produced work for the likes of Established & Sons, the city of Tokyo, and Nike.

Tamura, who lives and works in Brooklyn, was born into a creative family in Tokyo. Her grandmother and aunt are fashion designers, her mother and father interior and industrial designers, respectively. After studying communications and graphic design at Parsons School of Design, New York, she launched her own practice in Tokyo in 2009 before moving it into the New York apartment where she now lives.

Today, Tamura's work captures the power, delicacy, and poetry of nature. In "Rings" (2012), she lent a sense of time and timelessness to Artek's Stool 60 by depicting tree growth rings on its geometric seat. Her diaphanous, multimedia SunShower lounge for Lexus (2019) evoked a rain shower on a sunny day, using only fabric and light. Her designs make the minimal both expressive and warm. Flow(t) (2013–14) for WonderGlass consisted of several sculptural glass pendant lights, like an exploded chandelier. Its forms echoed the reflections of Venice in the water of its canals, hinting at the existence of an imaginary city in their depths.

Tamura also has an instinct for simplifying the complex. For Issey Miyake and Seiko, she designed the unisex, mechanical 1/6 watch (2019). Our increasing reliance on the high-tech alienates us from eons of hands-on human exploration of the world around us, so Tamura wanted to let the wearer feel the ticking of time. For Ambientec, the "Turn" families of precisely machined metal lanterns (2021) tapped the client's rigorous craft and cutting-edge technology to create waterproof, cordless, USB-charged lights in elemental and flawlessly curved forms.

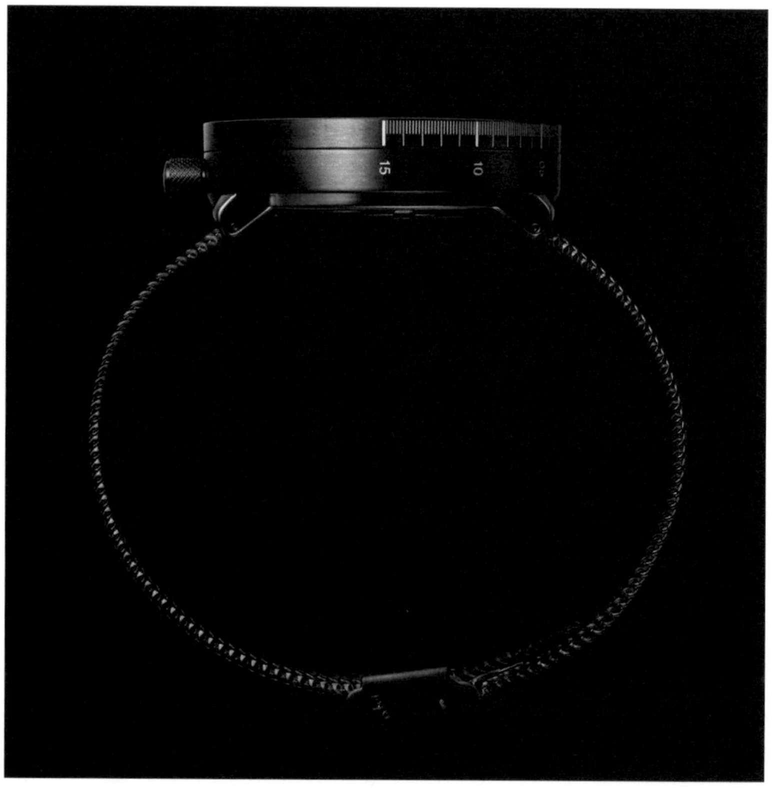

1/6 watch. Stainless steel, Hardlex. Issey Miyake x Seiko. 2019.

Turn lamps. Stainless steel, brass, or aluminum. Ambientec. 2019.

Turn+ lamp. Stainless steel, crystal glass diffuser. Ambientec. 2021.

Flow [t] lighting. Glass, metal. WonderGlass. 2013.

Dogon height-adjustable stool. Baltic birch plywood, ash. 2019.

JOMO TARIKU

MeQuamya Chair. Walnut. Fabricated by David Bohnhoff. 2019.

Raised in Kenya and Ethiopia, Jomo Tariku grew up among the eclectic objects brought home by his father, a diplomatic attaché. He studied industrial design at the University of Kansas, presenting his thesis about contemporary African furniture. By the time he launched his studio in 2017 in Springfield, Virginia, Tariku had worked as a janitor, a grocery stocker, a graphic designer, and a data scientist. Today, his handmade wooden furniture—inspired by his cultural and artisanal heritage—lives in the Afrofuturism Period Room at the Metropolitan Museum of Art in New York. The three-legged Nyala chair (2018), inspired by the horns of a mountain antelope, was one of five of his pieces used on the film sets of Marvel Studios' *Black Panther: Wakanda Forever* (2022).

During his childhood, after Tariku's parents made coffee, they would replace the pot on the mantel as a decorative object. He continues to see functional objects in this rich light. His Mukecha stool/table (2020) references traditional African mortars, small ones for grinding coffee beans and large ones that require family or neighbors to take turns grinding grain, accompanied by singing, which helps to synchronize the pounding of the mortar and pestle. The Meedo Chair (2021), with its toothed legs, smooth wooden curves (in sixteen layers of molded, laminated walnut veneer), and red along its sharp edges, was inspired by traditional African combs and the Afro pick of 1970s America, symbols of Black beauty and defiance.

Tariku is fascinated with traditional concepts, but layers his own meaning into his work. The Qwanta Totem Chair (2022) celebrates the traditional African birthing chair, which can be taken apart. Tariku reversed its mechanism and made the backrest a totem, a symbol that honors ancestors across Africa. His clients can choose their own totems, switching out the backrest for the one that is most meaningful to them.

Meedo Chair. Walnut veneer. Fabricated by David Bohnhoff. 2021.

TEENAGE ENGINEERING

field desk. Recycled anodized aluminum alloy, formica birch plywood. 2023.

The products designed by teenage engineering are the perfect synthesis of youthful enthusiasm and the deep knowledge and experience of master craftspeople. Founded in 2007 by Jesper Kouthoofd, David Eriksson, Jens Rudberg, and David Möllerstedt, the Stockholm studio is responsible for one of the most widely admired synthesizers in use. Its OP-1 field synthesizer, sampler, and sequencer was updated in 2022 with new reverb, new graphics, and FM broadcasting, among other features. Yet it's still fundamentally the same winsome gadget that won over musicians from Bon Iver to Reggie Watts when it debuted in 2011.

Over the years, it has been joined by such products as the OB-4 magic radio (2020), the CM-15 microphone (2023), and the TX-6 mixer (2022), all instantly recognizable as the output of teenage engineering. The rechargeable, bite-size 3½ in (90 mm) CM-15 microphone (2023), for instance, comes with a 1 in (25 mm) diaphragm capsule that ensures extraordinary quality of sound, and sports a charmingly retro square wire mesh, the throwback gesture a typical touch. The designers and engineers pack a wide selection of features into their gear, but eschew anything they deem superfluous or frivolous, including splashy branding or in-your-face, performative minimalism. The products have a variety of colors and typefaces, but within a purposefully limited range.

Perhaps the best explanation for the studio's continued innovation and success is that the minds behind teenage engineering are making things they themselves get a lot of pleasure from using. The studio has grown to a team of sixty, with some engineers doing double duty as Teenage Engineering Sound System, an in-house band that tests out the equipment in live performances. A sense of play and the determination to stick to the essentials coexist in every teenage engineering product, and anyone in possession of one of these devices has access to all the possibility the combination entails.

computer—1 case. Aluminum. 2021.

OB-4 magic radio and speaker. Various materials. 2020.

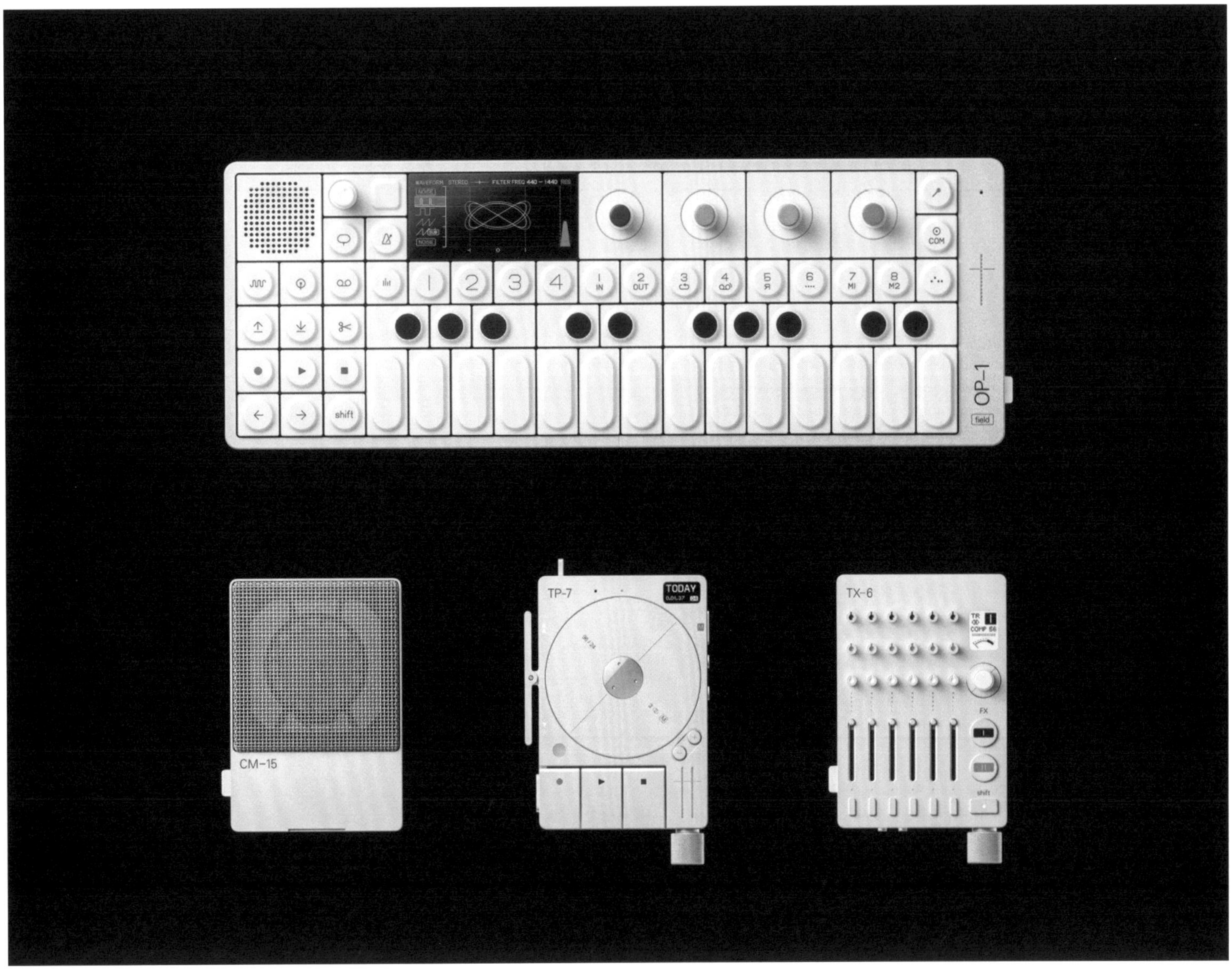

TX-6 mixer and audio interface, 2022; OP-1 field synthesizer, 2022; CM-15 microphone, 2023; TP-7 digital tape recorder, 2023.

THE AGENCY OF DESIGN

Air dehumidifers and fans. Various materials. Meaco. 2021.

The London-based The Agency of Design, founded by Rich Gilbert, Adam Paterson, and Matthew Emery-Laws, is a multidisciplinary outfit that uses design to create a cleaner, safer, more interesting world. Offering a range of services, including research, prototyping, and experiences for organizations, the trio behind The Agency have worked with multinational commercial clients including Samsung, Nespresso, eBay, and Barclaycard. Drawing on a team that includes coders and engineers, The Agency materializes vital, out-of-the-box ideas and makes them available in rather attractive boxes.

Some of The Agency's most fascinating projects are to be found at the cutting edge of healthcare technology. Take their 9 Hole Peg Test (2017), which is used to assess upper-limb function for people with multiple sclerosis, a disease of the central nervous system. Previous tests were costly, but The Agency of Design, in collaboration with researchers at Queen Mary University, London, brought the price of this critical object down to £5. The Agency's work on the PullClean door handle (2014) for Altitude Medical is likewise a stroke of fortune for anyone stepping foot into a hospital. Infections acquired at hospitals have long been an ordeal—one that the PullClean handle is designed to address. It incorporates a sanitizer dispenser at the base, and is also a smart device with built-in sensors that track sanitizer use, collecting statistics while encouraging a salubrious practice by integrating it seamlessly into the daily routine.

The Agency is no stranger to the domestic environment, designing an award-winning line of dehumidifiers, fans, air purifiers, air conditioners, and humidifiers for Meaco. And, crucially for designers tackling serious issues, the trio have a wonderful sense of levity and play. Their Optimist toaster (2013), made of recycled cast aluminum, foregoes the customary popping motion and instead features a rotating arm, inviting users to become the agents of their own breakfasts.

PullClean door handle. Aluminum, ABS, LDPE. Altitude Medical. 2014.

Blume lightbulb. Various materials. 2014.

The Optimist toaster. Various materials. 2013.

TOOGOOD

Puffy lounge chair. Natural canvas, stainless steel. Hem. 2020.

The British artist and designer Faye Toogood fits into no category neatly but excels in many. An early glimpse of the sculptor Barbara Hepworth set the young Toogood on a creative trajectory: she studied art history, worked in magazines, and finally founded her studio in 2008. The designer is invested in local manufacturing and her projects are produced domestically, but inspiration for the work comes from a list of forms that is as long as recorded history. Attracted to the best iteration of an object or idea, whether ancient or modern, Toogood exercises enormous freedom in her work.

Toogood's now-famous fiberglass Roly-Poly chair (2014) drew on her experience of pregnancy and motherhood. Four round plinths support a gently curving seat, clearly maternal but with room for significant variation: the Raw version of the chair calls to mind clay vessels and prehistory, while Water speaks of the sea and life on a cellular level, something fledgling and translucent. Toogood's more straightforwardly commercial pieces, such as the Puffy lounge chair that came of her partnership with Hem, also do not lack personality. A detachable canvas slung across a steel frame, the Puffy silhouette is appealingly casual—because precisely calculated to appear thus. Toogood is a master of the signifier: the unisex clothing line she produces with her sister Erica, a handsome alternative to flashy dressing, is a recalibration of the work clothes of tradespeople.

Toogood feels she is at her best when given a brief, yet the work made to order is memorable precisely because of her deep commitment to her own vision. Unconvinced that her objects are designs in the conventional sense, she organizes her work into assemblages, and believes that a designer, like an artist, must develop a personal alphabet of forms. Toogood's own striking abecedarium—archetypal and unconventional, soft and firm—is one future designers will learn by heart.

Roly-Poly chair. Raw fiberglass. 2014.

Dough ceramics. Glazed stoneware. Toogood. 2022.

Plot I table. Oak. 2022.

TRIBUTO

Venus table. Wood and volcanic stone. 2022.

Hammered copper, basketry, burnished clay, lava-stone carving, and metalwork are among a treasure trove of artisan techniques in Mexico that are given fresh life through the works of the design studio Tributo. Founded by the Mexican designer Laura Noriega, with her sister Gabriela, in Jalisco in 2013, Tributo designs and produces modern objects sleekly rooted in Mexico's rich tapestry of craftsmanship. From tables and chairs to kitchen tools, their contemporary products for daily life are created in collaboration with product designers and a string of master artisans specializing in a spectrum of generations-old skills.

Tributo's aim is to tap into the power of design as a tool to promote social, economic, and cultural development within Mexico's traditional artisan communities, with a geographical reach stretching from Jalisco and Oaxaca to Veracruz and Hidalgo. Laura Noriega spent a number of years studying and working in Milan before returning to Mexico to explore the creative possibilities of her homeland's artisan landscape. With Tributo's collections, she smoothly interconnects Mexico's traditional cartography of craftsmanship with a contemporary design narrative.

Your Skin (2012), crafted in Oaxaca and Jalisco, is an easy chair inspired by sensorial memories of Noriega's time in Japan, where she took part in a research program in Kyoto. The low chair consists of a light, solid structural frame of walnut or beech, with the "skin" being its textile seating, in such easily interchangeable materials as natural leather, cotton, or wool.

Other highlights include the Venus side table (2015), its circular top crafted from matte-black lava stone above a wooden base; the Tiripiti A lamp (2012), a clean-lined hammered copper pendant light made by the artisan Napoleón Pérez in the Michoacán region; and "La Noche" (2013), a collection of cheese knives crafted by the Ojeda family in Jalisco.

La Noche knives. Wood and stainless steel. 2013.

Your Skin chair. Wood and leather. 2015.

La Bonita chair. Aluminum and synthetic fabric. 2017.

Balance nightstand. Cedar. 2018.

MARIO TSAI

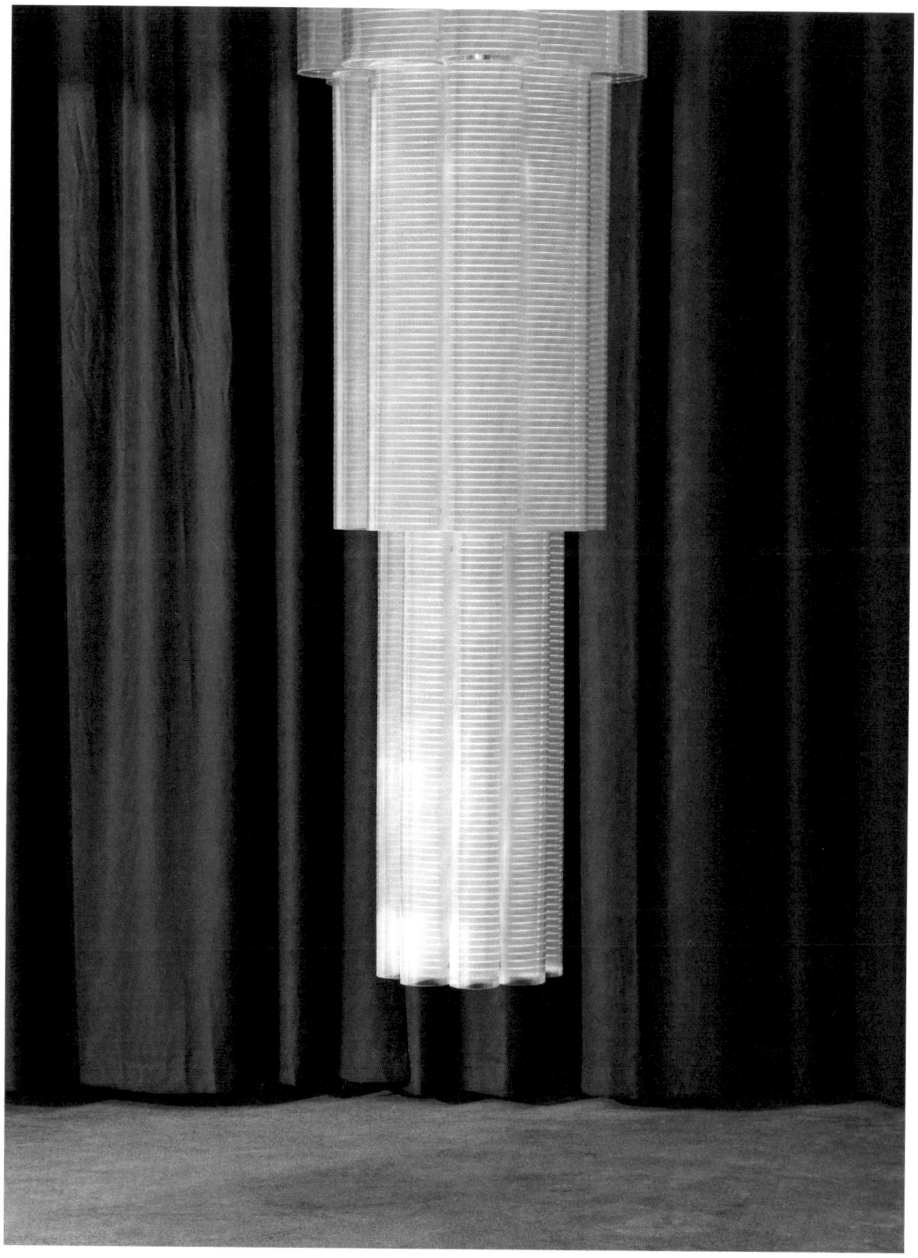

Light from Architecture Bloom chandelier. Aluminum, PET. 2023.

Mario Tsai's sturdy, appealing designs share a charming simplicity—not only of product, but also of process. After graduating from Beijing Forestry University in 2011, the designer worked in a factory as an engineer, focusing on efficiency and considering the best way to "execute ideas with the least amount of material and energy consumption." Since opening his own design studio in Hangzhou in 2014, Tsai has continued to research and experiment with sustainable production methods. Through his work with the studio, which offers a direct-to-consumer product line as well as consulting and art-direction, he aims for an aesthetic that he calls "soft minimalism," creating furniture, lighting, and spaces that are both utilitarian and inviting.

Although Tsai is inspired by naturally occurring examples of "extreme austerity and primeval simplicity," such as the landscape of the Gobi Desert in eastern Asia, his designs leaven their foundational, streamlined clarity with playfulness. His wooden Rong chair (2020), in colors from creamy white to red to neon or more tranquil laurel-green, is both frank and fun, with a circular seat and an angled rectangular back. Likewise, Tsai's "Rough" collection (2022) embraces imperfection, leaving visible the marks made during manufacture.

Tsai spent his childhood in the countryside, and silence and space still have an allure for him. Dreamed up in his mountainside studio, his modular Mazha Lighting System (2022), with crossing bars that recall the traditional Chinese folding stool, is a master achievement of functional and friendly design. The wiring of the lights is concealed within the threads used to suspend them, and their visible metal hinges are part of the circuitry. Infinitely adjustable, suited to spaces of any size, the lights are unobtrusive but remarkable, brightening both room and mood.

Light from Architecture Bloom chandelier. Aluminum, PET. 2023.

“Hardware Shop Project.” Various materials. 2021.

Rong benchair. Wood. 2020.

“Rough” collection. Wood. 2022.

“Origin” collection. Wood. 2021.

Mazha Lighting System. Lighting tubes, metal poles, wire. 2022.

MPHO VACKIER

It is a chair that tells a very particular story: its circular lines, woven backrest, and graphic textiles were inspired by the majestic elegance of the hairstyles traditionally worn by Ethiopia's Oromo people. The Oromo Chair (2018) is one of a string of creations dreamed up by the South African designer Mpho Vackier and her Kempton Park-based studio TheUrbanative, which collectively form something of a love letter to African hair stories.

Vackier, who launched her studio in 2017, explores the narratives that underpin the vibrant culture and heritage of her homeland through the prism of furniture and product design, all manufactured in South Africa. Her furniture combines layers of storytelling with African crafts and a Modernist undertone, all rooted in smooth functionality that is no doubt connected to her first career as an engineer. Her debut collection was ablaze with with geometric patterns inspired by the patterns of South Africa's Ndebele people, while the powerful culture of Indigenous African hair formed the creative backbone of the "African Crowns Collection" (of which the Oromo Chair is part).

There are also the cocooning, curved, coral-toned vertical lines of the Wambo Outdoor Pod (2022), a sculptural chair that celebrates the long braided hair of the Mbalantu women of early twentieth-century Namibia. And it's all about taking it easy when it comes to the Pumzika Couch (2022)—named after the Swahili word meaning "to rest or retire"—as reflected in its comfortably deep seat and puffy backrest, wrapped in a clean steel frame with organic lines.

Be they chairs, pods, mirrors, or couches, Vackier's furniture and products are ultimately vessels for exploring, questioning, and unraveling cultural representations in present-day African society.

"Homecoming" collection. Various materials. 2020–21.

WE+

Refoam stools and pillar. Styrofoam. 2023.

Discarded copper, waste Styrofoam, non-edible seaweed. All these alternative materials (and more) for designing and living are brought to life through the vision of Tokyo design studio we+. Founded in 2013 by Toshiya Hayashi and Hokuto Ando, we+ explores new forms of creative expression through meticulous research and experimentation, with a focus on the harmonious coexistence of nature and society.

The studio's varied projects reflect the diverse backgrounds of its members—which include designers, engineers, researchers, and writers—creating a refreshingly layered approach. Material explorations are key, as is reflected in Drought (2017), a starkly sculptural chair inspired, as they say, by the "cracked and weathered rocks of soil created by sun exposure." To achieve this effect, a wax prototype was mixed with a super-absorbent resin before being left to dry for a week, during which time it shrank extensively. The prototype was then replaced with bronze, using a lost-wax casting process. The result is a chair with a graphic silhouette and a weathered texture.

Papery sheets of *ita nori* seaweed, typically used for sushi, are the starting point of "Less, Light, Local," a research project unveiled at Milan Design Week 2023. This taps into an increase in non-edible seaweed waste in Japan, caused by rising ocean temperatures, and explores its potential as a new material. The result is a series of installations and lights made from the seaweed sheets, fusing simplicity with craftsmanship.

A playful approach to sustainability is another ingredient in we+'s output, embodied by the strongly contemporary, sculptural lines of the furniture in the "Refoam" collection (2023), which, from a distance, resembles marble. Closer inspection reveals that the material is in fact waste Styrofoam, rescued from treatment plants in Tokyo. Waste is also the main protagonist in "Remains" (2023), a research project that resulted in stone-like circular sculptures created from kiln-firing various leftover composite materials and debris from industrial recycling plants.

Drought chair. Bronze. 2017.

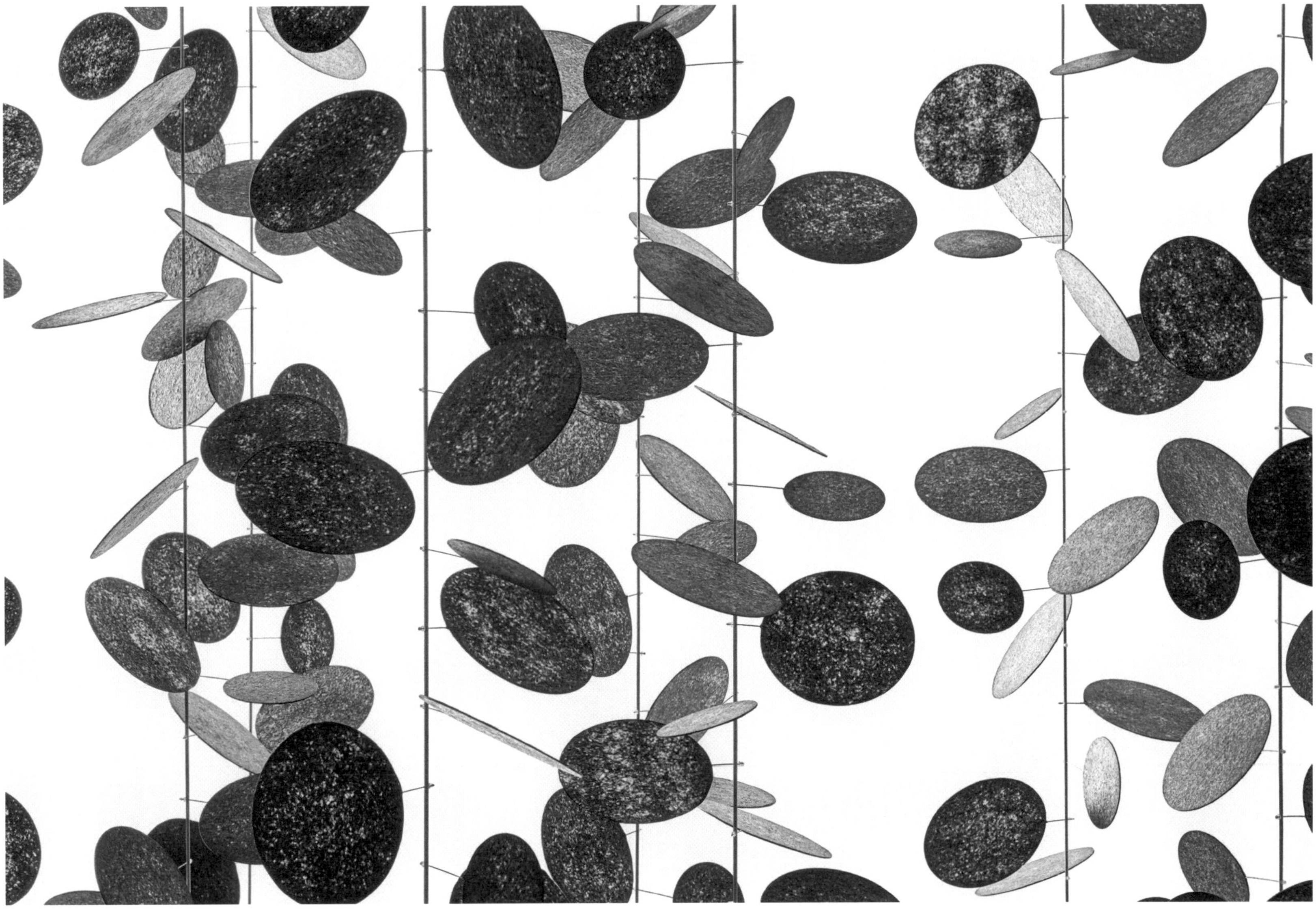

Less, Light, Local research project. Seaweed, stainless steel, acrylic. 2023.

"Haze" series of objects. Copper wire. 2022.

The Voice of Glass. Discarded window glass, paper. 2020.

ZAVIER WONG

The Common Table. Recycled wood, steel, brick, polystyrene, polycarbonate. 2021.

Zavier Wong describes himself as a gardener "in an industrial wilderness." He sees value in the discarded, defective, or generic, redeeming materials that have been lost and found again. Born in Singapore, Wong graduated in 2021 from the Design Academy Eindhoven, where his tutor was the Spanish artist Nacho Carbonell. He has stayed in the city, doing metalwork for the art and design practice Studio Job while working on his own interior objects and furniture design.

Wong enjoys "tinkering" with a range of materials and mediums, but is particularly drawn to those that are seen as imperfect, unwanted, or useless. He views this perceived weakness as an invitation to transform them, but also the viewer. As he "negotiates" with his materials, he gives them value and a voice. He offers the viewer a new way to see and experience the material: as perfect, wanted, and useful.

Wong's *The Common Table* (2021) consists of five tables that fit together, and explores ideas of individuality and togetherness. The tables are made of different found materials—brick, plastic, steel, Styrofoam, and wood—broken into pieces. They represent different "broken" people. Life can be hard and yet, for Wong, from hardship there is growth. *Junk to Funk!* (2020), meanwhile, questions perfection and imperfection. Wong fabricated a series of lounge tables from bricks and rebar rescued from two buildings undergoing demolition. He reassigned value to the worn, fragmented materials, creating coarse, asymmetric sculptures that are also functional. "That was during the beginning of the COVID pandemic, when there was a collective sense of things crumbling," he says, "so the material spoke to me, as a message of hope and restoration. Beauty from ashes."

Wong's work is expressive and textured, rough but refined, graphical, and balanced. The final form the material takes always follows its character and "behavior," but it's also meaningful to the designer himself.

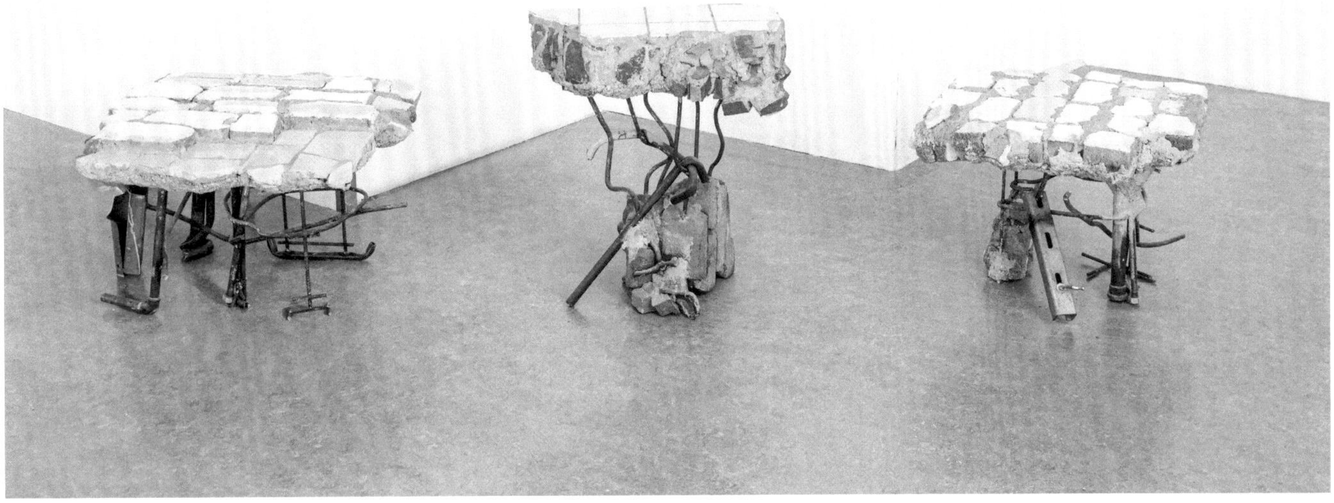

Junk to Funk tables. Brick, metal. 2020.

The Common Table. Recycled wood, steel, brick, polystyrene, polycarbonate. 2021.

BETHAN LAURA WOOD

Criss Cross Kite chandelier. Glass, brass, steel, cables, bulbs. With Pietro Viero. 2019.

The self-confessed "hoarder and collector" Bethan Laura Wood inhabits a world that is a jubilant collage of bold decoration, rendered in a rainbow of color, texture, material, and detail. This maximalism has become her design signature, with projects ranging from Valextra handbags for their Spring/Summer 2018 collection, through Christmas windows for Hermès and an award-winning tea set for Rosenthal.

Educated at the Royal College of Art in London, Wood draws inspiration from such celebrated artists and designers as Eduardo Paolozzi, Ettore Sottsass, and Nathalie Du Pasquier. Equally, she celebrates flea-market finds, and her approach mixes and mismatches with gleeful disregard for design rules.

Frequent limited-edition works with Nilufar gallery in Milan, for instance, ignited Wood's "Meisen" series (2021). This range of cabinets, desks, and dressers or dressing tables translates her beloved Meisen kimono into vibrant, jewel-like storage pieces. Tall Cabinet suggests the segmented body of an arthropod, its robust form poised atop skinny legs with exquisite details of inlaid brass and coated steel. Richly colored in tangerine, its doors feature an abstracted detail of Meisen silk, writ large in ALPI veneer.

In a *New York Times* house tour, references abound to Wood's favored Memphis Group designers. A similar energy can be traced in her Super Fake Rugs (2019) for cc-tapis. These colorful shards created from hand-knotted cotton, Himalayan wool, pure silk, and linen form sumptuous rugs in her hallmark confident colors. Although soft to the touch, their lithic, crystalline structures in Technicolor hues introduce vitality to interiors.

Wood's own appearance is a striking embodiment of her philosophy, with fantastical clothing, makeup, and accessories. Unsurprisingly, her spirited outlook and production have won loyal clients and many awards, and her work is in the permanent collections of the Victoria and Albert Museum and the Wellcome Trust in London, SFMOMA, and most recently the National Gallery of Victoria in Australia.

Toothpaste handbag. Brass, acetate. Valextra. 2018.

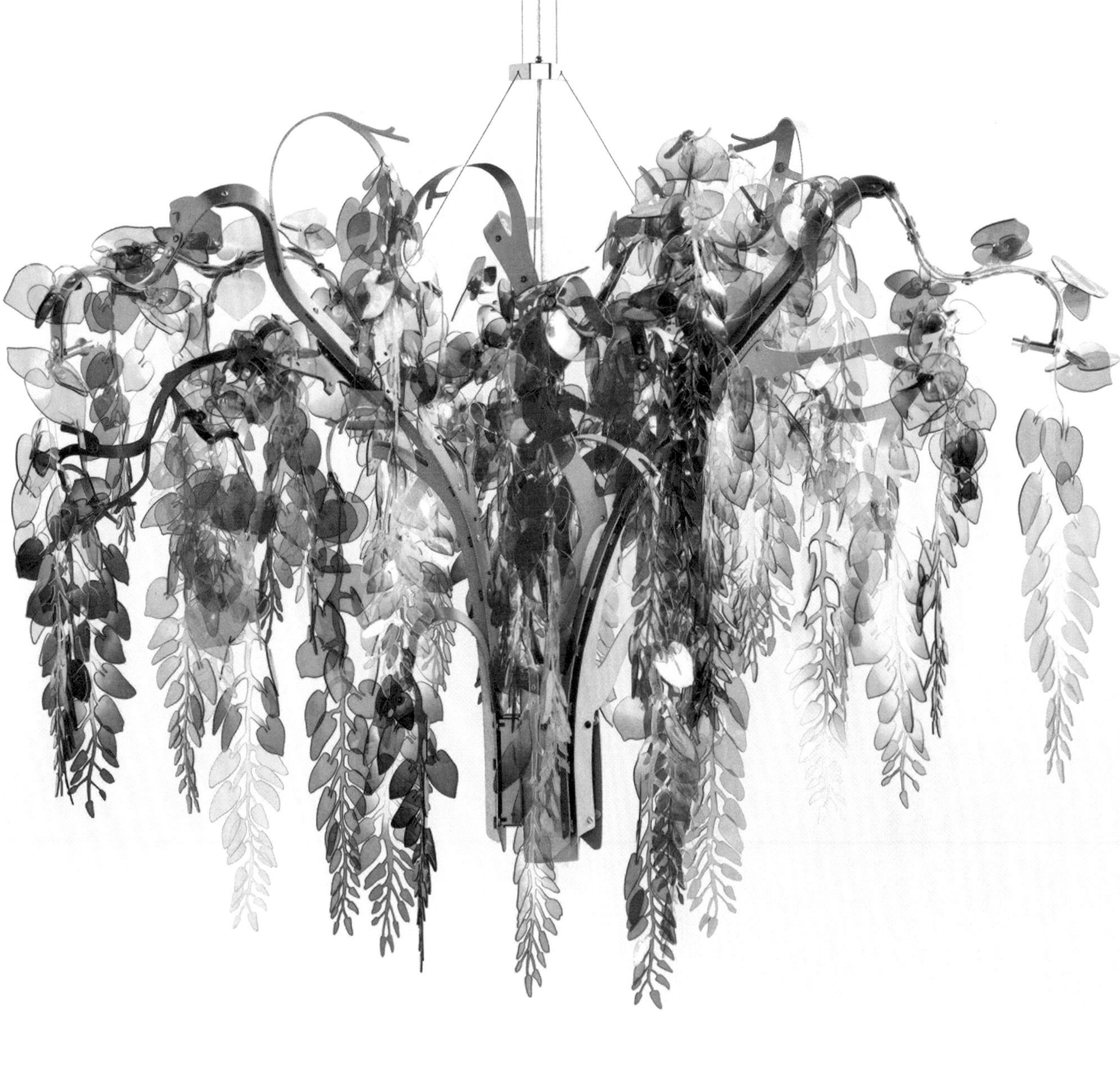

Wisteria chandelier. Aluminum, PVC, brass, cables, LED. With Neal Feay. 2020.

Meisen Caterpillar Cabinet. ALPIlignum veneer, wood, brass, powder-coated steel. 2022.

Meisen Tall Cabinet. ALPIlignum veneer, wood, brass, powder-coated steel. 2021.

Super Fake rug. Cotton, Himalayan wool, silk, linen. cc-tapis. 2019.

ZANELLATO/BORTOTTO

Lanterns. Leather, glass. Louis Vuitton. 2021.

The seriously serene designs of Zanellato/Bortotto, the Treviso-based studio of Giorgia Zanellato and Daniele Bortotto, are an invitation to relax and reflect. Having met as students at ECAL (École cantonale d'art de Lausanne), the two founded their studio in 2013, working on product and interior design as well as art-direction and the production of limited-edition pieces. The studio's output, uniformly luxurious, elegant, and subtle, is informed by Zanellato and Bortotto's desire to engage with the specificity of the places that inspire them. Their furniture, textiles, tiles, and other objects echo the colors, shapes, and histories of Italian cities, interpreting the emotions these places evoke in silk and copper, wood and gold.

The rugs and jacquard tapestries in the Venice-inspired "Acqua Alta" collection (2013), made by Zanellato/Bortotto for the city's venerable Rubelli company, are the result of repeated encounters with this historic site. The oval Giudecca rug (2016), a combination of cotton weave, Himalayan wool, and silk, hand-knotted in Nepal, is modeled on a photograph of water lapping at a set of Venetian steps. In muted blued and beiges, this Proustian backdrop for contemplation is both the outcome of an aesthetic experience and an experience in itself. Likewise, the oxidized ochre and sapphire gradients of the cabinets and sideboards in the designers' "Marea" collection (2018) evoke Rembrandt's chiaroscuro and J. M. W. Turner's near-abstract seascapes, endowing the space around them with a richness and depth beyond the literal.

Zanellato/Bortotto's signature elegance persists across the studio's collaborations with brands including Bulgari, Saba Italia, De Castelli, and Bolzan, yielding such stunning lines as the "Mangiafuoco"—fire-eater—collection (2023), created for Moroso. Vitreous powders applied to copper surfaces before firing create colorful rings on the metal. It's tempting, in these tables and trays, to see eyes, portals, or even the concentric rings of memory: vivid recollections of the past and foundations for future encounters.

Rotin chair and table. Teak, textile. Ethimo. 2013.

Mangiafuoco coffee tables. Fire enamel, copper, wood. Moroso. 2023.

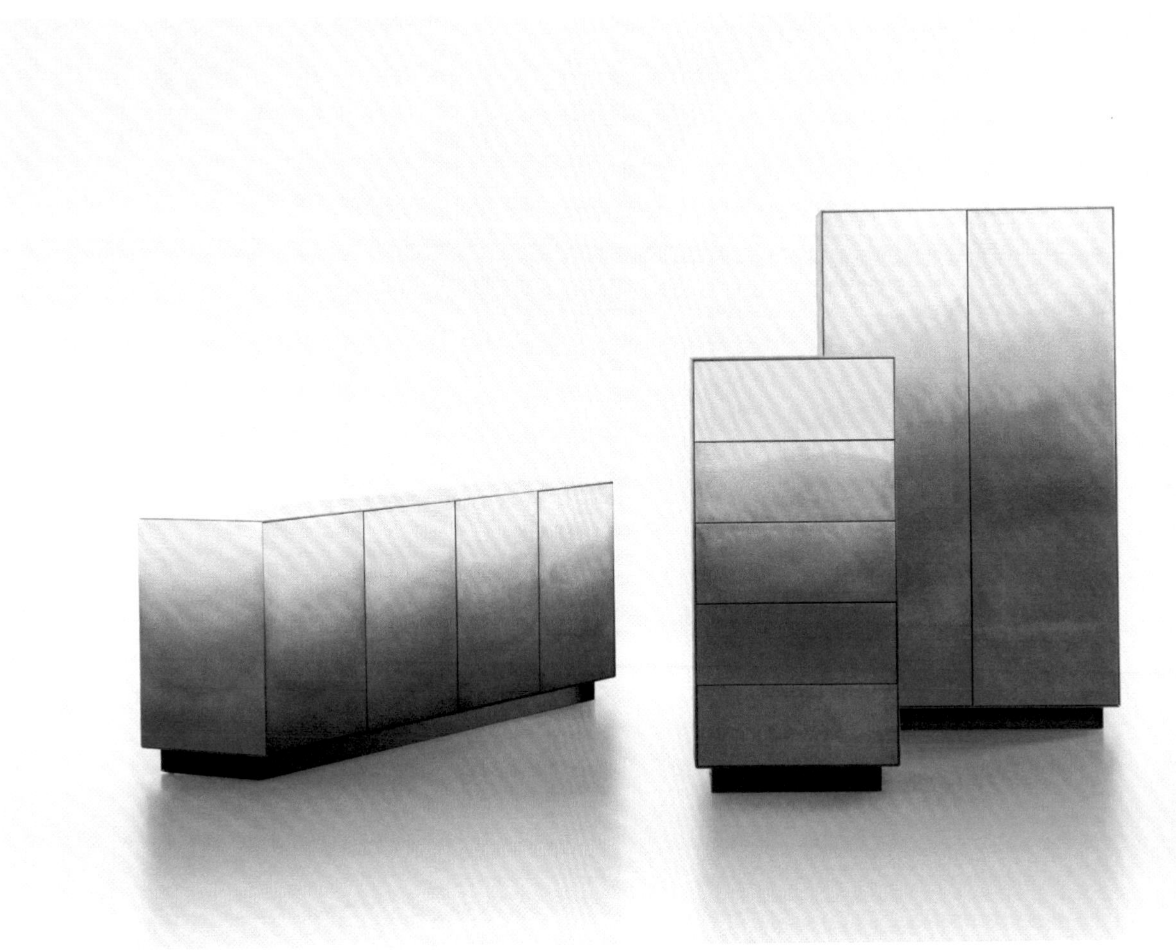

Marea cabinet, console, drawers. Brass, iron, copper. De Castelli. 2018.

ZAVEN

Enrica Cavarzan and Marco Zavagno founded Zaven in Venice in 2008. The studio is both agile and rooted in a professional network that is based in the Venetian Lagoon but reaches some of the most important players in the European design scene. Its network includes both commercial and institutional partners, underlining the studio's activity in the cultural and commercial arenas. Zaven mixes skills and perspectives from different worlds, particularly visual communications in relation to the most interesting trends in international contemporary art, and product design with a strongly handmade feel. The studio has a close working relationship with craftspeople and producers, particularly in the fields of glass, ceramics, and textiles, and Cavarzan and Zavagno personally study the manufacturing techniques and learn the limitations and potential of the various materials and production processes.

This way of working is enriched by academic activities, such as teaching at schools and universities. Always accompanied by analytical research and the in-depth study of contexts and typologies, Zaven's work has, over time, formed an extensive catalog of products. A collaboration with Zanotta, for instance, brought about the Za:Za sofa (2022), in which a structure of straps supports the upholstery.

Zaven has also developed important partnerships with galleries, editors, and museums. The Athletes floor lamps, for example, formed an installation for Nike for the 2016 Milan Design Week and were inspired by the beauty of an athlete in motion. In some cases, such collaboration has prompted the creation of limited-edition or exhibition pieces that later became mass-produced objects.

Zaven has also worked in the creative realm of exhibition design and site-specific installations. It has carried out projects for, among others, the Milan Triennale, the Design Museum Holon in Israel, the Museum für Kunst & Gewerbe Hamburg, Germany, and the Verso gallery in New York.

The Athletes floor lamps. Metal, strip bulb, Nike Flyknit fabric diffuser. Nike. 2016.

No Flags ceramic vessels. Ceramic. Verso. 2023.

Dune lamp. LED diffuser, cargo belts. WonderGlass. 2019.

No Flags desk. MDF, walnut, steel. Verso. 2023.

Za:Za sofa. Various materials. Zanotta. 2022.

If I Had Wings garments. Textile. With Anthony Knight for Kvadrat. 2020.

Biographies

AAKS
Akosua Afriyie-Kumi. Born 1986, Kumasi, Ghana. Based in Kumasi, Ghana. Established in 2014. **Press and Publications:** *Elle Decoration*, August 2022; *Vogue Italia*, May 2022; *Forbes Woman Africa*, 2016; *The Guardian*, December 2015; *The Times*, May 2015. **Clients include:** Anthropologie, Bloomingdales, J.Crew, John Lewis, Nordstrom, and United Arrows. **Award:** shortlist, Emerging Designer from Africa, *Vogue Italia*, 2015.
aaksonline.com @a.a.k.s

LINDSEY ADELMAN
Born 1968, New York. Based in New York and Los Angeles. Established in 2006. **Press and Publications:** *Elle Décor,* May 2023; *The New York Times,* April 2023; *Wallpaper**, October 2022; *Architectural Digest*, June 2020.
lindseyadelman.com @lindseyadelman

AGNES STUDIO
Estefania de Ros and Gustavo Quintana-Kennedy. De Ros born 1990, Guatemala City, Guatemala; Quintana-Kennedy born 1981, Guatemala City, Guatemala. Based in Guatemala. Established in 2017. **Press and Publications:** *Woman Made: Great Women Designers* (Phaidon, 2021); *Dwell*, September 2019; *Le Monde*, February 2019; *The New York Times T Magazine*, September 2018. **Exhibitions:** Ago Projects, Design Miami; Zona Maco; Objects with Narratives.
agnesstudio.co @agnesstudio.co

MICHAEL ANASTASSIADES
Born 1967, Athens, Greece. Based in London. Established in 1994. **Press and Publications:** *Artnet*, March 2023; *Dezeen*, March 2023; *An Interior*, November 2021; *Dezeen*, May 2019; *The New York Times*, May 2019. **Clients include:** Aboutwater by Fantini, Alessi, B&B Italia, Bang & Olufsen, Cassina, Flos, Gebrüder Thonet Vienna, Herman Miller, Karakter, Kettal, Lobmeyr, Molteni, Puiforcat, Roda, Salvatori, Sigmar London, Svenskt Tenn, and Valextra. **Awards:** Compasso d'Oro, 2020; Maison & Objet, 2020; The Design Prize, 2019; Designer of the Year, EDIDA, 2019; Royal Society of Arts (RSA); Royal Designer for Industry (RDI). **Exhibitions:** *Mirror Mirror: Reflections on Design,* Chatsworth House, Derbyshire, 2023; *My Circuit,* Six Acts, Milan, 2023; *Fringe,* Milan, 2023; *Silver Tongued,* SHOP Taka Ishii, Hong Kong, 2019*; Things That Go Together,* NiMAC, Nicosia, 2019.
michaelanastassiades.com @studiomichaelanastassiades

OMER ARBEL
Born 1976, Jerusalem. Based in Vancouver. Established in 2005. **Press and Publications:** *Design Edit*, October 2022; *West Coast North* (Figure 1 Publishing, 2022); *Architectural Digest Germany*, 2021; *Dezeen*, March 2021; *Omer Arbel* (Phaidon, 2021). **Awards:** Red Dot Design Award, 2022; winner, World Architecture Festival: Future Projects—House, 2019; *Wallpaper** Design Awards, 2019; Allied Arts Medal, Royal Architectural Institute of Canada, 2015; Good Design Award, Chicago Athenaeum Museum of Design, 2013. **Exhibitions:** *Material Experiments*, Victoria and Albert Museum, London, 2022; *75, 86, 91, 94—Architectural Experiments in Material and Form*, AEDES Architecture Forum, Berlin, 2020; *Omer Arbel 113*, Carwan Gallery, Athens, 2020; *Particles for the Built World*, Surrey Art Gallery, Canada, 2019; *Raw Design*, Museum of Craft and Design, San Francisco, 2018.
omerarbel.com @omerarbeloffice

INI ARCHIBONG
Born 1983, Pasadena, California. Based in Neuchâtel, Switzerland. Established in 2011. **Press and Publications:** *Surface*, April 2023; *Architectural Digest*, February 2023; *Forbes*, November 2022, *Wallpaper**, October 2022; *Financial Times*, June 2021. **Clients include:** Hermès, Knoll, Logitech, Sé Collections, and Vacheron Constantin. **Awards:** Good Design Award, 2022; Best Design Award, London Design Biennale, 2021. **Exhibitions:** *Mirror Mirror: Reflections on Design*, Chatsworth House, Derbyshire, 2023; *Before Yesterday We Could Fly: Afrofuturist Period Room*, Metropolitan Museum of Art, New York, 2021; *Speechless*, Dallas Museum of Art, 2019.
designbyini.com @iniarchibong

ATLASON STUDIO
Hlynur Atlason. Born 1974, Reykjavik. Based in New York. Established in 2004. **Press and Publications:** *The New York Times,* May 2023; *Wall Street Journal*, February 2022; *Design Milk*, February 2019. **Clients include:** Don Julio 1942, Estée Lauder, Heller, L.Ercolani, and MillerKnoll. **Award:** Smithsonian Cooper Hewitt National Design Award for product design, 2023.
atlason.com @atlason-studio

BARBER OSGERBY
Edward Barber and Jay Osgerby. Barber born 1969, Shrewsbury, UK; Osgerby born 1969, Oxford, UK. Based in London. Established in 1996. **Press and Publications:** *Wallpaper**, June 2023; *Il Giornale del Arte*, June 2023; *Il Sole 24 Ore*, June 2023; *The New York Times,* April 2023; *Financial Times*, April 2021; *Barber Osgerby: Projects* (Phaidon, 2017). **Clients include:** B&B Italia, Cassina, Fredericia, Marsotto Edizioni, and Rimowa. **Awards:** London Design Medal, 2015; OBE (UK), 2013; Royal Designers for Industry, 2007; Jerwood Prize, 2004. **Exhibitions:** *From Island to Island*, Studio Casoli, Filicudi, Italy, 2023; *Signals*, Galerie kreo, London, 2022; *Forecast*, London Design Biennale, Somerset House, London, 2016; *Double Space*, Victoria and Albert Museum, London, 2014.
barberosgerby.com @barberosgerby

BIG-GAME
Augustin Scott de Martinville, Grégoire Jeanmonod, and Elric Petit. Scott de Martinville born 1980, Paris; Jeanmonod born 1978, Lausanne, Switzerland; Petit born 1978, Etterbeek, Belgium. Based in Lausanne. Established in 2004. **Press and Publications:** *BIG-GAME: Everyday Objects* (Lars Müller Publishers, 2019); *NZZ*, November 2017; *Intramuros*, December 2015; *BIG-GAME Design Overview* (Stichting Kunstboek, 2008). **Clients include:** Alessi, HAY, IKEA, Karimoku New Standard, Muji, Muuto and Nespresso. **Awards:** Preis Schweiz Merit Award, 2015, Swiss Design Award, 2014, 2010 and 2006; Hublot Design Award, 2015; Good Design Award, 2014, *Wallpaper** Design Award, 2014. **Exhibitions:** *BIG-GAME BOX*, Karimoku Commons, Tokyo, 2023; *BIG-GAME Everyday Objects*, Mudac, Lausanne, 2019; *BIG-GAME Overview*, CID, Grand Hornu, Belgium, 2008.
big-game.ch @biggamedesign

AGUSTINA BOTTONI
Born 1984, Buenos Aires. Based in Milan, Italy. Established in 2016. **Press and Publications:** *La Repubblica*, November 2022; *Architectural Digest France*, March 2022; *Elle Decoration France*, December 2021; *Architectural Digest Mexico and Latin America*, December 2020; *Marie Claire Argentina*, September 2020; *Dezeen*, June 2018.

Clients include: Abet Laminati, Campari, Coincasa, IKEA, and Triennale di Milano. **Awards:** BIG SEE Wood Design Award, 2022; selected, 50 Best Designers, *Marie Claire Maison*, 2021; selected, Dwell 24: Two Dozen Up-and-Coming Designers, *Dwell*, 2018; Good Design Seal, Ministry of Industry Argentina, 2018. **Exhibitions:** *Assembly for Regeneration*, Fondazione Pistoletto, Biella, 2023; *Carpe(t) Diem*, Galerie Chevalier Parsua, Paris, 2021; *Super Superfici—The Spirit of Memphis (Reloaded)*, ADI Design Museum, Milan, 2021; *You Are Welcome*, Amelie Maison d'Art, Paris, 2019; *W. Women in Italian Design*, Triennale di Milano, 2016.
agustinabottoni.com @agustina.bottoni

BOUCHRA BOUDOUA
Born 1988, Casablanca, Morocco. Based in Casablanca and Marrakech, Morocco. Established in 2017. **Press and Publications:** *Konfekt*, June 2023; *Shoelifer*, January 2023; *Elle Decoration France*, June 2022; *Déco Actuelle*, August 2021; *Condé Nast Traveller*, January 2021; *British Vogue*, July 2019. **Clients include:** Conran Shop, Globus, La Mamounia, and A New Tribe.
bouchraboudoua.com @bouchraboudoua

RONAN & ERWAN BOUROULLEC
Ronan born 1971, Quimper, France; Erwan born 1976, Quimper. Based in Paris. Established in 1999. **Press and Publications:** *Le Monde*, March 2023; *Wallpaper**, October 2022; *Dezeen*, June 2022. **Editors:** Alessi, Cappellini, Kartell, Kvadrat, and Vitra. **Awards:** Best Seats, *Wallpaper** Design Awards, 2023; Compasso d'Oro (Italy), 2022. **Exhibitions:** *Mimèsis: Un Design Vivant*, Centre Pompidou-Metz, 2022–3; *Metalworks: Designing & Making*, Konschthal, Esch-sur-Alzette, 2022; *New Glass Now*, Toyama Glass Art Museum, 2022.
bouroullec.com @ronanbouroullec / @erwanbouroullec

RODRIGO BRAVO
Born 1981, Santiago. Based in Santiago. Established in 2005. **Press and Publications:** *Design Milk*, February 2022; *Wallpaper**, April 2021; *AD*, June 2019; *The New York Times*, September 2018. **Exhibitions:** *Friends like Family*, Matter, New York, 2020; *Beyond Language*, Chamber Projects, Venice, 2020; *Object of my Eye*, Matter, New York, 2019; *Quick Tiny Shows*, Buenos Aires, 2019; *Aesthetic Visions*, Milan Design Week, 2018; Boon Art & Design, Paris Design Week, 2018; Sight Unseen OFFSITE, NYCxDesign, New York, 2018; *Monoambiente #19*, Galería Monoambiente, Buenos Aires, 2017.
bravo.io @rodrigobravo / @bravo_estudio

THILO ALEX BRUNNER
Born 1977, Biel/Bienne, Switzerland. Based in Zürich, Switzerland. Established in 2006. **Awards:** Design Preis Schweiz, 2021; Design Preis Schweiz, 2017; German Design Award, 2015; Red Dot Design Award, 2014; Swiss Design Award, 2014; Design Preis Schweiz, 2013; Swiss Design Award, 2011.
thiloalexbrunner.ch / on.com

FABIEN CAPPELLO
Born 1984, Paris. Based in Guadalajara, Mexico. Established in 2010. **Press and Publications:** *Objetos de Resistencia* (Zaventem Publishing, 2021); *Sillas Callejeras* (Self Published, 2019). **Clients include:** Ago Projects, Coachella Music and Arts Festival, Hem, Lago/Algo, and Material Art Fair. **Exhibitions**: *Seeking Zohn*, MAK Center for Art and Architecture – Schindler House, Los Angeles, California 2023; *Conversation Pieces*, SFMOMA, San Francisco, California, 2022; *Objetos de resistencia*, Zaventem, Brussels, Belgica, 2021; *Artes y Oficios*, Ago Projects, Mexico City, Mexico, 2020; *Sillas Callejeras/Street Chairs*, The Jacobs Institute for Design Innovation, Berkeley, California, 2019.
fabiencappello.com @fabien.cappello

ALVARO CATALÁN DE OCÓN
Born 1975, Madrid. Based in Madrid. Established his first studio in 2004 and ACdO was established in 2009. **Press and Publications:** *TLmagazine*, February 2023; *Wallpaper**, 2023; *DOMUS*, 2021; *Shanghai Daily*, 2016; *Craft Becomes Modern: The Bauhaus in the making* (Bauhaus Dessau, 2011). **Award:** Spanish National Design Award, 2023.
acdo.es @acdo.es

MARISOL CENTENO
Born 1985, Mexico City. Based in Mexico City. Established Bi Yuu in 2012 and Estudio Marisol Centeno in 2016. **Press and Publications:** *Wallpaper**, October 2022; *Living, Corriere,* July 2019; *The New York Times*, October 2016. **Clients include:** Cartier, H&M, IKEA, Nike, and Tatiana Bilbao. **Exhibition:** *Hilando Rituales*, Museo Franz Mayer, Mexico City, 2023; *Nature by Design: Cochineal*, Cooper Hewitt, Smithsonian Design Museum, New York, 2019-22.
estudiomarisolcenteno.com / biyuu.mx
@estudio_marisolcenteno / @biyuumx

MICHEL CHARLOT
Born 1984, Lausanne, Switzerland. Based in Porto, Portugal. Established in 2011. **Clients include:** Camper, Kettal, Muji, and Vitra. **Award:** Swiss Design Awards, 2013.
michelcharlot.com @michelcharlot

PIERRE CHARPIN
Born 1962, Saint-Mandé, France. Based in Paris. Established in 1990s. **Press and Publications:** *Designboom*, March 2023; *Wallpaper**, August 2022; *Forbes*, August 2018; *Dezeen*, February 2016; *Pierre Charpin* (J. R. P. Ringier, 2014). **Clients include:** Alessi, HAY, Hermès, Ligne Roset, and Zanotta. **Award:** Creator of the Year, Maison & Objet, 2017. **Exhibitions:** *From the Studio*, Designart, Tokyo, 2017; *Créateur de l'année*, Maison & Objet, Paris, 2017; *Todo es de Color*, Musée des Arts Décoratifs et du Design, Bordeaux, 2017; *Atmosfera*, Kyoto, 2016; *Performance*, Forum, Kyoto, 2016.
pierrecharpin.com @atelierpierrecharpin

FRANK CHOU
Born 1986, Beijing. Based in Beijing. Established in 2012. **Press and Publications:** *Dezeen*, July 2023; *Town & Country*, September 2022; *Architectural Digest*, January 2022. **Clients include:** Antalis, Buick, BMW, COLMO, Dell, Fnji, HC28, Louis Vuitton, MINI, and Swire Properties. **Awards:** Lifestyle Designer of the Year, *GQ*, 2022; Designer of the Year, Robb Report China, 2022; Rising Talent Award, Maison & Objet, 2019; Young Talent of the Year, EDIDA, 2019; Special Mention Award, SaloneSatellite, 2016.
frankchou.com @frankchoudesignstudio

PAUL COCKSEDGE
Born 1978, London. Based in London. Established in 2004. **Press and Publications:** *British GQ*, September 2019; *Financial Times*, July 2019; *The New York Times*, May 2019. *Dezeen*, December 2022. **Clients include:** Hermès, Mercedes-Benz, MoMA, Swarovski, and V&A. **Exhibitions:** *Performance*, Friedman Benda, New York, 2021; *Slump*, Carpenters Workshop Gallery, London, 2020.
paulcocksedgestudio.com @paulcocksedge

MAC COLLINS
Born 1995, Nottingham, UK. Based in Nottingham. Established in 2018. **Press and Publications:** *Acne Paper*, June 2023; *Financial Times*, May 2023; *GQ*, April 2023; *Architectural Digest Italy*, January 2022; *The New York Times*, January 2022; *Wallpaper**, January 2022. **Clients include:** Benchmark Furniture, Design within Reach, and Vaarnii. **Awards:** Ralph Saltzman Prize, 2022; Emerging Designer of the Year, London Design Festival, 2021. **Exhibitions and Events:** *Runout*, Venice Biennale, 2023; *Global Tools*, Side Gallery, Barcelona, 2023; *To Be Held*, Carl Freedman Gallery, Margate, 2023; *Open Code*, Primary, Nottingham, 2022; *Radical Acts*, Harewood House, Leeds, 2022; *Discovered: Designers for Tomorrow*, Design Museum, London, 2021.
maccollins.com @maccollins__

STEFAN DIEZ
Born 1971, Freising, Germany. Based in Munich, Germany. Established in 2002. **Press and Publications:** *DOMUS*, September 2023; *Interni Magazine*, June 2023; *architekturblat*, March 2023; *Designboom*, March 2023; *Designwanted*, December 2022; *Architectural Digest*, November 2022; *DAMN*, 2022, *Disegno*, 2022; *Frame*, August 2022; *Ignant*, October 2022; *Dezeen*, June 2022; *Wallpaper**, October 2021; *Full House: Diez Office*, (Koenig Books, 2017). **Clients include:**

HAY, Herman Miller, Kaldewei, Magis, Midgard, Rosenthal, and Vibia. **Awards:** *AD100*, 2023; RDI Honorary Royal Designer for Industry, 2022; Archiproducts Design Award, 2022; Best in Class, Australian Good Design Award, 2022; Best Light, *Frame* Magazine Awards, 2022; Best of the Year Award, *Interior Design*, 2022; Designer of the Year, *AW Architektur & Wohnen*, 2022.
diezoffice.com @stefandiez

FRIDA FJELLMAN
Born 1971, Mariestad, Sweden. Based in Stockholm. Established in 2000. **Press and Publications:** *Dagens industri*, May 2023; *SvD Perfect Guide*, May and October 2021; *Elle Decor Spain*, March 2021; *Dezeen*, February 2021. **Clients include:** Art Basel, Forbes, Four Seasons, Kosta Boda, and Vitra. **Awards**: Lauritz Konsthantverkspris, 2018; selected, Top Ten Nordic Projects, *Form*, 2016; Craftist of the Year, *Residence Magazine*, 2009; Stockholm City Culture Award, 2007. **Exhibitions and Events:** *I Himlen*, Art Basel, Switzerland, 2022; *I Himlen på Frida Fjellman*, Ronneby Konsthall, Ronneby, 2021; *Crystal Atmosphere*, Hostler Burrows, New York, 2018; *Une Touche Postmoderniste*, Sotheby's, Stockholm, 2017; *I Himlen på Frida Fjellman*, Gustavsberg Konsthall, Värmdo, and Ekilstuna Konstmuseum, Ekilstuna, 2015–16.
fridafjellman.com @fridafjellmanwork

FORMAFANTASMA
Andrea Trimarchi and Simone Farresin. Trimarchi born 1983, Sicily, Italy; Farresin born 1980, Vicenza, Italy. Based in Milan, Italy, and Rotterdam, the Netherlands. Established in 2009. **Press and Publications:** *Dezeen*, June 2023; *Domus*, June 2023; *TL Magazine*, June 2023; *Wallpaper**, May 2023; *GQ*, October 2022. **Clients include:** Cassina, Fendi, Flos, Lexus, and Max Mara. **Awards:** Designers of the Year, *Wallpaper** Design Awards, 2021; Designer of the Year, *Dezeen* Design Awards, 2020; Milano Design Award, 2019; Hublot Award, 2018; Designer of the Year, EDIDA, 2017. **Exhibitions:** *Oltre Terra*, National Museum of Oslo, 2023; *Sub Rosa*, ARCH Athens, 2022; *Cambio*, Serpentine Galleries, London, 2020; *Nervi in the Making*, MAXXI, Rome, 2019; *The Stranger Within*, MAK, Vienna, 2013.
formafantasma.com @formafantasma

FRONT
Sofia Lagerkvist and Anna Lindgren. Lagerkvist born 1976, Eskilstuna, Sweden; Lindgren born 1974, Stockholm, Sweden. Based in Stockholm. Established in 2003. **Press and Publications:** *TL Magazine*, February 2023; *Wallpaper**, January 2023; *Dezeen*, November 2022; *Financial Times*, September 2022. **Clients include:** Friedman Benda, Galerie kreo, Tom Dixon, Vestre, and Vitra. **Awards:** Årets Designer, *Elle Decor* Awards Sverige, 2023; Best in Lighting, EDIDA, 2023; Best Rock Formations, *Wallpaper** Design Awards, 2023; Bruno Mathsson Award, 2023; New Born Classic, Bukowskis, 2019. **Exhibitions and Events:** *Design by Nature*, Vandalorum, Värnamo, 2023; Guest of honor, Stockholm Furniture Fair, 2023; *Objects of Desire: Surrealism and Design 1924 – Today*, Design Museum, London, 2022–3; *Forest Wanderings*, Teatro Filodrammatici, Milan Design Week, 2022; *Things, Spaces, Interactions*, M+ Hong Kong, 2021.
frontdesign.se @frontdesign

NAOTO FUKASAWA
Born 1956, Kōfu, Yamanashi Prefecture, Japan. Based in Tokyo. Established in 2003. Established "Super Normal" with Jasper Morrison in 2006. Founded Design Science Foundation in 2022. He sits on the advisory board of Muji, is the art director of Maruni, and is a professor in the Integrated Design Department of Tama Art University. **Press and Publications:** a number of books, most recently *Naoto Fukasawa: EMBODIMENT* (Phaidon, 2018). **Clients include:** B&B Italia, Boffi, Emeco, Erco, Herman Miller, Maruni, Molteni, and Muji. **Awards:** Royal Designer for Industry, Royal Society of Arts; Isamu Noguchi Award, 2018. **Events:** ; Judging committee for LOEWE Craft Prize, 2017–; Chairman of The Nihon Mingei-kan, The Japan Folk Crafts Museum, 2012–.
naotofukasawa.com @naoto_fukasawa_design_ltd

GAMFRATESI
Stine Gam and Enrico Fratesi. Gam born 1975, Copenhagen; Fratesi born 1978, Pesaro, Italy. Based in Copenhagen. Established in 2006. **Press and Publications:** *Dezeen*, June 2023; *Forbes*, April 2023; *Wallpaper**, April 2023; *Design Milk*, June 2022; *Domus*, June 2020. **Clients include:** Bang & Olufsen, De Padova, HAY, Kvadrat, and Louis Poulsen. **Awards:** AD100, 2020, 2021, and 2022; International Designer of the Year, EDIDA, 2020; Bruno Mathsson Award, 2018; Best Designer, *Elle Decoration Japan*, 2017; Finn Juhl Prize, 2015.
gamfratesi.com @gamfratesi

MARTINO GAMPER
Born 1971, Merano, Italy. Based in London. Established in 2000. **Press and Publications:** *100 Chairs in 100 Days and its 100 Ways* (Dent-De-Leone, 2012). **Clients include:** Moroso, Prada, and Valextra. **Awards:** OBE (UK), 2023; Best Use of Colour, *Wallpaper** Design Awards, 2011; Moroso Award for Contemporary Art, 2011; Best Alchemist, *Wallpaper** Design Awards, 2008; Furniture Award, Brit Insurance Designs of the Year, 2008. **Exhibitions:** *100 Chairs in 100 Days*, Wellington City Gallery, 2017; *Middle Chair*, The Modern Institute at Pollock House, Glasgow, 2017; *100 Chairs in 100 Days*, RMIT, Melbourne, 2016; *100 Chairs in 100 Days*, MIMOCA, Marugame, 2015; *Design Is a State of Mind*, Museion, Bolzano, 2015.
martinogamper.com @martinogamper

KONSTANTIN GRCIC
Born 1965, Munich, Germany. Based in Berlin. Established in 1991. **Press and Publications include:** *Domus*, April 2023; *Konstantin Grcic: New Normals* (Buchhandlung Walther König, 2022); *Wallpaper**, May 2017; *Konstantin Grcic Abbildungen/Figures* (Lars Müller Publishers, 2016). **Clients include:** Artek, Flos, Issey Miyake, Muji, Venice Architecture Biennale, and Vitra. **Awards include:** gold, German Design Award, 2013 and 2023; Compasso d'Oro (Italy), 2001, 2011, and 2016. **Exhibitions:** *New Normals*, Haus am Waldsee, Berlin, 2022; *L'Immaginazione al Potere*, MAXXI, Rome, 2020; *Night Fever*, Vitra Design Museum, Weil am Rhein, 2018; *Animal Farm*, Magis, Milan, 2017; Konstantin Grcic – Panorama, Vitra Design Museum, 2014.
konstantin-grcic.com @konstantingrcicdesign

GT2P
Guillermo Parada, Tamara Pérez, Sebastián Rozas, and Victor Imperiale. Parada born 1981, Santiago; Pérez born 1981, Diriamba, Nicaragua; Rozas born 1978, Santiago; Imperiale born 1986, Puerto Varas, Chile. Based in Santiago. Established in 2009. **Press and Publications:** *Wallpaper**, February 2021; *TL Magazine*, May 2018; *Dezeen*, November 2016. **Clients include:** Capellini, Friedman Benda, IQHQ, and Marca Chile. **Awards:** Las Salinas Park Urban Park Contest, 2021; Miami Design District Annual Commission, 2020. **Exhibitions:** *The Design Triennale*, Cooper Hewitt, New York, 2019–20; *Raw Design*, Museum of Craft and Design, San Francisco, 2019; *gt2P: Manufactured Landscapes*, Friedman Benda, New York, 2018; Suple Connecting Form: Manufactured Landscapes Bench on show in the gardens of the Design Museum, London, 2017–18; *Creating the Contemporary Chair*, National Gallery of Victoria, Melbourne, 2017.
gt2p.com @gt2p

GUNJAN GUPTA
Born 1974, Mumbai, India. Based in New Delhi. Established Studiowrap in 2006 and Ikkis in 2019. **Press and Publications:** *Elle Decor India*, October 2021; *Architectural Digest India*, October 2019; *Wallpaper**, January 2019; *House & Garden*, December 2018; *Vogue India*, 2017. **Exhibitions and Events:** jury member, Le French Design 100, Paris, 2022; *Here We Are: Women in Design*, Vitra Design Museum, Weil am Rhein, 2021; Kochi Art Biennale, 2016; Triennale Design Museum, Milan, 2016; Venice Architecture Biennale, 2016.
gunjangupta.in / ikkis.in @gunjanguptastudio / @ikkis.21

JAIME HAYON
Born 1974, Madrid. Based in Valencia, Spain. Established in 2001. **Press and Publications:** *Jaime Hayon* (Gestalten, 2022); *Architectural Digest*, October 2017; *Wallpaper**, May 2017. **Clients include:** &Tradition, B. D. Barcelona, Cassina, Fritz Hansen, and Magis.

Awards: Best Playground, *Wallpaper** Design Awards, 2021. **Exhibitions:** *InfinitaMente*, Centre del Carme Cultura Contemporània, Valencia, 2023; *New Beginnings*, Galerie kreo, Paris, 2023; *Chez Soi*, Galerie kreo, London, 2022; *Step by Step*, Galerie kreo, Paris, 2022; *Cosmotik Jungle*, L21 Gallery, Majorca, 2021; *Chromatico*, Galerie kreo, Paris, 2018; *Game ON*, Galerie kreo, Paris, 2015.
hayonstudio.com @jaimehayon

MOISÉS HERNÁNDEZ
Born 1983, Mexico City. Based in California and Mexico City. Established in 2014. **Press and Publications:** *Dezeen*, March 2021; *Design Milk*, September 2020. **Clients include:** Comex, Diario, HAY, Mexa, and Pirwi. **Award:** Good Design Award, Chicago Athenaeum, 2020.
moises-hernandez.com @anothermoises

MARLÈNE HUISSOUD
Born 1990, Haute Savoie, France. Based in Paris. Established in 2013. **Press and Publications:** *Interior Design*, September 2020; *Icon*, September 2019; *Science of the Time*, September 2019; *Financial Times*, March 2019. **Clients include:** cc-tapis, London Design Festival 2020, Les Nouveaux Commanditaires, Science Museum, London, and SFER IK Museum. **Awards:** Greater London Enterprise Awards, 2022; AD100, The Game Changers, 2021; Wood Awards—Bespoke Category, 2020; Most Innovative Design Studio, Business Excellence Awards, 2018; Most Innovative Experimental Artist of the Year, Global Excellence Awards, 2018.
marlene-huissoud.com @marlenehuissoud

YINKA ILORI
Born 1987, London. Based in London. Established in 2015. **Press and Publications:** *Dezeen*, June 2023; *Architectural Digest*, May 2023; *Financial Times*, February 2023; *Wallpaper**, December 2022; *Pricegore and Yinka Ilori: Dulwich Pavilion* (Park Books, 2021). **Clients include:** Adidas, Bombay Sapphire, Courvoisier, Lego Group, Somerset House, and Universal Music. **Exhibitions:** *KNIT!*, Kvadrat, Copenhagen, 2020; *Home Affairs*, Now Gallery, London, 2015; *If Chairs Could Talk*, The Shop at the Bluebird, London, 2015; *Making Africa*, Vitra Design Museum, Weil am Rhein, 2015; *This Is Where It Started*, Whitespace Gallery, Lagos, 2014.
yinkailori.com @yinka_ilori

INDUSTRIAL FACILITY
Sam Hecht and Kim Colin. Hecht born 1969, London; Colin born 1961, San Jose, California. Based in London and California. Established Industrial Facility in 2002 and Future Facility in 2016. **Press and Publications:** *Chairs: 100 Masterpieces* (Welbeck, 2023); *Chair: 500 Designs that Matter* (Phaidon, 2018); *Industrial Facility* (Phaidon, 2018); *Industrial Design A–Z* (Taschen, 2016); *Usefulness in Small Things* (Rizzoli, 2010). **Clients include:** Google, Herman Miller, Mattiazzi, Muji, and Novo Nordisk. **Award:** Royal Designers for Industry, 2008 (Hecht) and 2015 (Colin). **Exhibitions:** *Parts list*, Galería Santa Cole, Barcelona 2022; *Beauty as Unfinished Business*, Saint-Étienne International Design Biennale, 2015; *Some Recent Projects*, Design Museum, London, 2008; *Found/Made/Thought*, Israel Museum, Jerusalem, 2005.
industrialfacility.co.uk @industrialfacility

ISPA (NIKE)
ISPA is a Nike design team. Established in 2018. **Press and Publications:** *Hypebae*, June 2023; *Designboom*, April 2023; *Hypebeast*, January 2023; *GQ*, May 2022; *Dezeen*, April 2022.
nike.com @nike / @teamteamteamteamteamteamteam

MARIA JEGLIŃSKA-ADAMCZEWSKA
Born 1983, Fontainebleau, France. Based in Warsaw and France. Established in 2012. **Press and Publications:** *Vogue Polska Living*, November 2022; *Faz Magazine*, April 2022; *Le Monde*, April 2022; *Design Hotels*, September 2021; *Raum und Wohnen*, April/May 2021. **Clients include:** Hermès, Kvadrat, Ligne Roset, Saint-Étienne International Design Biennale, and Vitra. **Exhibitions:** *Connected*, Design Museum, London, 2020; *L'été à Hyères*, Villa Noailles, Hyères, 2020; *In Circulation*, Museum of Applied Arts, Budapest, 2019; *Social Seating*, Fiskars Village Art & Design Biennale, 2019; *Ways of Seeing/Sitting*, Łódź Design Festival, 2012.
mariajeglinska.eu @mariajeglinska

HELLA JONGERIUS
Born 1963, De Meern, Utrecht, the Netherlands. Based in Berlin. Established in 1993. **Press and Publications:** *Eindhovens Dagblad*, February 2023; *Financial Times*, October 2022; *NRC Magazine*, April 2022; *Kinfolk*, December 2021; *Wallpaper**, May 2021. **Clients include**: KLM, Maharam, United Nations, and Vitra. **Exhibitions:** *Woven Cosmos*, Gropius Bau, Berlin, 2021; *Entrelacs: Une Recherche Tissée*, Lafayette Anticipations, Paris, 2019; *Breathing Colour*, Design Museum, London, 2017; *Die Neue Sammlung*, Pinakothek der Moderne, Munich, 2017.
jongeriuslab.com @hellajongerius

MISHA KAHN
Born 1989, Duluth, Minnesota. Based in New York. Established in 2013. **Press and Publications:** *Casually Sauntering the Perimeter of Now: Misha Kahn* (Apartamento, 2023); *Süddeutsche Zeitung*, April 2022; *Designboom*, June 2022; *Wallpaper**, February 2020; *Surface*, May 2019. **Exhibition:** *Misha Kahn: Glancing Blows,* The Page Gallery WEST, Seoul, South Korea, 2023; *Misha Kahn: Staged,* Friedman Benda, Los Angeles, 2023; *Misha Kahn: Style Without Substance,* Friedman Benda, New York, 2022; *Under the Wobble Moon: Objects from the Capricious Age,* Museum Villa Stuck, Munich, 2022; *Misha Kahn: Startling the Echoes,* Objective Collection, Shanghai, China, 2021; *Watermelon Party: Misha Kahn at The Little House,* Dries van Noten, Los Angeles, 2021.
mishakahn.com @mishakahn

CHARLOTTE KIDGER
Born 1992, Nottingham, UK. Based in London. Established in 2018. **Press and Publications:** *Elle Decoration*, September 2021; *Architectural Digest India*, 2020; *Forbes*, August 2020; *Dezeen*, August 2018; *House & Garden*, August 2018. **Clients include:** Adidas, Browns Fashion, Converse, COS, Red Deer, and Selfridges. **Awards:** Best Element of Surprise, *Wallpaper** Design Awards, 2023; finalist, Design Blok Prague Diploma Section, 2019; finalist, Cræftiga, 2018; finalist, HIX Art Award, 2018. **Exhibitions:** *300 Objects*, London Craft Week, 2020; *Collectible Art Fair*, Brussels, 2020; *Liberty Makers*, London Craft Week, 2019; *Re. Use, Re. Think, Re. Imagine*, Hauser & Wirth, Bruton, 2019; *Ventura Future*, Salone del Mobile, Milan, 2018.
charlottekidger.com @charlottekidger

MINJAE KIM
Born 1989, Seoul. Based in New York. Established in 2020. **Press and Publications:** *Apartamento*, Spring/Summer 2022; *Cero*, August 2021; *Architectural Digest*, May 2021; *Pin-Up*, Spring/Summer 2021; *Milk*, February 2021. **Exhibitions:** *IYKYK (If You're Korean You Know)*, Nina Johnson Gallery, Miami, 2022–3; MyoungAe Lee in Conversation with Minjae Kim, Matter, New York, 2022; *I Was Evening All Afternoon*, Marta, Los Angeles, 2021.
minjae.kim @mnjae.kim

KITT.TA.KHON
Teerapoj Teeropas with Suwan Kongkhunthian. Teeropas born 1989, Bangkok, Thailand Kongkhunthian born 1949, Chaingmai, Thailand. Based in Bangkok. Established in 2019. **Press and Publications:** *Financial Times*, September 2022. **Awards:** winner, Product Design, IFDA Award, 2022; winner, Furniture Design, Design Excellence Award, 2021; winner, Product Design, Golden Pin Design Award, 2021. **Exhibitions:** *D17/20*, Bangkok Design Week, 2020; *Design in Southeast Asia*, Galerie Joseph, Paris, 2020.
kitt-ta-khon.com @kitt.ta.khon

JORIS LAARMAN
Born 1979, Borculo, the Netherlands. Based in Zaandam, the Netherlands. Established in 2004. **Press and Publications:** *Joris Laarman Lab* (August Editions, 2017). **Clients include:** Droog, Flos, Swarovski, and Vitra. **Awards:** International Elle Deco Award, 2008; Woon Prize, 2007; Red Dot Design Award, 2006. **Exhibitions:** *Mirror Mirror:*

Reflections on Design, Chatsworth House, Derbyshire, 2023; *Joris Laarman Lab: Gradients*, Kukje Gallery, Seoul, 2018; *Joris Laarman Lab: Design in the Digital Age*, High Museum of Art, Atlanta, Museum of Fine Arts, Houston, Cooper Hewitt, New York, Groninger Museum, Groningen, Autostadt, Wolfsburg, 2015–18.
jorislaarman.com @jorislaarmanlab

MAX LAMB
Born 1980, St Austell, UK. Based in London. Established in 2007. **Press and Publications:** *Wallpaper**, March 2023; *Dezeen*, October 2022; *Financial Times*, September 2022; *The New York Times*, March 2016. **Exhibitions:** *Mirror Mirror: Reflections on Design*, Chatsworth House, Derbyshire, 2023; *Max Lamb: Special Delivery*, Salon 94 Design, New York, 2019; *Max Lamb: Exercises in Seating*, Art Institute of Chicago, 2018; *Poème Brut*, Design Museum Gent, Ghent, 2018; *Re-Considering Canon*, Design Museum, London, 2018.
maxlamb.org

FERNANDO LAPOSSE
Born 1988, Paris. Based in Mexico City. Established in 2015. **Press and Publications:** *TL Magazine*, June 2023; *Vogue*, June 2023; *Wallpaper**, March 2022. **Clients include:** Bentley, Daum Cristallerie, Selfridges, Tom Dixon, and Toogood. **Awards:** finalist, Hublot Design Prize, 2018; winner, Future of Food Design, 2017; selected, 70 Ones to Watch, Design Council UK, 2015. **Exhibitions:** *Food: Bigger than the Plate*, Victoria and Albert Museum, London, 2019; *Nature*, Cooper Hewitt, Smithsonian Design Museum, New York, 2019; *Transmutaciones*, Archivo de Diseño, Mexico City, 2019; *Material Consequences*, London Design Festival, 2018; *Saponaceous*, Pocko Gallery, London, 2015.
fernandolaposse.com @fernandolaposse

LAUN
Rachel Bullock and Molly Purnell. Bullock born 1985, Detroit, MI, USA; Purnell born 1982, Madison, WI, USA. Based in Los Angeles. Established in 2018. **Press and Publications:** *Elle Decor*, March 2023; *Sunset Magazine*, March 2023; *Dwell*, October 2022; *Architectural Digest China*, April 2022; *Woman Made: Great Women Designers* (Phaidon, 2021). **Exhibitions:** *California Designed*, Long Beach Museum of Art, 2020; *Inside/Out*, William Vale Hotel, New York, 2019.
launlosangeles.com @launlosangeles

KWANGHO LEE
Born 1981, Guri, South Korea. Based in Seoul and Jeju, South Korea. Established in 2007. **Press and Publications:** *Architectural Digest*, October 2022; *Surface*, October 2022; *Wallpaper**, September 2022. **Clients include:** Bottega Veneta, Dior, Hem, and Vaarnii. **Awards:** Designer of the Year (shortlist), Wallpaper*, UK, 2023; Designer of the Year, MADE, São Paulo, 2017; Young Craftsman of the Year, YÉOL—Society for Korean Cultural Heritage, 2013; Artist of the Year, Korean Ministry of Culture, Korea, 2011; nomination Designer of the Future, Design Miami/ Basel, 2009. **Exhibitions:** *Infinite Expansion*, Salon 94 Design, New York, 2023; *Antifragile*, Leeahn Gallery, Daegu, Korea, 2021; *Composition in blue*, Leeahn Gallery, Seoul, Korea, 2020; *10 Years*, Victor Hunt, Brussels, 2016.
kwangholee.com @_kwangho_lee

SHAHAR LIVNE
Born 1989, Tel Aviv, Israel. Based in the Netherlands. Established in 2017. **Press and Publications:** *The New Stijl* (Staat and MENDO, 2022); *Axis Japan*, December 2022; *Domus,* November 2017*, ELLE Decor NL*, 2020*; Financial Times,* September 2018*; Icon,* Winter 2020*; Wallpaper*,* February 2018. **Clients include:** Balenciaga, Cooper Hewitt Design Museum, Design Miami/Basel, NAT2, and NEOM. **Awards:** finalist, Prince Bernhard Award for Design, 2023; Winner, *Dezeen* Awards Emerging Design Studio of the Year, 2020; Winner, EcoCoin Award, Next Nature Network, 2020; *Icon* Magazine 100 Most Influential Creatives in the World, 2019–20; Creative Hero Award for Social Impact, 2019. **Exhibitions:** *Food*, Design Museum Holon, 2023; *IT'S OUR F***ING BACKYARD DESIGNING MATERIAL FUTURES,* Stedelijk Museum, 2022*; Prince Bernhard Award Exhibit, Design Museum Den Bosch, 's-Hertogenbosch, 2023; PLANET LOVE. Climate Care in the Digital Age,* Museum of Applied Arts (MAK), Vienna, 2022*; At the Coalface: Design in a Post-Carbon Age*, CID, Grand Hornu, 2022.
shaharlivnedesign.com @_studioshaharlivnedesign_

PETER MABEO
Born 1971, Gaborone, Botswana. Based in Botswana. Established Mabeo brand in 2006 and Mabeo Studio in 2013. **Press and Publications:** *Elle Decor France*, April 2022; *Architectural Digest France*, March 2022; *L'Officiel*, December 2021; *La Repubblica*, November 2021; *Architectural Digest*, May 2020. **Clients include:** Fendi and Wales Bonner.
mabeofurniture.com @mabeofurniture

INDIA MAHDAVI
Born 1962, Tehran, Iran. Based in Paris. Established in 2000. **Press and Publications:** *The New York Times T Magazine*, September 2023; *Magma*, June 2023; *Frame*, Special Issue 2023; *India Mahdavi* (Chronicle Chroma, 2021); *The New Yorker*, March 2018; *PIN-UP*, Spring Summer 2016. **Clients include:** De Gournay, Dior, Louis Vuitton, Nespresso, and Svenskt Tenn. **Awards:** AD100, 2023; Designer of the Year, *Wallpaper** Design Awards, 2023; Lifetime Achievement Award, *Frame* Magazine Awards, 2022.
india-mahdavi.com @indiamahdavi / @indiamahdavieditions

PHILIPPE MALOUIN
Born 1980, Montreal, Canada. Based in London. Established in 2008. **Press and Publications:** *Dezeen*, May 2023; *The Times*, May 2023; *Surface*, April 2023; *Wallpaper**, April 2023; *Design Milk*, February 2023. **Clients include:** De Sede, Flos, Hem, Iittala, Ishinomaki, and Marsotto Edizioni. **Awards:** Best of Year, Residential Seating, Interior Design, 2022; Designer of the Year, *Wallpaper** Design Awards, 2018.
philippemalouin.com @philippemalouin

CECILIE MANZ
Born 1972, Odsherred, Denmark. Based in Copenhagen. Established in 1998. **Clients include:** Bang & Olufsen, Duravit, Fritz Hansen, Iittala, Maruni, and Nils Holger Moormann. **Awards:** Honorable Award, Danish National Banks Foundation, 2021; Chevalier des Arts et des Lettres (France), 2019; Designer of the Year, Maison&Objet Paris, 2018; E. Kold Christensen's Award of Honor, 2003. **Exhibitions:** *Transpose: A Hint of Colour*, Maruni Showroom, Tokyo, 2023; *Transpose: Turning Ideas Around*, BaBaBa Gallery, Tokyo, 2023; *The Needle in the Haystack*, Danish Architecture Center, Copenhagen, 2021–2.
ceciliemanz.com @ceciliemanz

SABINE MARCELIS
Born 1985, Alkmaar, the Netherlands. Based in Rotterdam, the Netherlands. Established in 2013. **Press and Publications:** *Vogue*, May 2023; *Vogue Living*, March 2023; *EST Living*, January 2023; *Wallpaper**, August 2022; *Stir*, June 2022. **Clients include:** Audi, Fendi, Hem, IKEA, and Isabel Marant. **Awards:** Designer of the Year, EDIDA, 2023; Designer of the Year, *Monocle*, 2023; Designer of the Year, *Wallpaper** Design Awards, 2020; Newcomer of the Year, The Design Prize, 2019; Young Designer of the Year, EDIDA, 2019. **Exhibition:** *Colour Rush!*, Vitra Design Museum, Weil am Rhein, 2022–3.
sabinemarcelis.com @sabine_marcelis

NIFEMI MARCUS-BELLO
Born 1988, Lagos. Based in Lagos, Nigeria. Established in 2017. **Press and Publications:** *Domus*, April 2023; *Wallpaper**, December 2022; *Dezeen*, February 2022; *British Vogue*, June 2021; *HYPEBEAST*, September 2020. **Clients include:** Chalete African, Design Miami, and Tiwani Gallery. **Awards:** Emerging Designer of the Year, Monocle Design Awards, 2023; HUBLOT LVMH Design Prize, 2022; Life-Enhancer of the Year Award, *Wallpaper** Design Awards, 2021. **Exhibition:** *Oriki (Act I): Friction Ridge*, Marta, Los Angeles, 2023.
nmbello.com @nmbello1

MARZ DESIGNS
Coco Reynolds. Born 1985, Perth, Australia. Based in Byron Bay, Australia. Established in 2010. **Press and Publications:** *Woman Made: Great Women Designers* (Phaidon, 2022). **Award:** Temple & Webster People's Choice Award, 2014.
marzdesigns.com @marzdesigns

MASH. T DESIGN STUDIO
Thabisa Mjo. Born 1987, Eastern Cape province, South Africa. Based in Sandton, South Africa. Established in 2013. **Press and Publications:** *Wallpaper**, August 2022. **Clients include:** Beauty Ngxongo, Houtlander, and Qaqambile Bead Studio. **Awards:** Most Beautiful Object in South Africa, 2019; South African Designer of the Year, 2019; Nando's Hot Young Designer Talent Search, 2015. **Exhibitions and Events:** *Sacrosanct*, Milan Design Week, 2019.
mashtdesignstudio.com @mashtdesignstudio

MATERRA-MATANG
Ophélie Dozat and Lucien Dumas with the collaboration of Lou-Poko Savadogo. Dozat born 1993, Paris; Dumas born 1993, Paris. Based in Paris. Established in 2022. **Press and Publications:** *Les Presses du Réel*, 2022; *France Culture*, October 2021; *Liberation*, October 2021; *The Parisian*, October 2021; Article Terroir, biennale of architecture and of landscape, Versailles 2022. **Awards:** Tectona Design Parade Prize, 2023; Dotation Fondation Carmignac 2023; winner, Faire Paris, Pavillon de l'Arsenal, 2020; shortlist, Young Talent Architecture Award, EU Mies Awards, 2020. **Exhibitions and Events:** Residency, Villa Médicis, 2023–24, Académie de France, Roma *Colloque ¡Viva Villa!*, La Gaîté Lyrique, Paris, 2023; Biennale Émergences, CND, Pantin, 2023; Cité des Arts x Académie des Beaux-Arts, Paris, 2023; Villa Noailles, Design Parade Toulon, 2023; La Galerie du Vivant, Modern Art Fair, Paris, 2022.
materra-matang.com @materra_matang

CASEY MCCAFFERTY
Born 1989, New York. Based in Fair Lawn, New Jersey. Established in 2013. **Press and Publications:** *Elle Décor*, April 2023; *Galerie Magazine*, March 2023; *Sight Unseen*, June 2022; *Surface*, June 2022; *Architectural Digest*, April 2021. **Clients include:** Burberry, Kelly Behun, and Kelly Wearstler. **Exhibitions and Events:** *Snake Eyes*, Egg Collective, New York, May 2023; Design Miami, Gallery FUMI, November 2022; *Transcendence*, The Future Perfect, Los Angeles, August 2022; *Power of Myth*, Nino Mier, Los Angeles, June 2022.
casey-mccafferty.com @casey_mccafferty

CHRISTIEN MEINDERTSMA
Born 1980, Utrecht, the Netherlands. Based in Asperen, the Netherlands. Established in 2004 in Rotterdam. **Press and Publications:** *TL Magazine*, May 2023, *Wallpaper**, October 2022, *Financial Times*, May 2019; *Dezeen*, November 2016. **Awards:** Best Product, Dutch Design Awards, 2016; Future Award, Dutch Design Awards, 2016; winner, Play Category, Index Award, 2009. **Exhibitions:** *Christien Meindertsma – Onder de Wol*, Cuypershuis, Roermond, the Netherlands, 2023; *Make Good*, Victoria and Albert Museum, London, 2023 *Fertile Grounds*, Fries Museum, Leeuwarden, 2022; *De Zachte Stad*, DDW, Eindhoven, 2022; *Another Crossing*, Fuller Craft Museum, Plymouth, 2021; *Long Live Fashion*, Textile Museum, Tilburg, 2021; *Another Crossing*, The Box, Plymouth, 2020.
christienmeindertsma.com

MIMINAT DESIGNS
Miminat Shodeinde. Born 1994, London. Based in London. Established in 2015. **Press and Publications:** *Interior Design*, January 2023; *Woman Made: Great Women Designers* (Phaidon, 2022); *Kinfolk*, 2023; *Architectural Digest*, Middle East, December 2022; *Elle Decoration*, May 2022; *Financial Times*, April 2022; *Surface*, February 2022. **Exhibition:** *Discovered: Designers for Tomorrow*, Design Museum, London, 2021.
miminat.com @miminat_designs

MISCHER'TRAXLER STUDIO
Katharina Mischer and Thomas Traxler. Mischer born 1982, Sankt Pölten, Austria; Traxler born 1981, Linz, Austria. Based in Vienna. Established in 2009. **Press and Publications:** *BIO25 Faraway, So Close* (Motto, 2017); *Happening 2: Design for Events* (Frame, 2017); *Miroir Miroir* (Infolio, 2017); *Nomadic Furniture 3.0: New Liberated Living?* (Niggli, 2017); *Shedding Light* (Corraini Edizioni, 2017). **Clients include:** Design Miami, Hermès, Kvadrat, Maison Perrier Jouët, and PCM Design. **Awards:** Swarovski Design Medal, 2016; Young Talent Award, Be-open Foundation, 2014; Designer of the Future Award, Design Miami/Basel and W Hotels, 2011. **Exhibitions:** *Design by Time*, Gregg Museum of Art & Design, Raleigh, North Carolina, 2020; *Kleureyck: Van Eyck's Colours in Design*, Design Museum Gent, Ghent, 2020; *MADE IN: Crafts—Design Narratives*, Museum of Arts and Crafts, Zagreb, 2020; *Walden*, Schloss Hollenegg for Design, Hollenegg, 2020; *MAK Design Lab*, MAK, Vienna, 2019.
mischertraxler.com @mischertraxler.studio

NICOLE MONKS
Born 1981, Noongar Country (Subiaco), Australia. Based in Worimi and Awabakal Country (Newcastle), Australia. Established in 2012. **Press and Publications:** *Artlink*, March and June 2018; *Habitus*, March and September 2017; *Artichoke*, March 2017. **Clients include:** Australian National Maritime Museum, Carriageworks, Lendlease, Northern Beaches Council, Royal North Shore Hospital, and University of Technology Sydney. **Awards:** winner, European Healthcare Design, Interior Design and the Arts 2023; winner, Exhibition Projects —Galleries Small, Museums and Galleries of NSW IMAGinE Award, 2021; UNSW Art & Design Indigenous Professional Development Award, 2014.
nicolemonks.com @nicole_monks

JASPER MORRISON
Born 1959, London. Based in London. Established in 1986. **Press and Publications:** *Wallpaper**, July 2023; *Wall Street Journal*, October 2020; *A Book of Things* (Lars Müller Publishers, 2015); *The Good Life* (Lars Müller Publishers, 2014); *Super Normal* (Lars Müller Publishers, 2006); *A World Without Words* (Lars Müller Publishers, 1998). **Clients include:** Cappellini, Emeco, Flos, Maruni, Mattiazzi, and Vitra. **Awards:** CBE (UK), 2020; Compasso d'Oro (Italy), 2020.
jaspermorrison.com @jasper.morrison

JONATHAN MUECKE
Born 1983, Cody, Wyoming. Based in Minneapolis. Established in 2010. **Press and Publications:** *Core77*, April 2023; *Dezeen*, April 2023; *Pin-Up*, Spring/Summer 2022; *Newcity Design*, May 2022. **Award:** Knight Fellowship, 2015. **Exhibitions:** *Jonathan Muecke: Objects in Sculpture*, Art Institute of Chicago, 2022; *Volume 80*, Volume Gallery, Chicago, 2022.
jonathanmuecke.com @jonathanmuecke

MULLER VAN SEVEREN
Fien Muller and Hannes Van Severen. Muller born 1978, Lokeren, Belgium; Van Severen born 1979, Ghent, Belgium. Based in Ghent. Established in 2011. **Press and Publications:** *Dezeen*, May 2023; *Architectural Digest France*, April 2023; *Le Monde*, April 2020. **Clients include:** Centre Pompidou, HAY, Hermès, and Kvadrat. **Awards:** Designer of the year, Maison & Objet, 2023; Best Design Studio of the Year, *Dezeen* Awards, 2022; Best Designer, IDEAT Design Awards, 2022; *AD100*, 2021. **Exhibitions:** *Ten Years of Muller Van Severen*, Design Museum Gent, Ghent, 2021; *Design! Muller Van Severen at Villa Cavrois*, Croix, 2020.
mullervanseveren.be @mullervanseveren

NENDO
Oki Sato. Born 1977, Toronto, Canada. Based in Tokyo and Milan, Italy. Established in 2002. **Press and Publications:** *Design Milk*, May 2023; *Dezeen*, May 2023; *Wallpaper**, April 2023; *nendo: 2016–2020* (Phaidon, 2021); *nendo* (Phaidon, 2019); *Nendo in the Box* (Adp, 2015). **Clients include:** Baccarat, Cappellini, Cartier, DePadova, Issei Miyake, and TOYOTA. **Awards:** Designer of the Year, Maison & Objet, 2015; Best Domestic Design, Wallpaper, 2012;

Designer of the Year, EDIDA, 2012. **Exhibitions:** *Break to Make*, Milan Design Week, 2023; *nendo: Breeze of Light*, Milan Design Week, 2019; *nendo: Forms of Movement*, Milan Design Week, 2018; *nendo: Invisible Outlines*, CID, Grand Hornu, 2017; *nendo: Invisible Outlines,* Milan Design Week, 2017.
nendo.jp @nendo_official

EREZ NEVI PANA
Born 1983, Bnei Brak, Israel. Based in Tel Aviv, Israel. Established in 2015. **Press and Publications:** *Designboom*, July 2021; *Dezeen*, October 2020; *TL Magazine*, August 2020; *Surface*, October 2019. **Exhibitions and Events:** *Crystalline*, National Gallery of Victoria, Melbourne, 2020–1; *Nature: Cooper Hewitt Design Triennial*, Smithsonian Design Museum and the Cube Design Museum, New York and Kerkrade, 2019–20; *Beazley Designs of the Year*, Design Museum, London, 2018–19.
ereznevipana.com @ereznevipana

CAROLIEN NIEBLING
Born 1984, Maastricht, the Netherlands. Based in Zürich, Switzerland. Established in 2014. **Press and Publications:** *Elephant Magazine*, August 2019; *Frame*, November–December 2017; *The Sausage of the Future* (Lars Müller Publishers, 2017); *Le Monde*, July 2017; *Dezeen*, March 2017. **Clients include:** Design Indaba, ECAL, IKEA, Louis Vuitton, and MIT. **Awards:** Swiss Design Awards, 2019; nominee, Swiss Design Awards, 2018; Grand Prix, Design Parade, Villa Noailles, 2017; Hublot Design Prize, 2017; Silver Hare, Die Besten, Hochparterre, 2017. **Exhibitions:** *Urgent Legacy: Future Proof Plating*, House of Switzerland, Salone del Mobile, Milan, 2023; *Ask Me if I Believe in the Future: Plating up the Future*, Museum für Kunst und Gewerbe, Hamburg, 2022; *FOOD: Bigger than the Plate, The Sausage of the Future*, Victoria and Albert Museum, London, 2019; *Broken Nature: Design Takes on Human Survival, The Sausage of the Future*, Milan Triennale, 2019; *Glass Oriented Design: The Beauty of Water Plants*, CID, Grand Hornu, 2019.
carolienniebling.net @carolienniebling

OBJECTS OF COMMON INTEREST
Eleni Petaloti and Leonidas Trampoukis. Petaloti born 1982, Thessaloniki, Greece; Trampoukis born 1981, Thessaloniki, Greece. Based in New York and Athens. Established in 2016. **Press and Publications:** *Dezeen*, April 2023; *Hypebeast*, April 2023; *STIRworld*, January 2023; *Wallpaper**, January 2023; *Artnet*, December 2022. **Awards:** AD100, 2022; Designers of the Year, *Wallpaper** Design Awards, 2022; Design Prize for Experimentation, Designboom Awards, 2021. **Exhibitions:** *Ask Me If I Believe in the Future*, Museum für Kunst und Gewerbe, Hamburg, 2022; *Why Now?*, Spotti Milano, 2022; *Future Archaeology*, Etage Projects, Copenhagen, 2021; *Hard, Soft, and All Lit Up with Nowhere to Go*, Noguchi Museum, New York, 2021; *Volax*, Carwan Gallery, Athens, 2021.
objectsofcommoninterest.com @objects_of_common_interest

JONATHAN OLIVARES
Born 1981, Boston, USA. Based in Los Angeles, USA. Established in 2006. **Press and Publications:** *Wallpaper**, April 2023; *Global Design News*, November 2022; *Jonathan Olivares: Selected Works* (powerHouse Books, 2018); *Surface*, April 2018. **Clients include:** Blum & Poe, Camper, Hem, Kvadrat, and Vitra. **Award:** Compasso d'Oro (Italy), 2011.
jonathanolivares.com

HUGO PASSOS
Born 1982, Setúbal, Portugal. Based in Copenhagen and Porto, Portugal. Established in 2007. **Press and Publications:** *Dezeen*, June 2023; *Design Milk*, January 2023; *Berlingske*, August, 2022; *Domus* n. 1045, April 2020; *Monocle* no.100, February 2017; *Icon* no.101, December 2011; *i-D* no.307, 2010. *Interior Design*, June 2023; *Design Milk*, January 2023. **Clients include:** Crane Cookware, Fredericia, Monocle, Nikari, and Skagerak/Fritz Hansen.
hugopassos.com @_hugopassos_

PEDRO PAULØ-VENZON
Born 1990, Tijucas, Brazil. Based in Florianópolis, Brazil. Established in 2013. **Press and Publications:** *Sight Unseen*, May 2020; *Dezeen*, December 2018; *The New York Times*, March 2018; *Architectural Digest India*, July 2017. **Clients include:** Cheval Blanc Paris, Kelly Wearstler, MATTER Made, Objekto, Peter Marino, and Viccarbe. **Awards:** selected, *Casa Vogue* Design Award, 2019; longlist, Emerging Designer of the Year, Ultimate *Dezeen* Awards, 2018; selected, Museu da Casa Brasileira, 2018; gold, A' Design Award and Competition, 2017; selected, Officine Panerai Next Generation Designer of the Year, *Wallpaper** Design Awards, 2017.
pedrovenzon.com @pedropaulovenzon

JULIE RICHOZ
Born 1990, Yverdon-les-Bains, Switzerland. Based in Paris. Established in 2015. **Press and Publications:** *Das Ideal Heim*, 2019; *Le Monde*, 2018; *Icon Design*, 2016; *TL Magazine*, 2016; *The Weekender*, 2015. **Clients include:** Alessi, Galerie kreo, HAY, Louis Poulsen, Louis Vuitton, and Tectona. **Awards:** Swiss Design Awards, 2019; Bourse Leenaards, 2016; finalist, Hublot Design Prize, 2016; Swiss Design Awards, 2015; Grand Prix, Design Parade, 2012.
julierichoz.com @julierichoz

DANIEL RYBAKKEN
Born 1984, Oslo. Based in Gothenburg, Sweden. Established in 2008. **Press and Publications:** *Dezeen*, February 2023; *Hypebeast*, February 2023; *Designboom*, March 2021; *Interior Design*, April 2019. **Clients include:** Artek, Givenchy, HAY, Karimoku, Luceplan, and Vitra. **Awards:** Torsten and Wanja Söderberg Prize, 2017; Compasso d'Oro (Italy), 2016 and 2014; selected, Top 20 Designers in the World Under the Age of 40, *Wallpaper** Design Awards, 2015.
danielrybakken.com @danielrybakken

INGA SEMPÉ
Born 1968, Paris. Based in Paris. Established in 2000. **Clients include:** Alessi, HAY, Iittala, Kvadrat, Ligne Roset, Magis, Tectona, and Wästberg. **Award:** Design of the Year, Stockholm Furniture Fair, 2011; Grands Prix de la Création de la Ville de Paris 2002. **Exhibition and events**: *In line with Inga Sempé,* Arabia Design Centre, Helsinki 2022-23; Fellow at the Villa Medici, Rome, 2000–01 for a year's residency for creation; *Tutti Frutti*, Villa Noailles, Design Parade 12, Hyères, France, 2017; *Inga Sempé*, Musée des Arts Décoratifs, Paris, France, 2003.
ingasempe.fr @ingasempe

SOFT BAROQUE
Nicholas Gardner and Saša Štucin. Gardner born 1988, Melbourne, Australia; Štucin born 1984, Kranj, Slovenia. Based in Ljubljana, Slovenia. Established in 2013. **Publications:** "Natural Order & Violent Hobbies" for ZHdK, 2021; "Tag Poems" for MACRO, 2020; "Gallery Infrastructure Catalogue" for Museum für Gestaltung Zürich, 2020; "Liquid Tension" for Superposition, 2020. **Clients include:** Balenciaga, Hem, Kiko Kostadinov, and Marsèll. **Exhibitions:** *Performance Anxiety*, Etage Projects, Copenhagen, 2023; *Inox Detox*, Barbati Gallery, Venice, 2023; *Clear Cut, Cave in*, Room 6×8, Beijing, 2022; *We Walked the Earth* (with Uffe Isolotto), Danish Pavilion, Venice Biennale, 2022; *Sun City*, Marsèll, Milan, 2021; *Total Space*, Museum für Gestaltung, Zürich, 2020; *World of Ulteriors*, Etage Projects, Copenhagen, 2019.
softbaroque.com @softbaroque

SINA SOHRAB
Born 1990, Tehran. Based in Madrid. Established in 2021. **Press and Publications:** *Capsule*, April 2023; *PIN-UP*, November 2022; *Architectural Digest Germany*, June 2021; *Domus*, September 2020; *Elle Decor Spain*, January 2020; *Wallpaper**, February 2019. **Clients include:** Cooper Hewitt Smithsonian Design Museum, Kvadrat, Museo Nacional de Artes Decorativas (Madrid), Normann Copenhagen, and Zucchetti.Kos. **Awards:** Red Dot Design Best of the Best Award, 2021; *Wallpaper** Design Awards, 2019; selected, Young Guns, *Dwell*, 2017; ICFF Editors' Award, 2016. **Exhibitions:** *Exposición de Bienes*, Museo Nacional de Artes Decorativas, Madrid, 2022; *Slanted/Enchanted*, Erin Stump Projects, Toronto, 2022; *Knit!*, Kvadrat, Ebeltoft, 2020;

The Sculptor and the Ashtray, Noguchi Museum, New York, 2020; *The Ashtray Show*, Fisher Parrish Gallery, New York, 2018.
sinasohrab.com @sinasohrab

SOMIAN DESIGN
Jean Servais Somian. Born 1971, Adiake, Côte d'Ivoire. Lives and works in Grand-Bassam and Paris. Established in 2002. Also Founder of the Young Designer Workshop. **Press and Publications:** *France 24*, April 2023; *The New York Times*, March 2023; *CNN*, December 2022; *Forbes Afrique*, August 2022; *Elle Decoration*, June 2022; *TV5 Monde*, April 2021; *Génération Africaine, La force du design* (Langages du Sud, 2019); *Contemporary Design Africa* (Thames & Hudson, 2015). **Awards:** Object Award, Beirut Design Fair, 2019; Design Award, Abidjan Now, Archibat 2013. **Exhibitions and Events:** PAD Paris, 2023; Design Miami/Basel, June 2022; Révélations International Biennial of Crafts and Creation, Paris, June 2022; Unique Design x Miami, June 2021; Floor One 9 Exhibition, Art Twenty-One, Lagos, October 2020; Babitopie, Dakar, December 2019; Africa Africa Exhibition, Palazzo Litta, Milan, October 2018; Dakar Biennal, May 2008.
somiandesign.com @somiandesign

GEORGE SOWDEN
Born 1942, Leeds, UK. Based in Milan, Italy. Established in 1981. **Press and Publications:** *Architectural Digest*, March 2023; *The Guardian*, March 2023. **Clients include:** Alessi, Bodum, Guzzini, Olivetti, and Swatch. **Exhibitions:** *Materialism—Memphis*, Post Design Gallery, Milan Design Week, 2018; *The Heart of the Matter*, Assab One Milano, Milan Design Week, 2017.
georgesowden.com @george_sowden

STEPHEN BURKS MAN MADE
Stephen Burks. Born 1969, Chicago. Based in New York. Established in 2000. **Press and Publications:** *Stephen Burks: Shelter in Place* (Yale University Press, 2022); *Now Make This* (Phaidon, 2018); *Stephen Burks Man Made* (Studio Museum in Harlem, 2011); *The Global Africa Project* (Prestel, 2010); *Boxed and Labelled: New Approaches to Packaging Design* (Gestalten, 2009). **Clients include:** Calvin Klein, Cappellini, Harry Winston, MASS Design Group, Roche Bobois, and Swarovski. **Awards:** Best Outdoor Living, *Wallpaper** Design Awards, 2022; Archiproducts Design Awards, Salvatori, 2021; Gold Delta Award, ADI-FAD, 2020; National Design Award, Smithsonian Cooper Hewitt, 2015; nominee, 100 Most Wanted Designers, *Wallpaper** Design Awards, 2015. **Exhibitions:** *Stephen Burks: Shelter in Place*, High Museum of Art, Atlanta, 2022; *Stephen Burks Man Made Material Compositions*, 1:54 Contemporary African Art Fair, London, 2016; *Stephen Burks Noir*, The Armory Show, New York, 2016; *The Others*, Southern Guild, Cape Town, 2016; *Stephen Burks: Man Made*, Studio Museum, Harlem, 2011.
stephenburksmanmade.com @stephenburksmanmade

STUDIO BRYNJAR & VERONIKA
Brynjar Sigurðarson and Veronika Sedlmair. Sigurðarson born 1985, Reykjavik; Sedlmair born 1985, Immenstadt, Germany. Based in Immenstadt, Germany. Established in 2011. **Press and Publications:** *Macguffin 3: The Rope*, 2017; *Lafayette Anticipations* 2016; *Field Essays: Things that Happened* (Onomatopee, 2015). **Clients include:** CIRVA, Galerie kreo, Ornamenta 24, Swarovski, and Thomas Eyck. **Awards:** Torsten and Wanja Söderberg Prize, 2018; Swarovski Designers of the Future Award, Design Miami/Basel, 2016; Swiss Design Awards, 2015. **Events and Exhibitions:** *Animated Geology*, 44th edition of the Tedenser (Tendencies) exhibition series, Moss, Norway, 2020; *Brynjar Sigurðarson*, Design Museum, Helsinki, 2019; *Reservation*, Hafnarborg, Hafnarfjörður, 2019; *Brynjar Sigurðarson*, Röhsska Museet, 2018; *Silent Village Collection*, Galerie kreo, 2014; *U-JOINTS*, Milan Design Week, 2018; *Joining Forces with the Unknown*, Lafayette Anticipations, 2016.
biano.is @studiobrynjarandveronika

STUDIO JUJU
Priscilla Lui and Timo Wong. Lui born 1983, Singapore; Wong born 1982, Singapore. Based in Singapore. Established in 2009. **Press and Publications:** *Wallpaper**, April 2023; *Financial Times*, September 2022; *The New York Times T Magazine*, September 2018. **Clients include:** Desalto, Foundry, Industry+, Land Transport Authority of Singapore, Living Divani, OCBC Bank, and W Hotels. **Awards:** Design of the Year, Singapore President's Design Awards, 2014; Designers of the Future, Design Miami/Basel, 2011.
studio-juju.com @studio_juju

STUDIO LANI
Lani Adeoye. Born 1989, London. Based in Lagos, Nigeria, and New York. Established in 2017. **Press and Publications:** *Wallpaper**, October 2022; *Architectural Digest*, March 2022; *1000 Design Classics* (Phaidon, 2021); *Designing Design Education* (IF Design Foundation, 2021); *Woman Made: Great Women Designers* (Phaidon, 2021). **Clients include:** Bacchus, Google, Netgear, Philips Auction House, and YouTube. **Awards:** "Designing for Our Future Selves" Award, SaloneSatellite, 2022; silver award, European Product Design Awards, 2018; winner, NYC's Wanted Design's Launch Pad—Furniture, 2017. **Exhibitions:** *Time Space*, Venice, 2023; SaloneSatellite, Milan, 2022; *40 Innovative Women*, Los Angeles Design Festival, 2020; London Craft Week, 2020; *Africa by Design*, Ghana Club, Accra, 2019.
studio-lani.com @studiolani

STUDIO URQUIOLA
Patricia Urquiola and Alberto Zontone. Urquiola born 1961, Oviedo, Spain; Zontone born 1970, Udine, Italy. Based in Milan, Italy. Established in 2001. **Press and Publications:** *Dezeen*, May 2023; *Wallpaper**, April 2023; *Stir*, January 2023; *Designboom*, October 2022; *Surface*, October 2022. **Clients include:** Agape, Alessi, Boffi, Flos, Georg Jensen, and Kvadrat. **Awards include:** IIDA Titan Award, 2015; German Design Award, 2011; Medalla de Oro al Mérito en las Bellas Artes, 2011; the Order of Isabella the Catholic awarded by His Majesty the King of Spain King Juan Carlos I, 2011; EDIDA Designer of the Year, 2005. **Exhibitions:** *Patricia Urquiola: Nature Morte Vivante*, Madrid Design Festival, 2020; *Patricia Urquiola: Between Craft and Industry*, Philadelphia Museum of Art, 2017.
patriciaurquiola.com @patricia_urquiola

TAF STUDIO
Gabriella Lenke and Mattias Ståhlbom. Lenke born 1974, Gällivare, Sweden; Ståhlbom born 1971, Norrköping, Sweden. Based in Stockholm. Established in 2002. **Press and Publications:** *Design Milk*, April 2023; *The Times*, February 2023; *House Beautiful*, December 2021; *Dezeen*, May 2016. **Clients include:** Artek, Fogia, Gärsnäs, Muuto, and Vandalorum. **Award:** Bruno Mathsson Award, 2017.
tafstudio.se @studiotaf

NAO TAMURA
Born 1976, Tokyo. Based in New York. Established in 2009. **Press and Publications:** *Room*, December 2022; *Domus*, February 2021; *Frame*, November–December 2020; *Dezeen*, August 2020; *Axis*, December 2015. **Clients include:** Artek, Iittala, Issey Miyake, Lexus, Nike, and Panasonic. **Awards:** IF Design Award, 2013; Red Dot Design Award, 2013; gold, Industrial Design Excellence Awards, 2002; first prize, SaloneSatellite Award, 2010.
naotamura.com @nownao

JOMO TARIKU
Born 1968, Nairobi. Based in Springfield, Virginia. Established in 2017. **Press and Publications:** *Fine Woodworking*, May/June 2023; *The New York Times*, March 2023; *House Beautiful*, February 2023; *Elle Decor France*, June 2022; *Disegno*, April 2021. **Clients include:** Marvel Studios, Megalopolis, MoMA Design Store, and Sheila Bridges Design, Inc. – One Observatory Circle (Vice President's Residence). **Awards:** Bikila Award, 2023; BADG Makers Award, 2022. **Exhibitions and Events:** Clark Art Institute, Williamstown, 2023; CADA Panel Discussion, Miami, 2022; DesignMiami, Wexler Gallery, Philadelphia, 2022; *What Is New What Is Next*, New York, 2022; *Before Yesterday We Could Fly: An Afro-Futurist Period Room*, Metropolitan Museum of Art, New York, 2021.
jomofurniture.com @jomotariku

TEENAGE ENGINEERING
David Eriksson, Jesper Kouthoofd, David Möllerstedt, and Jens Rudberg. Eriksson born 1978, Norrland, Piteå, Sweden; Kouthoofd born 1970, Göteborg, Sweden; Möllerstedt born 1974, Göteborg, Sweden; Rudberg born 1973, Rone, Gotland, Sweden. Based in Stockholm. Established in 2007. **Press and Publications:** *MusicRadar*, July 2023; *Design Milk*, June 2023; *Domus*, May 2023; *Wired*, May 2023; *MusicTech*, March 2023. **Award:** Good Design Award, Japan Institute of Design Promotion, 2017.
teenage.engineering @teenageengineering

THE AGENCY OF DESIGN
Rich Gilbert, Adam Paterson, and Matthew Emery-Laws. Gilbert born 1983, Reading, England; Paterson born 1988, Edinburgh, Scotland; Emery-Laws born 1985, Oxford, England. Based in London. Established in 2011. **Clients include:** UK Department of Energy and Climate Change, Design Museum, London, eBay, HP, Lenovo, and Samsung.
agencyofdesign.co.uk @agencyofdesign

TOOGOOD
Faye Toogood. Born 1977, Rutland, UK. Based in London. Established in 2008. **Press and Publications:** *ICON Eye Magazine*, April 2023; *M Le Monde*, April 2023; *World of Interiors*, April 2023; *WSJ. Magazine*, April 2023; *Faye Toogood: Drawing, Material, Sculpture, Landscape* (Phaidon, 2022). **Clients include:** Carhartt WIP, Dover Street Market, Hermès, Mulberry, and Selfridges. **Exhibitions:** *Mirror Mirror: Reflections on Design*, Chatsworth House, Derbyshire, 2023; *Assemblage 7*, Friedman Benda, Los Angeles, 2022; *Clay Court* for Qatar Museums, National Theatre, Qatar, 2022; *Downtime*, NGV Triennial, Melbourne, 2020–1.
t-o-o-g-o-o-d.com @t_o_o_g_o_o_d

TRIBUTO
Laura and Gabriela Noriega. Laura born 1980, Guadalajara, Mexico; Gabriela born 1981, Guadalajara, México. Based in Jalisco, Mexico. Established in 2013. **Press and Publications:** *Designboom* 2022; *AD100 Architectural Digest México,* 2021; *Guadalajara Inspiration City WGSN* 2021; *Interni Magazine* 2017; *Elle Decoration México* 2015.
tributo.mx @tributomx

MARIO TSAI
Born 1988, Qianjiang, China. Based in Hangzhou, China. Established in 2014. **Press and Publications:** *Dezeen*, November 2022; *Wallpaper**, October 2022; *Financial Times*, May 2019. **Clients include:** The Beast, Ferm Living, Shangxia, Woud, and Zaozuo. **Awards:** shortlist, Designer of the Year, *Wallpaper** Design Awards, 2022; Best Lighting, EDIDA China, 2020; Emerging Designer, IDEAT Future Award, 2020; Rising Talent, Paris Maison&Objet, 2019; Young Design Talent, EDIDA China, 2019. **Exhibitions:** *Designew*, Shengzhen Creative Week, 2021; *Unfinished*, Hangzhou, 2021; *Poetic Light*, SH x Ontimeshow, 2020; *Sustainable Reaction*, Mario Tsai Studio x Design Shanghai, 2020; *From the Structures*, Milan Design Week, 2019.
mariotsai.studio @mariotsai.studio

MPHO VACKIER
Born 1982, Johannesburg, South Africa. Based in Kempton Park, South Africa. Established in 2017. **Press and Publications:** *Design Milk*, September 2022; *Visi*, July 2022; *Woman Made: Great Women Designers* (Phaidon, 2021); *Financial Times*, July 2019. **Clients include:** Investec, Nando's, Nike Shapa Soweto, South African National Parks, and WeWork. **Awards:** Industry Stewardship Award, 2022; Designer of the Year, 100% SA Design Awards, 2019; nominee, Most Beautiful Object in South Africa, Design Indaba, 2019; winner, South African Department of Trade and Industry Design Competition, 2018.
theurbanative.com @theurbanative

WE+
Toshiya Hayashi and Hokuto Ando. Hayashi born 1980, Toyama, Japan; Ando born 1982, Yamagata, Japan. Based in Tokyo. Established in 2013. **Press and Publications:** *DAMN*, Summer 2023; *AXIS*, September 2022; *Frame*, April 2022; *Room*, April 2021; *ICON DESIGN*, December 2019; *Dezeen*, May 2017. *Financial Times*, November 2018. **Clients include:** Hermès, Issey Miyake, Panasonic, Shiseido, and Sony. **Awards:** shortlist, *Dezeen* Awards, 2022; Emerging Design Studio of the Year Public Vote, *Dezeen* Awards, 2022.
weplus.jp @weplus.jp

ZAVIER WONG
Born 1993, Singapore. Based in Eindhoven, the Netherlands. Established in 2021. **Press and Publications:** *DAMN*, Winter 2023; *Financial Times*, January 2023; *Crafts Magazine*, Fall/Winter 2022; *Financial Times*, September 2022; *Design Anthology Asia Edition*, Issue 20, 2019. **Exhibitions:** *New Year Group Exhibition*, Priveekollektie, Heusden, 2023; *Made in Eindhoven*, Yksi Expo, Eindhoven, 2022; *New Year Group Exhibition*, Priveekollektie, Heusden, 2022; *No Space for Waste*, Isola Design District, Milan, 2022; *PAD London 2022*, Priveekollektie Gallery, London, 2022.
zavierwong.net @zavierwong_

BETHAN LAURA WOOD
Born 1983, Stockport, Manchester, UK. Based in London. Established in 2011. **Press and Publications:** *Vogue Hong Kong*, June 2023; *The Clamor of Ornament: Exchange, Power, and Joy from the Fifteenth Century to the Present* (Drawing Center, 2022); *What Is Design? 100 Definitions* (Hurtwood Books, 2022); *More Is More: Memphis, Maximalism and New Wave Design* (teNeues Publishing, 2019); *Women Design: Pioneers from the Twentieth Century to Today* (Frances Lincoln, 2018). **Clients include:** Dior, Design Miami, Hermès, Peter Pilotto, and Poltronova. **Awards:** Design Awards Best Afternoon Tea, *Wallpaper** Design Awards, 2021; Outstanding Product, German Design Awards, 2021; winner, Tableware, EDIDA Design Awards, 2021; winner, Floor Covering, EDIDA, 2019; winner, Floor Covering, EDBDA, 2019. **Exhibitions:** *Conversation Pieces*, Museum of Modern Art, San Francisco, 2022; *Miss Dior Exhibition: 12 Women Artists*, Château de La Colle Noire, Montauroux, 2021; *Ornate*, Nilufar Gallery, Milan, 2021; *Bags: Inside Out*, Victoria and Albert Museum, London, 2020.
bethanlaurawood.com @bethanlaurawood

ZANELLATO/BORTOTTO
Giorgia Zanellato and Daniele Bortotto. Zanellato born 1987, Venice, Italy; Bortotto born 1988, Pordenone, Italy. Based in Treviso, Italy. Established in 2013. **Press and Publications:** *Architectural Digest France*, July 2023; *Cultured Magazine*, July 2023; *Sight Unseen*, June 2023; *Domus*, May 2023; *Elle Decor Italy*, May 2023. **Clients include:** cc-tapis, Ethimo, Galleria Luisa delle Piane, Louis Vuitton, Moroso, and Rubelli. **Awards:** Good Design Award, 2018; NYCxDESIGN Prize, *Interior Design*, 2016; Red Dot Design Award, 2016; nominee, Young Talent of the Year, *Elle Decor Italy*, 2015.
zanellatobortotto.com @zanellatobortotto

ZAVEN
Enrica Cavarzan and Marco Zavagno. Cavarzan born 1977, Castelfranco Veneto, Italy; Zavagno born 1977, Trieste, Italy. Based in Venice, Italy. Established in 2008. **Press and Publications:** *Financial Times*, June 2022. **Clients include:** Knoll, Kvadrat, Mercedes, Palazzo Grassi—Pinault Collection, and Verso. **Awards:** *AD100 Italy*, 2023; Archiproduct Design Award, 2022; Best of Year Design Award, 2022; Red Dot Design Award, 2021; IF Design Award, 2019. **Exhibitions:** *No Flags*, Verso, New York, 2023; *Ask Me If I Believe in the Future*, Museum für Kunst und Gewerbe, Hamburg, 2022; *U-Joints, Knots & Knits*, Fiskars Village Art & Design Biennale, 2022; *Past Forward*, Museo Archeologico, Venice, 2021; *U-Joints, Adhesives and Fusion*, Winterthur Trade Museum, 2021.
zaven.net @_zaven_

Index

Page numbers in *italics* refer to illustrations

Picture credits

T = top C = center B = bottom

AAKS: 6M.Productions, Courtesy of AAKS 14T, 15, Cara Johnson Photography, Courtesy of AAKS 14B; **Lindsey Adelman:** Black & Steil, Courtesy of Lindsey Adelman Studio 16T, Lauren Coleman, Courtesy of Lindsey Adelman Studio 16B, © Aaron Leitz 17T, © Stephan Julliard / Tripod Agency 17B, Matteo Imbriani, Courtesy of Lindsey Adelman Studio 18–19; **Agnes Studio:** Victor Martinez, Courtesy of Agnes Studio 20, 21, 22T, 22B, 23; **Michael Anastassiades:** Courtesy of Michael Anastassiades 24T, 24B, 27, Michele Branca Piero Fasanotto, Courtesy of Michael Anastassiades 25, Jeppe Sørensen, Courtesy of Michael Anastassiades 26L, Claudia Zalla, Courtesy of Michael Anastassiades 26R; **Omer Arbel:** Fahim Kassam, Courtesy of Omer Arbel 28T, Kate Williams, Courtesy of Omer Arbel 28B, 29; **Ini Archibong:** © Joël von Allmen, Courtesy of L.M.N.O. Creative 30T, Andreas Zimmermann Fotografie, Courtesy of L.M.N.O. Creative 30B, 31; **Atlason Studio:** Billie, Courtesy of Atlason 32T, Hlynur Atlason, Courtesy of Atlason 32B, 33T, 33B, 34–35; **Barber Osgerby:** © Eva Herzog, Courtesy of Barber Osgerby 36T, © David Brook, Courtesy of Barber Osgerby 36B, Courtesy of Barber Osgerby 37T, 37B; **BIG-GAME:** Younès Klouche, Courtesy of BIG-GAME 38T, Courtesy of BIG-GAME 39TL, Arnaud Childéric / Kalice.fr, Courtesy of BIG-GAME 39TR, Masaaki Inoue, Courtesy of BIG-GAME / Model: Joel Shohei 39B; **Agustina Bottoni:** Roberto Nino Betancourt, Courtesy of Agustina Bottoni Studio 40T, 41T, 41B, Vincent Thibert, Courtesy of Agustina Bottoni Studio 40B; **Bouchra Boudoua:** Courtesy of Bouchra Boudoua 42, 43T, 43B; **Ronan & Erwan Bouroullec:** © Claire Lavabre / Studio Bouroullec 44T, 45TL, © Studio Bouroullec 44B, 45TR, 45B; **Rodrigo Bravo:** Carlos Molina, Courtesy of Bravo 46T, 47T, 47 BL, Andrés Maturana, Courtesy of Bravo 46B, Felix Niikado, Courtesy of Bravo 47BR; **Thilo Alex Brunner:** © Ingmar Swalue, Courtesy of On AG 48T, 48B, 51T, 51B, © Detlef Schneider, Courtesy of On AG 49, © On 50; **Fabien Cappello:** Rodrigo Alvarez, Courtesy of Studio Fabien Cappello 52T, Erik Wåhlström, Courtesy of Studio Fabien Cappello 52B, Jasper Morrison Shop, Courtesy of Studio Fabien Cappello 53TL, Mariana Achach, Courtesy of Studio Fabien Cappello 53TR, Rodrigo Alvarez 53B; **Alvaro Catalán de Ocón:** © Alfonso Herranz+Alicia, Courtesy of ACdO 54T, © Anette Aulestia, Courtesy of ACdO 54B, © ACdO 55, 56T, © Amir Shams, Courtesy of ACdO 56B, © GAN, Courtesy of ACdO 57; **Marisol Centeno:** Estudio Marisol Centeno 58 Mariana Achach, Courtesy of Estudio Marisol Centeno 59L, Bi Yuu, Courtesy of Estudio Marisol Centeno 59R, Mauricio Alejo, Courtesy of Estudio Marisol Centeno 60–61; **Michel Charlot:** Courtesy of Michel Charlot 62T, 62B, 63T, 63B; **Pierre Charpin:** © Pierre Antoine, Courtesy of Atelier Pierre Charpin 64T, 65BR, © Ligne Roset, Courtesy of Atelier Pierre Charpin 64B, © Alexandra de Cossette, Courtesy of Atelier Pierre Charpin 65T, © Maxime Tetard – Les Graphiquants, Courtesy of Atelier Pierre Charpin 65BL, © HAY, Courtesy of Atelier Pierre Charpin 66–67; **Frank Chou:** © FRANK CHOU COLLECTION 68, 69TL, 69TR, 69B; **Paul Cocksedge:** © Paul Cocksedge 70T, 70B, 71T, 71B, © Adrien Dirand 72–73; **Mac Collins:** Jussi Puikkonen, Courtesy of Mac Collins 74T, David Cleveland, Courtesy of Mac Collins 74B, 75T, Jason Yates, Courtesy of Mac Collins 75B; **Stefan Diez:** Daniela Trost, Courtesy of Diez Office 76, 78T, 78BL, 78BR, © Fabian Frinzel, Courtesy of Diez Office 77T, © Gerhardt Kellermann, Courtesy of Diez Office 77BL, © Midgard, Courtesy of Diez Office 77BR, © Vibia, Courtesy of Diez Office 79; **Frida Fjellman:** Svenskt Tenn, Courtesy of Frida Fjellman 80T, Alain Potignon, Courtesy of Frida Fjellman & Hostler Burrows 80B, Patrick Miller, Courtesy of Frida Fjellman 81; **FormaFantasma:** © George Darrell, Courtesy of Formafantasma 82T, © Ikon, Courtesy of Formafantasma 82B, 83, © Gregorio Gonella, Courtesy of Formafantasma 84–85; **Front:** Courtesy of Front Design & Moooi 86T, © Alexandra de Cossette, Courtesy of Front Design & Galerie kreo 86B, 88T, 88B, 89B, Alessandro Paderni, Courtesy of Front Design & Moroso 87T, 87B, 89T; **Naota Fukasawa:** Courtesy of HAY 90T, Courtesy of Molteni&C 90B, Wen Studio, Courtesy of B&B Italia 91; **GamFratesi:** Poltrona Frau, Courtesy of GamFratesi 92T, Petra Kleis, Courtesy of GamFratesi 92B, Hiroshi Iwasaki, Courtesy of GamFratesi 93T, GUBI, Courtesy of GamFratesi 93B, Irina Boesma, Courtesy of GamFratesi 94, Tuala Hjarnø, Courtesy of GamFratesi 95; **Martino Gamper:** © Mattia Lotti, Courtesy of Martino Gamper Studio 96T, © Izzy Leung, Courtesy of Martino Gamper Studio 96B, © Paolo Riolzi, Courtesy of Martino Gamper Studio 97, © Angus Mill, Courtesy of Martino Gamper Studio 98–99; **Konstantin Grcic:** Santi Caleca, Courtesy of Konstantin Grcic Design 100T, Florian Böhm, Courtesy of Konstantin Grcic Design 100B, Federico Cedrone, Courtesy of Konstantin Grcic Design 101; **GT2P:** Felix Speller, Courtesy of Friedman Benda 102, Kris Tamburello, Courtesy of Anava Projects 103, gt2P, courtesy Friedman Benda 104, 105TL, 105TR, 105B; **Gunjan Gupta:** Ikkis 106T, 106B, Studio Wrap 107TL, 107TR, Courtesy of Studio Wrap 107B; **Jaime Hayon:** © Klunderbie, Courtesy of Hayonstudio 108, 109T, BD Barcelona, Courtesy of Hayonstudio 109B, Ceccotti Collezione. Courtesy of Hayonstudio 110–11; **Moisés Hernández:** Courtesy of Moisés Hernández 112T, 113, Santiago Vega, Courtesy of Moisés Hernández 112B; **Marlène Huissoud:** Studio Marlène Huissoud 114T, 114C, Valentin Russo, Courtesy of Studio Marlène Huissoud 114B, SFER IK Museion, Courtesy of Studio Marlène Huissoud 115; **Yinka Ilori:** © Andy Stagg 116, © Veerle Evens 117, © Mark Cocksedge 118–19; **Industrial Facility:** Industrial Facility 120, 121T, 121 BL, Gerhardt Kellermann, Courtesy of Industrial Facility 121BR, Kristalia SpA, Courtesy of Industrial Facility 122–23; **ISPA (Nike):** Courtesy of Nike 124T, 125TL, 125TR, 125B, 126, © Kyoko Nishimoto / BUAISOU 124B, © Nicholas V. Ruiz 127; **Maria Jeglińska-Adamczewska:** Courtesy of Maria Jeglińska-Adamczewska Office for Design and Research 128, © David Cleveland, Courtesy of Maria Jeglińska-Adamczewska Office for Design and Research 129T, © Robert Świerczyński, Courtesy of Maria Jeglińska-Adamczewska Office for Design and Research 129B; **Hella Jongerius:** © Laura Fiorio, Courtesy of Hella Jongerius / Jongeriuslab 130T, © Luke Hayes, Courtesy of Hella Jongerius / Jongeriuslab 130B, © Vitra, Courtesy of Hella Jongerius / Jongeriuslab 131T, 131B; **Misha Kahn:** Julian Calero, Courtesy of Friedman Benda and Misha Kahn 132T, 133B, Timothy Doyon, Courtesy of Friedman Benda and Misha Kahn 132B, 133TL, Daniel Kukla, Courtesy of Friedman Benda and Misha Kahn 133TR, 134–35; **Charlotte Kidger:** Charlotte Kidger 136T, 136B, 137; **Minjae Kim:** Clément Pascal, Courtesy of Minjae Kim 138T, Sean Davidson, Courtesy of Minjae Kim 138B, 139; **Kitt.Ta.Khon:** Sirisak Chantorn, Courtesy of Kitt.Ta.Khon 140T, 140B, 141T, 141B; **Joris Laarman:** Leonard Fäustle, Courtesy of Joris Laarman Studio 142T, 142B, 144, Friedman Benda Gallery, Courtesy of Joris Laarman Studio 143, Chatsworth Estate, Courtesy of Joris Laarman Studio 145; **Max Lamb:** Dimitri Bähler, Courtesy of Max Lamb 146T, 147TL, Courtesy of Max Lamb 146B, 147TR, Angus Mill, Courtesy of Max Lamb 147B; **Fernando Laposse:** Luis Gomez, Courtesy of Fernando Laposse 148T, Courtesy of Fernando Laposse 148B, 149T, 149BL, 149BR; **LAUN:** Ye Rin Mok, Courtesy of LAUN 150T, 150B, 151, 152, Little League Studio, Courtesy of LAUN 153; **Kwangho Lee:** Salon 94 Design, New York, Courtesy of Kwangho Lee 154, 155T, 155B; **Shahar Livne:** Alan Boom, © Shahar Livne Design 156, 157, © Shahar Livne Design Studio 157TR, Barbara Medo, Courtesy of Shahar Livne Design 157B; **Mabeo:** Robin Hill, Courtesy of Mabeo Studio 158T, 158–59, 159T; **India Mahdavi:** Courtesy of India Mahdavi Studio / IMH 160, 161TL, 161TR, 161B; **Philippe Malouin:** © Jonas Marguet 162T, Courtesy of Flos 162B, Courtesy of The Breeder 163, Toaki Okano Photography, Courtesy of Resident 164–65; **Cecilie Manz:** Yoneo Kawabe / Maruni 166T, Jeppe Sørensen / Cecilie Manz Studio 166B, Bang & Olufsen 167TL, Jeppe Sørensen / Bang&Olufsen 167TR, Cecilie Manz Studio 167B; **Sabine Marcelis:** Mathijs Labadie, Courtesy of Studio Sabine Marcelis 168T, Pim Top, Courtesy of Studio Sabine Marcelis 168B, 170T, 171, Rami Mansour, Courtesy of Studio Sabine Marcelis 169, Ed Reeve, Courtesy of Studio Sabine Marcelis 170B; **Nifemi Marcus-Bello:** Guy Ferguson, Courtesy of nmbello Studio 172, Ọlájídé Ayẹni, Courtesy of nmbello Studio 173T, 173B; **Marz Designs:** Aaron Chapman, Courtesy of Marz Designs 174T, Lawrence Furzey, Courtesy of Marz Designs 174B, 175; **Mash.T Design Studio:** Sarah de Pina, Courtesy of Mash.T Design Studio 176T, 176C, 176B, 177; **Materra-Matang:** Arthur Crestani, Courtesy of Materra-Matang 178, 179T, 179B; **Casey McCafferty:** Joseph Kramm, Courtesy of Casey McCafferty 180T, 180B, 181; **Christien Meindertsma:** Mathijs Labadie, Courtesy of Christien Meindertsma 182T, 182B, 183, 184, 185; **Miminat Designs:** Courtesy of Miminat Designs 186T, 187T, 187B, Edvinas Bruzas, Courtesy of Miminat Designs 186B; **mischer'traxler studio:** Faruk Pinjo, Courtesy of mischer'traxler studio 188T, Leonard Hilzensauer, Courtesy of mischer'traxler studio 188B, Francesco Allegretto, Courtesy of mischer'traxler studio 189T, Jara Varela for PCM Design, Courtesy of mischer'traxler studio 189B, Jure Horvat, Courtesy of mischer'traxler studio 190–91; **Nicole Monks:** Bseated, Courtesy of Nicole Monks 192T, Boaz Nothman / Australia Design Centre, Courtesy of Nicole Monks 192B, 139B, Fourth Street Studio, Courtesy of Nicole Monks 193T; **Jasper Morrison:** Jasper Morrison Studio 194, Marc Eggimann, Courtesy of Jasper Morrison 195T, Hay, Courtesy of Jasper Morrison 195BL, Miro Zagnoli, Courtesy of Jasper Morrison 195BR; **Jonathan Muecke:** Courtesy of Jonathan Muecke 196, 197T, 197B, Jeroen Verrecht, Courtesy of Jonathan Muecke 198–99; **Muller Van Severen:** Frederik Vercruysse, Courtesy of Muller Van Severen 200, Fien Muller, Courtesy of Muller Van Severen 201T, 202T, 202B, 203T, 203B, © Reform, Courtesy of Muller Van Severen 201B; **nendo:** Akihiro Yoshida, Courtesy of nendo 204T, 205T, Masahiro Ohgami, Courtesy of nendo 204B, Hiroshi Iwasaki, Courtesy of nendo 205B, 206–207; **Erez Nevi Pana:** Dor Kedmi, Courtesy of Erez Nevi Pana 208T, Daniel Kukla, Courtesy of Erez Nevi Pana 208B, Klau Rothkegel, Courtesy of Erez Nevi Pana 209T, 209B; **Carolien Niebling:** Jonas Marguet, Courtesy of Carolien Niebling 210T, 210B, Carolien Niebling 211TL, 211TR, 211BL, 211BR; **Objects of Common Interest:** Piercarlo Quecchia / DSL Studio, Courtesy of Objects of Common Interest 212T, 212B, © Alejandro Ramirez Orozco, Courtesy of cc-tapis 213T, Marco Arguello, Courtesy of Objects of Common Interest 213B; **Jonathan Olivares:** Daniele Ansidei, Courtesy of Jonathan Olivares 214T, 214B, 215B, Casper Sejersen, Courtesy of Jonathan Olivares 215T; **Hugo Passos:** Hugo Passos & Julien Renault, Courtesy of Hugo Passos 216T, 216B, Fredericia Furniture, Courtesy of Hugo Passos 217, Skagerak, Courtesy of Hugo Passos 218–19; **Pedro Paulø-Venzon:** Pedro Paulø-Venzon Studio / pedrovenzon.com 220T, 220B, 221T, 2251; **Julie Richoz:** Florian Böhm, Courtesy of Julie Richoz 222T, © Alexandra de Cossette, Courtesy of Julie Richoz 222B, Fernando Etulain, Courtesy of Julie Richoz 223TL, Francis Amiand, Courtesy of Julie Richoz 223TR, © Luke Evans, Courtesy of Julie Richoz 223B; **Daniel Rybakken:** Daniel Rybakken 224, 225BL, 225BR, Kalle Sanner & Daniel Rybakken 225T; **Inga Sempé:** © Inga Sempé 226T, 227L, 227R, © Iittala, Courtesy of Inga Sempé 226B; **Soft Baroque:** Soft Baroque 228T, 229T, 229C, 229B, 230L, 230R, 231, Daniel Kukla, Courtesy of Friedman Benda and Soft Baroque 228B, Corporate Marble 234L; **Sina Sohrab:** Delfino Sisto Legnani / DSL Studio, Courtesy of Sina Sohrab 232, Sean Davidson, Courtesy of Sina Sohrab 233TL, 233TR, Lana Ohrimenko, Courtesy of Sina Sohrab 233B; **Somian Design:** Gaël Gellé, Courtesy of Jean Servais Somian 234, 235T, 235B; **George Sowden:** Alice Fiorilli, Courtesy of SOWDEN 236T, 237, Delfino Sisto Legnani / DSL Studio, Courtesy of SOWDEN 236B; **Stephen**

Burks Man Made: Caroline Tompkins, Courtesy of Stephen Burks Man Made 238T, 238B, 239, 240–41; **Studio Brynjar & Veronika:** Brynjar Sigurðarson, Courtesy of Studio Brynjar & Veronika 242T, 242B, 245C, 245B, Emile Barret, Courtesy of Studio Brynjar & Veronika 243, Fabrice Gousset, Courtesy of Studio Brynjar & Veronika 244, 245T; **Studio Juju:** Studio Juju 246, 247T, 247BL, 247BR, 248–49; **Studio Lani:** Emmanuel Oyeleke, Courtesy of Studio-Lani 250T, 250B, 251T, 251B; **TAF Studio:** Karin Björkquist, Courtesy of TAF Studio 252T, Gärsnäs, Courtesy of TAF Studio 252B, Artek, Courtesy of TAF Studio 253T, Henrik Lundell 253B; **Nao Tamura:** littala, Courtesy of Nao Tamura 254T, Seiko, Courtesy of Nao Tamura 254B, Hiroshi Iwasaki, Courtesy of Nao Tamura 255TL, Daniel Kai Hirao, Courtesy of Nao Tamura 255TR, Koroda Takeru, Courtesy of Nao Tamura 255B; **Jomo Tariku:** Jomo Tariku 256T, 256B, 257; **teenage engineering:** Courtesy of teenage engineering 258T, 258B, 259T, 259B; **The Agency of Design:** The Agency of Design 260T, 260B, 261T, 261B; **Toogood:** © Heiko Prigge 262T, Angus Mill, Courtesy of Toogood 262B, 263B, Matthew Donaldson, Courtesy of Toogood 263T; **Tributo:** Santiago Vega, Courtesy of Tributo 264T, 264B, 265TL, 265TR, Pablo Fernandez del Valle, Courtesy of Tributo 265B; **Mario Tsai:** Mario Tsai, Courtesy of Mario Tsai Studio 266T, 266B, 269B, Mario Tsai Studio 267T, 267B, Chen Hua, Courtesy of Mario Tsai Studio 268T, Xu Xiaodong, Courtesy of Mario Tsai Studio 268B, 269T; **Studio Urquiola:** Alejandro Ramirez Orozco, Courtesy of Studio Urquiola 270, Leonardo Duggento, Courtesy of Studio Urquiola 271TL, 271TR, Francesco Dolfo, Courtesy of Studio Urquiola 271B; **Mpho Vackier:** Aart Verrips-South Africa, Courtesy of TheUrbanative 272–73; **we+:** Masayuki Hayashi, Courtesy of we+ inc. 274T, 274B, 275T, 275B; **Zavier Wong:** Courtesy of Zavier Wong 276T, 276B, 277T, 277B; **Bethan Laura Wood:** Emanuele Tortora, Courtesy of Bethan Laura Wood 278T, 280L, 280R, Valextra, Courtesy of Bethan Laura Wood 278B, Perrier-Jouët, Courtesy of Bethan Laura Wood 279, cc-tapis, Courtesy of Bethan Laura Wood 281; **Zanellato/Bortotto:** Philippe Lacombe, Courtesy of Zanellato/Bortotto Studio 282, Massimo Gardone, Courtesy of Zanellato/Bortotto Studio 283TL, Alessandro Paderni, Courtesy of Zanellato/Bortotto Studio 283TR, AlbertoParise, Courtesy of Zanellato/Bortotto Studio 283B; **Zaven:** Zaven 284, © Fran Parente, Courtesy of Zaven 285TL, 286T, Omar Sartor, Courtesy of Zaven 285B, Zanotta, Courtesy of Zaven 286B, © Luke Evans, Courtesy of Zaven 287.

Writers

DANIELLE DEMETRIOU
Danielle Demetriou is a British writer and editor based in Japan since 2007. She writes about design, architecture, art, and culture for magazines and newspapers, including *Wallpaper**, *Architectural Review*, *Design Anthology*, and the *Daily Telegraph*. Previous Phaidon book projects include contributions to *Japanese Interiors* (2022) and Peter Marino's *The Architecture of Chanel* (2021). She lives in Kyoto.

VERA KEAN
Vera Kean lives in New York, where she writes about art and design.

KELSEY KEITH
Kelsey Keith is the brand creative director at Herman Miller, a contributor at *Elle Decor*, and the former editor-in-chief of *Curbed* and deputy editor at *Dwell*.

SHONQUIS MORENO
A journalist and former editor of *Frame*, *Surface*, and *Dwell* magazines, Shonquis Moreno writes about architecture, interiors, design, and travel. Having lived in New York, Paris, and Istanbul, she is currently based in the San Francisco Bay Area.

REBECCA ROKE
Rebecca Roke is a writer, editor, and educator, with more than two decades' experience writing about architecture and design for clients and publishers worldwide. Her first Phaidon book, *Nanotecture* (2016), won acclaim, and was followed by *Mobitecture* (2017). She has also written books for Thames & Hudson, Prestel, and Laurence King, alongside private writing commissions. Rebecca is completing her doctorate at RMIT University with a focus on new forms of collective housing; she also teaches architectural design, history, and theory.

MARCO SAMMICHELI
Curator of the design, fashion, and crafts sector at the Milan Triennale and Superintendent of Museo del Design Italiano, Marco Sammicheli has curated exhibitions in Italy, Switzerland, and Denmark and contributed to catalogs for cultural institutions and private galleries in Europe and the Middle East. A former columnist for *Wallpaper** and *Il Sole 24 Ore*, he has contributed to various international magazines.

Danielle Demetriou: Omer Arbel 28, Rodrigo Bravo 46, Fabien Cappello 52, Marisol Centeno 58, Pierre Charpin 64, Stefan Diez 76, Naoto Fukasawa 90, Konstantin Grcic 100, gt2P 102, Moisés Hernández 112, Marlène Huissoud 114, Mash.T Design Studio 176, Muller Van Severen 200, Nendo 204, Objects of Common Interest 212, Pedro Paulø-Venzon 220, Studio Brynjar & Veronika 242, Tributo 266, Mpho Vackier 272, we+ 274. **Vera Kean:** AAKS 14, Agnes Studio 20, Ini Archibong 30, BIG-GAME 38, Agustina Bottoni 40, Bouchra Boudoua 42, Thilo Alex Brunner 48, Frank Chou 68, Mac Collins 74, Frida Fjellman 80, Front 86, Martino Gamper 96, Gunjan Gupta 106, Max Lamb 146, Kwangho Lee 154, Nifemi Marcus-Bello 172, Miminat Designs 186, Jasper Morrison 194, Erez Nevi Pana 208, Carolien Niebling 210, Soft Baroque 228, Somian Design 234, George Sowden 236, Studio Lani 250, TAF Studio 254, teenage engineering 260, The Agency of Design 262, Toogood 264, Mario Tsai 268, Zanellato/Bortotto 282. **Kelsey Keith:** Introduction 8–11; **Shonquis Moreno:** Lindsey Adelman 16, Atlason Studio 32, Yinka Ilori 116, ISPA (Nike) 124, Misha Kahn 132, Joris Laarman 142, LAUN 150, Shahar Livne 156, Cecilie Manz 166, Sabine Marcelis 168, Casey McCafferty 180, Christien Meindertsma 182, Jonathan Muecke 196, Jonathan Olivares 214, Daniel Rybakken 224, Stephen Burks Man Made 238, Studio Juju 246, Nao Tamura 256, Jomo Tariku 258, Zavier Wong 276. **Rebecca Roke:** Michael Anastassiades 24, Barber Osgerby 36, Ronan & Erwan Bouroullec 44, Alvaro Catalán de Ocón 54, Paul Cocksedge 70, Formafantasma 82, Jaime Hayon 108, Industrial Facility 120, Hella Jongerius 130, Charlotte Kidger 136, Minjae Kim 138, Kitt.Ta.Khon 140, Fernando Laposse 148, Mabeo 158, India Mahdavi 160, Marz Designs 174, Materra-Matang 178, Nicole Monks 192, Julie Richoz 222, Inga Sempé 226, Sina Sohrab 232, Studio Urquiola 252, Bethan Laura Wood 278. **Marco Sammicheli:** Michel Charlot 62, GamFratesi 92, Maria Jeglińska-Adamczewska 128, Philippe Malouin 162, mischer'traxler studio 188, Hugo Passos 216, Zaven 284.

Phaidon Press Limited
2 Cooperage Yard
London E15 2QR

Phaidon Press Inc.
111 Broadway
New York, NY 10006

phaidon.com

First published 2024

ISBN 978 1 83866 769 6

A CIP catalogue record for this book is available from the British Library and the Library of Congress.

Commissioning Editor: Emilia Terragni
Project Editor: Sophie Hodgkin
Production Controller: Lily Rodgers
Design: Apartamento Studios

The Publisher would like to thank all the nominators, designers, and writers for their invaluable contributions—we are indebted to you for your expertise and creativity. In addition, we would like to thank Jane Birch, Emma Caddy, Philippe Dionne Bussières, Rosanna Fairhead, Angelika Pirkl, and Phoebe Stephenson for their contributions to the book.

Printed in China

LINDSEY ADELMAN
MICHEL CHARLOT
FRANK CHOU
PIERRE CHARPIN
MICHAEL ANASTASSIADES
AAKS
OMER ARBEL
NAOTO FUKASAWA
STEFAN DIEZ
PAUL COCKSEDGE
ATLASON STUDIO
AGNES STUDIO
INI ARCHIBONG
FRONT
GUNJAN GUPTA
BIG-GAME
GT2P
BARBER OSGERBY
GAMFRATESI
THILO ALEX BRUNNER
AGUSTINA BOTTONI
INDUSTRIAL FACILITY
MARIA JEGLIŃSKA-ADAMCZEWSKA
ISPA (NIKE)
BOUCHRA BOUDOUA
KONSTANTIN GRCIC
FABIEN CAPPELLO
KITT.TA.KHON
RONAN & ERWAN BOUROULLEC
RODRIGO BRAVO
MAX LAMB
CHARLOTTE KIDGER
MISHA KAHN
MARISOL CENTENO
ALVARO CATALÁN DE OCÓN
LAUN
JORIS LAARMAN
KWANGHO LEE

MAC COLLINS

FORMAFANTASMA

FRIDA FJELLMAN

PHILIPPE MALOUIN

CECILIE MANZ

SABINE MARCELIS

JAIME HAYON

MARTINO GAMPER

NIFEMI MARCUS-BELLO

CASEY MCCAFFERTY

YINKA ILORI

MATERRA-MATANG

MOISÉS HERNÁNDEZ

MIMINAT DESIGNS

HELLA JONGERIUS

NENDO

JONATHAN MUECKE

MISCHER'TRAXLER

MINJAE KIM

MARLÈNE HUISSOUD

SOMIAN DESIGN

GEORGE SOWDEN

SHAHAR LIVNE

STEPHEN BURKS MAN MADE

STUDIO LANI

INDIA MAHDAVI

MABEO

NAO TAMURA

TRIBUTO

FERNANDO LAPOSSE